WOMEN'S CHANGING LANDSCAPES

LIFE STORIES FROM THREE GENERATIONS

WOMEN'S ISSUES PUBLISHING PROGRAM

WOMEN'S
CHANGING
LANDSCAPES

◆

LIFE STORIES FROM
THREE GENERATIONS

EDITED BY

Greta Hofmann Nemiroff

SECOND
STORY
Press

WOMEN'S ISSUES PUBLISHING PROGRAM

SERIES EDITOR: BETH MCAULEY

CANADIAN CATALOGUING IN PUBLICATION DATA

Main entry under title:
Women's changing landscapes:
life stories from three generations

Includes bibliographical references.
ISBN 1-896764-24-X

1.Women – Canada – History – 20th century. 2. Women – Canada –
Biography. I. Nemiroff, Greta Hofmann, 1937-

HQ 1453.W6575 1999   305.4'0971   C99-931765-2

*Royalties from the sale of this book are being donated
to the Canadian Women's Studies Association*

Edited by Beth McAuley

Copyright © 1999 Greta Hofmann Nemiroff

Front Cover: Original Photograph by Chum McLeod

*Second Story Press gratefully acknowledges the assistance of the Ontario Arts
Council and the Canada Council for the Arts for our publishing program.
We acknowledge the financial support of the Government of Canada
through the Book Publishing Industry Development Program and the
multiculturalism program of the Department of Canadian Heritage
for our publishing activities.*

Canadä

Printed in Canada

Published by
SECOND STORY PRESS
*720 Bathurst Street, Suite 301
Toronto, Ontario
M5S 2R4*

CONTENTS

QUÉBEC

Nova Scotia

Women's Changing Lives
*Linda Christiansen-Ruffman, Angela Dinaut, Colleen McMahon,
Brenda Lee Regimbal, Paula Veinot 259*

Questions for General Study
Appendix
Contributors' Notes

ACKNOWLEDGEMENTS

This project was designed and facilitated, in 1995, by the Changing Landscapes Project Co-ordinating Committee comprising Professors Linda Christiansen-Ruffman, Huguette Dagenais, Keith Louise Fulton, Greta Hofmann Nemiroff, Christine St.Peter and Eliane Silverman. In addition, they compiled and edited the report that resulted from this collaboration.

In this initial stage, the project was supported by a grant from the Women's and Youth Affairs Division of the Commonwealth Secretariat as part of their program "Three Generations, Two Genders, and One World." We would not have known about it had Huguette Labelle, President of the Canadian International Development Agency and Chancellor of the University of Ottawa, not drawn our attention to it. Both Eleni Stamiris, Director, and Nusrat Husain, Senior Project Officer, of the Women's and Youth Affairs Division of the Commonwealth Secretariat were most helpful. Anne Burgess of the Office of Research Services of Carleton University managed the initial financing of the project. Heather McAfee and Elizabeth Turcotte worked on the graphics for the report and created the maps that are included in this book. Above all, Hélène Boudreault, Assistant to the Joint Chair of Women Studies at Carleton University and the University of Ottawa, was a truly indispensable participant in every step of the process.

In 1999, the Project Co-ordinating Committee revised the initial report in preparation for this publication by Second Story Press. *Women's Changing Landscapes* could never have been completed without the wisdom, tact and editing skills of Beth McAuley, who shepherded this work through its many stages. She must be saluted for tenacity, good humour and endless professional know-how. The commitment of Second Story Press to this project is deeply appreciated.

INTRODUCTION

Greta Hofmann Nemiroff

◄○►

IN THE YEARS AND MONTHS preceding the Fourth UN World Conference on Women in Beijing, women throughout the world were preparing projects in honour of this event and to celebrate the end of a twenty-year period in which women's issues had been brought to such conferences every five years. In 1994, as Joint Chair of Women's Studies at Carleton University and the University of Ottawa, I was sent an announcement from the Women's and Youth Affairs Division of the Commonwealth Secretariat in London, expressing their interest in supporting research projects in Commonwealth countries on the theme of "Three Generations, Two Genders and one World." It was their hope that such studies would "generate in-depth information on changing gender ideology and practice over a period of three generations — grandparents, parents and youth." The projects were to be inspired by and dedicated to the World Conference being held in the Fall of 1995 and to be undertaken by "a team of university students" who would "record their own stories and then interview their own parents and grandparents." This project was intended to familiarize interested readers with the diversity of women's lives and achievements in the Commonwealth countries.

The project piqued my interest and challenged me for several reasons. As a teacher of Women's Studies, I have always been fascinated by the anecdotal information students bring to the field from their own experience and that of the women in their lives. I myself had struggled to do justice to the lives and experiences of women in Canada when Robin Morgan invited me to write the section on Canada for *Sisterhood is Global*,[1] an anthology of writings celebrating the end of the UN Decade of Women. This process had made me aware of how difficult it is to capture and convey the complexity and diversity of women's lives in Canada. It is a huge country with many cultural and regional differences, composed of numerous discrete Aboriginal cultures, as well as many cultures imported by immigrants from all parts of the world. Moreover, Canada is in a constant state of flux; Canadians are continually recreating ourselves as demographic changes inform our cultural landscape. I wanted to develop a means of gathering information that would dynamically communicate how women in Canada have experienced social changes within their lifetimes. It seemed to me that the voices of women talking about their lives would give the most authentic sense of women's lives in Canada. Capturing their thoughts and tone would, in my opinion, give a more textured and authentic sense of women's experience of the twentieth century in Canada than what could be gleaned from statistical surveys. As well, the project would give students the chance to learn interviewing skills, to improve their writing skills, to deepen their knowledge of their own families and to experience the joys and vicissitudes of group work. Finally, I myself have conducted numerous workshops on autobiographical writing and am always struck by the insights people gain as they account for their lives. It is a fascinating experience both for the "autobiographer" and for witnesses to the process.

The Beijing deadline, however, did not allow for the participation of a large group of women or for a search for a group of women who precisely reflected the demographic composition of Canada, although it was important to have regional representation.[2] I was fortunate to know many Women's Studies professors and scholars across the country, and I contacted those I thought would be most interested in this kind of a project. To my delight, the first five women I contacted agreed to participate in it. They are Christine St. Peter, University of Victoria; Eliane Silverman, University of Calgary; Keith Louise Fulton, University of Winnipeg; Huguette Dagenais, Laval University; and Linda Christiansen-Ruffman, St. Mary's University in Halifax. I would participate from Carleton University and the University of Ottawa in Ontario.

Aside from experience in the teaching and researching of Women's Studies, our team of faculty members had been educated in the disciplines of Anthropology, English Literature, History, Philosophy of Education and Sociology. I wrote and circulated among my colleagues a draft proposal for the project, which was then refined by their contributions. It was submitted to, accepted, and supported by the Commonwealth Secretariat. We began work in January 1995, with only six months to complete the work.

Our plan was the following: each professor would find five to seven women students interested in participating in such a project. Together, through teleconferencing, pooling our knowledge about interviewing techniques and oral history, and through discussion with our students, we would design a questionnaire for intergenerational interviews. In each region, participants would individually interview three generations of a family, one of whom would be themselves, and write approximately five to seven pages to account for their findings. Each group would work together on an introduction on the situation of women in their region. We agreed to look for a diversity of students that could represent the composition of the population in the region and in Canada as a whole. We wanted a wide representation spanning social class, sexual orientation, race, ethnicity and occupation. The faculty members met regularly through teleconferencing. Each regional group set up its own schedule, protocols and approach to the project. We agreed not to expect uniformity in content, methodology or style; we expected every section of the book to be unique in that it reflected the taste and textual decisions of a particular group of people. In the report, the section from Québec was written in French and each section was preceded by an abstract written in the "other language."[3]

Our teleconferences were informative, mutually supportive and often fun. Although some of the group members knew one another, initially I was the only person who knew all members of the group. We had six teleconferences and finally all met for a group breakfast before giving a presentation on this project at the Canadian Women's Studies Association at the Learned Societies in Montréal, in June 1995.

As with all "best laid plans," this one did not fully conform to our original outline. The faculty members, with in-put from our students, fabricated a long and arduous questionnaire that attempted to satisfy everyone's criteria. In practice, however, people adapted it to their own situations. We developed a "tip sheet" on interviewing techniques as well as a release form for the interviewees.[4]

Finally, twenty-four students and six teachers participated in the project; seventy-five women across the country were interviewed. In almost every region there were drop-outs, much to the discouragement of us all. However, each drop-out reminded us how the pressures arising from many women's difficult life situations place projects like this one beyond their reach. Always, we were aware of the speed with which the project had to be completed and regretful that although we were able to provide many interesting accounts of how three generations of women had experienced change in their lives, we were not able to provide a more finely tuned representation of women in Canada.

All the participants learned a great deal in this process. It was fascinating to witness women naming their experiences and describing them in their own unique voices. While each region may have its own particular history of feminist consciousness and action, there are many common themes across the country that were reflected in the interviews: the socialization of girls; access to contraception; the influence of religious orthodoxies; the experience of motherhood; women's paid and unpaid labour; violence against women; and the importance of education for women.

Of particular note is the diminishing importance of organized religion in regulating the lives of women in Canada. The Québec interviews illustrate how the interrelated issues of religion and fertility shaped women's lives two generations ago. Over time, in Québec as elsewhere, the authority of men seems to have diminished. On the whole, women have worked very hard, sometimes working themselves into illness and shortened lives. Narratives from other regions indicate that while many women have rich spiritual and creative lives, often their spirituality thrives beyond the reach of organized religion, especially among the youngest generation of women in these stories. Education was also a recurring theme over the three generations. So many of the oldest women were prevented from pursuing their education by family duties, marriage or poverty. Their ambitions to be teachers or nurses could often only be realized in the lives of their daughters or granddaughters, or both. The youngest generation, however, see broad educational and career opportunities for themselves, well beyond traditional "women's work."

This was not an easy project to carry through. Ethical questions confounded each of the six groups of women. What does one do with confidentiality? What about terrible family secrets? How does one go about not identifying those who do not wish to be named, but still want their stories to be included? What does one do with privileged information that might hurt others within a family? How does one ask questions that may seem tactless or indiscrete? Sometimes the interviewers were privileged to hear family secrets that had been kept from previous generations. These issues were addressed within the local groups and in the teleconferences. Ultimately, each individual and each group had to address and resolve their ethical questions as they saw best.

Neither was it simple to write the introductions to the sections of this book. How does one communicate accurately what specific regions are like and what they mean to the women who inhabit them? This is especially difficult because women, on the whole, have not been written into the official histories of our regions. Hence, we had to account for place and history through the eyes and bodies of our grandmothers, mothers, ourselves and our daughters. Although we attempted to acknowledge the presence of people we could not include — those whose words we had not heard directly for this project — each group was left to resolve this challenge in its own way.

Editing itself presents serious problems, especially when there is a surfeit of engaging material. What must one include or leave out? The writers had to reduce very rich and compelling material to five- or seven-page accounts. Some interesting anecdotes had to be sacrificed. The usual way of resolving this problem was by identifying themes and addressing them cross-generationally. The Alberta group addressed themes as a group rather than as individuals.

It was not always easy to arrange group meetings. However, the participants made the project a priority and managed to find ways of fitting it into their busy lives. The Manitoba group taped their meetings to send to their member in Churchill, Manitoba. The Victoria group met at Christine St. Peter's house on Sunday afternoons around a table set for tea and cake. The group in Calgary ended its work in an intensive two-day meeting. The Ottawa group met over potlucks at the dinner hour. While the project commenced in a burst of energy, the school year ended and some members had to leave Ottawa to find work before it was finished. The Halifax group was an entire sociology class. Because of time, availability and distance, the women in Québec worked on their own. However, in her introduction, Huguette Dagenais mentions that in her twenty-three years as a university professor, she has "rarely encountered as much enthusiasm on the part of students for a project, especially for a demanding project that had neither credit nor financial remuneration attached to it."

All faculty members involved in this project have learned a great deal. Linda Christiansen-Ruffman has said that she learned again how important an aspect of feminist pedagogy it is to understand that the researcher is in a process of discovery, in a situation of flux. Huguette Dagenais found that the students needed to learn interview methodology that took into account the qualitative nature of the information elicited, the necessity to adapt to the style of the interviewee, sometimes to return to subjects that had seemed difficult at the beginning, and to understand that in the process of being interviewed, people often reinterpret their own lives. Eliane Silverman was interested in the convention that has formed around telling one's life story. She wondered if women simply reproduce the way men tell their life stories and suggested that the themes and "salient events" of women's lives are not the same as the ones in men's lives. Perhaps, if left to their own devices, women would tell a different kind of life story than the ones we elicited. I was struck with how difficult it was for some of the students to give life to the "voices" of their mothers and grandmothers, how impoverished our spoken and written languages have become and how much skill it takes to elicit, recognize and reproduce the uniqueness of each person's voice. Christine St. Peter found that the students were eager for the opportunity to publish: the product mattered intensely to them. Ana Torres, the Guatemalan contributor from British Columbia, said: "You have no idea what this means to my grandmother to be a part of a Canadian story!" Keith Louise Fulton was interested in how women process the accounts given to us by "women we love or want to love." She also wanted to understand the women who dropped out of the project and what it was in their lives that prevented them from finishing commitments.[5]

It is now five years since the notice from the Commonwealth Secretariat crossed my desk in Ottawa. Some Canadian women's groups are gearing up for the Beijing Plus Five conference to take place at the United Nations in New York, in June 2000. In Québec, the Fédération des femmes du Québec has initiated a World March for Women that will culminate in a huge demonstration at the United Nations in October 2000. Many of the struggles mentioned in this book have not been resolved in Canada or elsewhere in the world; in other places women are engaged in serious struggles for the most basic rights. Many feminist organizations in Québec and Canada work in solidarity within Canada and with feminists throughout the world.

Five years later, the professors who worked on the report are still in contact with one another; however, many of the students are harder to find, since they have dispersed into the next chapters of their lives. As the general editor, I have been heartened and supported in this project by the generosity and perseverance of my colleagues in preparing this book for publication by Second Story Press.

"My students are so in love with the words of their mothers," Christine St. Peter said at our presentation. I think this sentiment is probably shared by many of the authors in this book. The interviewers were often surprised by stories they had not heard before, by insights, attitudes and values they did not know their mothers, grandmothers or daughters had. They showed immense appreciation of the accomplishments and strengths of their foremothers, and sometimes humour at the contradictions they heard, especially in relation to feminism. The experience of interviewing the women in their families or in families they know well, of working with a group of women whom they might not have known before, and of accounting for their region from a woman's point of view was both stimulating and validating.

It is especially pleasing that *Women's Changing Landscapes* will not only be read by individuals interested in the unique voices of these women, but that it will also be read and reflected upon by students in Women's Studies courses. Surely many of the issues made alive through these personal accounts will touch upon the lives of students reading them. I hope that the contents of the book will stimulate discussion, debate and, most of all, enjoyment of the knowledge and artistry of the women who have shared their lives with us.

Notes

1. Robin Morgan, ed., *Sisterhood is Global* (New York: Doubleday, 1984).

2. Time restraints necessitated working with a small group. It is regrettable that we did not include representation from Saskatchewan, New Brunswick, Prince Edward Island and Newfoundland/Labrador.

3. Greta Hofmann Nemiroff, ed., *Changing Landscapes: Three Generations of Canadian Women Tell Their Stories / Paysages en mouvements: Trois générations de femmes au Canada recontent leur histoire* (Ottawa: The University of Ottawa, 1996).

4. Although different questionnaires were developed in French and in English, they all covered the same general themes: demographic particulars, family life, relationships, education, paid and unpaid work, social and political participation.

5. The preceding paragraph is a reconstruction of some of the remarks made by each of the professors at our presentation at the 1995 Learned Societies in Montréal.

BRITISH COLUMBIA

Terrace

Haida Gwaii/
Queen
Charlotte
Islands

Kooteny
National Park

Nakusp
Graham's Landing
Calgary, Alberta
New Denver
Slocan
Kootenay

P.O.W. camp, Ontario
Lake
Superior

Ottawa, Ontario

Victoria

Nelson

Vancouver
Trail

Hamilton, Ontario

Vernon

RENEGOTIATING BRITISH COLUMBIA

Christine St. Peter and Theresa Newhouse

—◄◦►—

BRITISH COLUMBIA, CANADA'S WESTERNMOST province, is a place rife with extremes, contradictions and paradoxes. The complexity and diversity of British Columbia's geography — mountain ranges, glaciers, fertile river deltas, deserts, rain forests, oceanscapes and grasslands — have shaped the imaginations and life possibilities of the people who inhabit its spaces. And this geography, never a neutral feature, finds a match in the diversity among the population. Despite the name of the province, and of its capital city (Victoria), British Columbia is no longer a place dominated by British immigrants. Although this ethnic group accounted for over 70 percent of the population in 1931, by 1991 only a quarter of British Columbia's 3.3 million people identified their (often distant) origins as British.[1] Now recent immigrants add hundreds of national and ethnic groups, each with its own history of achievement, oppression and resistance. All of this immigration is built, of course, upon pre-existing First Nations' civilizations, whose archeological traces in the province date back over ten thousand years.

If ethnic demographics have shifted dramatically over the course of provincial history, the province has experienced a similar shift in the demographics of gender. While First Nations people had equivalent gender divisions prior to contact with Europeans,[2] non-Aboriginal settlement was originally overwhelmingly male. In the late nineteenth century, non-Aboriginal men outnumbered non-Aboriginal women three to one.[3] As historian Jean Barman asserts, it was "a truly male culture," with men still outnumbering women two to one as late as the First World War.[4] This gender imbalance has had profound effects on the lives of British Columbia's women, most of whom have been written out of the dominant history of the province. The purpose of this chapter is to share narratives of women who, with only a few exceptions, have been known solely within their domestic and local settings, their stories erased from the public record. The six stories that follow this introduction, while by no means representative of the full range of diversity in the province, attempt to reflect some of the extremes, contradictions and paradoxes found in British Columbia. We offer the stories in the same order as the families' arrivals.

At the time of the first European contact with the Haida and Nuu-chah-nulth Nations on the Pacific Coast in the 1770s, nearly half of Canada's Aboriginal or First Nations people lived in the area that now comprises British Columbia, with ten major groups speaking thirty-four different languages. The province itself was established in 1871 upon the unceded land of these First Nations people.[5] The first of our stories is also one of the first in chronological time in this region, that of women from Haida Gwaii (the Queen Charlotte Islands) in the family of Roberta Kennedy.

A remarkable feature of this story is how far back the living family history went at the time she wrote her narrative. Although our group task was to interview three generations of women, Roberta Kennedy had five living generations of women in her lineage, from her centenarian great-grandmother to her young daughter. One of the participants, Roberta's Naanii Lavinia White, is a well-respected global activist in Aboriginal issues, so when Roberta Kennedy makes the following statement, she knows how destructive colonization and active resistance can be embodied in one woman's life: "After European contact with the Haida people in British Columbia, things began to change for our women. The Haida women were the traders before the Europeans came. The white men did not like this arrangement so our men took over the trading. It was the start of the European patriarchal influence on my people who had traditionally been matrilineal with women occupying powerful social positions. Later, Europeans made laws specifically to restrict the First Nations women all across Canada."

These patriarchal, assimilationist, even genocidal laws included such measures as granting Indian Status only to Aboriginal men and their wives and children. Non-Aboriginal women marrying Aboriginal men automatically acquired status, but any Aboriginal woman marrying a non-Aboriginal man lost her status, as did her children. Despite this unjust law, only revised in 1985, and a myriad of other injustices that persist, Aboriginal women and men have survived, as we see in Roberta Kennedy's story. But much that was destroyed may never be recovered. The 1991 census, for example, tells us that of the 37,370 First Nations women now living in British Columbia, only 2,385 can still speak their mother tongues — a brutal legacy of the province's residential school system that continued for Aboriginal girls and boys in this province even into the 1980s.[6]

In the latter half of the 1800s, British Columbia began to fill up slowly with migrants lured by the promise of economic development and jobs. The building of the provincial arm of the Canadian Pacific Railway, promised to the province by the Canadian government in return for joining Confederation in 1871, drew male workers from across the nation and the ocean. So did opportunities for work in such primary resource sectors as fishing, mining and forestry. Here we find one of the ironies of British Columbia's economic development: most of the male labourers from China, Japan and India who emigrated to the province in the last decades of the 1800s and the beginning of the 1900s had originally intended to be temporary sojourners, until they had earned enough money to return home to families or future marriages. But when they were paid only half the wages of white workers, they were unable to save enough to return, and many thus became permanent settlers. What is more important, it was to British Columbia, rather than to other areas of Canada, that most of these immigrants had moved. "In 1901 the province contained almost twenty thousand out of the twenty-two thousand Asian residents in Canada, by 1911 over three-quarters of the total of almost forty thousand."[7]

White settlers in British Columbia were loathe to admit more Asian immigrants and prevailed upon the Canadian government to create racist measures to bar further immigration. In the beginning of the twentieth century, Sikh men who had emigrated from India attempted to bring their wives to Canada. Like their husbands, these women were British subjects, yet they faced a series of "contrived rules and policies fabricated to justify their exclusion."[8] Not until 1919 did the Indian government secure an agreement that permitted South Asian women to enter Canada.

In the case of Chinese immigrants, extortionist Head Taxes were levied on those attempting entry — $50 in 1885, $100 in 1900, and a whopping $500 in 1903. Then in 1923, the *Chinese Immigration Act,* commonly known as the *Exclusion Act,* forbade the entry into the country of almost all categories of Chinese, an Act not rescinded until 1947. Yuen-Fong Woon's recent novel, *The Excluded Wife,* is based on the actual lives of women refused entry during this period. In her introduction, she points out how external forces, such as diplomatic relations between China and Canada, as well as events within both countries, had very adverse influences on "the identity and images of Chinese-Canadians, the inter-generational dynamics of their families, and the sociopolitical structures, cultural life, and personal relations within their community."[9] It is appalling to see history repeating itself when, in 1995, the Canadian government re-introduced a Head Tax that applies to all incoming immigrants.

The second of our stories, told to writer Nancy Pang, gives stark evidence of the effects of this history on one family of Chinese-Canadian women born in Victoria (the oldest was born in 1908). As Nancy Pang writes: "Kwei-yun was forced to deal with the burden and pain of sexism, poverty and racism in a white and male-dominated society." She also faced extreme oppression within her own culture where, as Kwei-yun's daughter, Xiao-fa,[10] says: "Females were treated as slaves and the males were the slave-drivers." Nancy Pang analyzes how the institutionalized racism and poverty imposed by the larger society created a hierarchy of oppression in which "the abused became the abuser." The three generations of women, including the youngest, university graduate Michele whose life is radically different from that of her grandmother and mother, explore the "interconnecting question of self-image, cultural identity and social roles" among Chinese-Canadian women.

In the case of the Japanese immigrants, Canada "bowed to British Columbia pressure to limit their immigration by entering into the Lemieux-Hayashi Gentlemen's Agreement of 1908, which limited the number of labourers entering Canada to 400 per year." While this resulted in fewer Japanese men entering Canada, it accelerated the immigration of women. Some of these women were the wives of earlier immigrants, who were accompanied by their children, but by 1924 there were 6,240 women who, after an exchange of photos with prospective husbands, came as "picture brides." As Audrey Kobayashi explains, "The cruelty for the young bride consisted … in placing her, a young girl of eighteen or so who had never been away from her village, on a ship to a strange place where she would be required to work hard, to endure the prejudice of a hostile white community, and to bring up her family away from the familiarity of her native environment and the friends and family who would normally support her through the first trials of marriage."[11]

The third of our stories retells the experiences of the women in the family of Michiko (Midge) Ayukawa. Her mother came to Canada in 1922 with her new husband, who had returned to Japan to seek a wife ten years after he had first joined his father in Canada in 1912. Midge Ayukawa tells of the backbreaking labour of her parents and other Japanese immigrants, and of the added burdens suffered by the wives. Without contraception, these women bore many children. During labour they were frequently only attended by their husbands and often delivered their babies in wilderness shacks. This devastating reproductive labour was in addition to the heavy manual labour and poverty the women had to share equally with their men. But the hardships of these newcomers did not ease with time. Instead, with the beginning of the Second World War, the Canadian government removed all Japanese-Canadians — 73 percent of whom were actually Canadian citizens — from the British Columbia coast, confiscated their property and incarcerated them, either in the camps of interior British Columbia and Northern Ontario or on the sugar beet farms of Alberta and Manitoba. Midge Ayukawa and her family suffered this fate. Her story focuses on the experiences of the girls and women in their Slocan Valley camp and on the historic post-war fight for redress undertaken by Japanese women and men in alliance with non–Japanese-Canadian supporters, a struggle not won until 1988. She speaks, too, of her earlier sense of shame that came from internalizing the hatred she and other Japanese-Canadians had experienced, and of her desire to assimilate into the post-war white majority. But her story also recounts her recovery and that of her adult daughters of an identity that now takes pride in their Japanese heritage. In the case of Midge Ayukawa, this includes extensive study of, and publication about, the experiences of Japanese-Canadian immigrants.[12]

While these minority groups experienced unique hardships in a racist society, historian Jean Barman points out that "whatever the individuals' ethnicity or race, the actual process of adjustment was never easy."[13] To

Barman's "whatever," we might add "whenever." For example, in a study of German and Italian women immigrating to Vancouver between 1947 and 1961, we learn of women choosing emigration as a way to "adventure, freedom, travel and independence," only to find their very identities shaken by their "disillusioning experiences in the exploitative and stigmatizing occupation of domestic service in Vancouver," a situation that required myth-making as a way of restabilizing their sense of self and reconciling tensions between the "real and the ideal."[14]

While there has been a persistent prejudice in favour of white British immigrants, class discrimination has existed even towards members of that group. Early in the twentieth century, for example, "English immigrants from poor or working-class backgrounds were often disparaged. For a time, 'No English Need Apply' signs were commonplace in parts of British Columbia."[15] The family in the fourth of our stories comes from this kind of background: a mixed-heritage family from the British Isles arriving from Eastern Canada via wagon train and settling in a Northern resource-based town dominated economically and socially by the Consolidated Mining and Smelting Company (Cominco). Because of the organization of labour in such towns, class antagonism with strict separation of workers and bosses was, and continues to be, fundamental to people's sense of identity, as is narrated by the mother and grandmother of Anonymous. Furthermore, the single-industry resource towns, with their boom-and-bust economies, are places in which women have always found it difficult to find paid work, so are doubly dependent, both on the company and on their husbands.[16]

This political economy is given concrete shape in several of our stories, but takes centre stage in the story by Anonymous, where we discover a community deeply conservative in social and familial values. This conservatism was built on the base of the heterosexual family structure. The older two generations of women, born in the 1920s and 1950s respectively, did not see this as a negative experience. Indeed, the mother of Anonymous, entering adulthood in the 1970s era of second-wave feminism, speaks of distrusting the women's movement for not valuing enough the traditional women's roles that she thought provided the emotional stability and cohesion of the community. But Anonymous, a young woman in her twenties, struggles between her own commitment to her family's values and their small-town roots in Terrace, and her need for the space to create her own identity, particularly when as a university student in Victoria she comes out as a lesbian.

This storyteller, with her lesbian-feminist analysis, hides her identity under a pseudonym women writers have used for centuries: Anonymous. This camouflage is not because the young lesbian fears outing herself — she has been openly and unashamedly "out" — but rather because of her mother's deep sense of privacy about *all* family business. Our writing collective found this veiling very difficult to accept, fearing that readers would attribute the secrecy exclusively to fear of homophobic backlash. And yet here, as with our Chinese-Canadian family who also requested anonymity, we respected the families' reasons, even as we regretted the reality of their experiences that had created an acute sense of vulnerability.

The women of our fifth narrative are also British, but they descend from generations of educated, middle-class teachers. Stacey Morrison's great-grandparents immigrated from England, via Mexico, to a remote farmstead in British Columbia's interior in 1927, seeking a physically healthy environment for their children. There they became subsistence farmers, sending their children to a one-room school. High school was a distant boat ride away; university was in another world. The high value placed on education persisted from generation to generation, however, even though the family continues to choose remote villages as their most congenial habitat. Stacey found both comfort and constraint in her natal village of New Denver. The community is situated in the midst of breathtakingly beautiful mountains, yet it is separated within by class lines and historical racial divisions that included the imprisonment of the Japanese-Canadians during the Second World War.

White immigrants may have had privileged status among the other settlers when they arrived in British Columbia, but *white women* did not have equal status with white men. White women only won the vote provincially in 1917 (federally in 1918) and, in fact, were not considered "persons" under the law until 1929. Men had the legal right to control women's lives — even down to such details as the right of men to give a twelve-year-old daughter away without the mother's consent.[17] Male legislators consistently denied women the vote through a half-century of suffrage agitation. Dorothy Davis, Maria Grant, Helen Gregory MacGill and Florence Hall are some of the women who fought for the vote through organizations such as the Women's Christian Temperance Union and the Political Equality League (with its publication, *The Champion*).[18] Yet when white women began to achieve numerical parity and finally achieved the franchise provincially, they did not engage in franchise struggles for other groups in the province: Chinese-Canadians and Indo-Canadians were granted the vote only in 1947, Mennonites in 1948, Japanese-Canadians and First Nations people in 1949, and the Doukhobors in 1952. The 1931 census report reveals the kind of racist thinking that marked not just British Columbia but the country as a whole: Europeans are minutely differentiated by nationality, while all other groups are lumped into two categories, "Asiatic" and "other."

This kind of blinkered vision marked a good deal of the political work done not just by men but also by feminists and progressive labour activists as well, evidence of the contradictions referred to in the beginning of this chapter. Such a contradiction occurred in the Mothers' Pension campaign, which began in the province in 1901, under the aegis of middle-class women from Vancouver's Local Council of Women and the University Women's Club, both determined to establish the right of support for widows, deserted and unwed mothers. In 1914, working-class labour activist Helena Gutteridge convinced the provincial Trades and Labour Congress to join this struggle, and with the support of many charity, labour and religious organizations, the provincial government adopted the policy in 1920, under the direction of Mary Ellen Smith, the province's first woman MLA (Member of the Legislative Assembly). With its insistence on including unwed mothers among the "suitable" recipients, the British Columbia legislation was the most progressive on the continent, providing more pensions per capita than anywhere else in North America.[19] And yet this apparently progressive action combined within it a reactionary, even racist, contradiction, as the supporters of the Pension refused to extend it to immigrants who were non-British subjects. [20]

We discover a similar kind of contradiction in British Columbia's reproductive and sexual politics — the feminist struggle for women's control of their own fertility and sexuality. An early example occurs in the battle for birth control, which found its first Canadian defenders in British Columbia within the thriving socialist movement that was a "spawning ground for a host of radical movements" in the early decades of the twentieth century.[21] It was to Vancouver, at the invitation of two prominent socialist-feminist activists, Laura Jamieson, of the Women's International League for Peace and Freedom, and Helena Gutteridge of the Trades and Labour Council, that the American contraception campaigner Margaret Sanger first came to Canada to aid in the fight to decriminalize the teaching of birth control methods.[22] The socialist feminists in the province went on to establish the first birth control league in Canada in the 1920s and one of the country's first clinics in the 1930s.[23] Despite the progressive nature of the reproductive politics of socialist feminists, however, British Columbia, along with its neighbour Alberta, passed bills permitting the "forcible sterilization of the mentally ill and retarded" in the late 1920s and 1930s, the same period that saw the passage of similar laws in Nazi Germany.[24] In other words, we find simultaneously in British Columbia both the most progressive and the most reactionary of political movements; indeed, some of the supposedly progressive initiatives carried out as an integral part of their campaign were features intended to benefit some at the expense of others.

The 1930s in British Columbia reveal the Depression-bound poverty and limitation found elsewhere in Canada, a condition experienced by the oldest generation of women in our stories. As one of them says, "I would have liked to have been a nurse but there was no money, absolutely no money. There were no jobs, you couldn't get a job for anything. I did do housework, ten dollars a month — I'm not saying a day, a month ... I did that all through high school to get all my books ... and that was the last of the education in the Kootenays ..." This personal recollection illustrates precisely the gendered pattern of work not just in the Depression, but also after the Second World War.

Although women and men shared poverty and lack of opportunities during the Depression, it was difficult to make the authorities recognize that unemployed women also needed relief work even though 14 percent of the British Columbia labour force was female in 1931. These women, typically confined to "women's" jobs, earned on average between one-half and two-thirds of what men earned.[25] But even among women's groups there was no unanimity about how to alleviate this situation. The need of relief work for unemployed *men* was the concern of the Mothers' Council of Vancouver in the 1930s,[26] while the plight of unemployed *single women* (who formed 76 percent of the female workforce in 1931)[27] became the focus of the middle-class Local Council of Vancouver. The socialist Committee on Trades and Professions for Women, however, demanded work for all unemployed women and men, single, married, divorced or widowed.[28] Of course, the beginning of the Second World War, with its mobilization of men into the Armed Forces, also saw a massive entry of women into the paid workforce, including such traditional male workplaces as the shipyards. In 1939 when Canada was still in the throes of the Great Depression, only 17 percent of women were in gainful employment and more than one-third of these had jobs as domestic servants. Five years later, in 1944, the number of women working full-time had doubled, but as historian Ruth Roach Pierson argues, "post-war policy-makers were by and large blind to the contradiction between the imposition on women of home responsibilities and the promise of equality in the marketplace."[29] Indeed, their schemes were designed to "perpetuate a sex-stereotyped and sex-segregated labour market ... that rested to a significant degree on the retirement of tens of thousands of women to domesticity" in the 1950s and 1960s.[30] In British Columbia, for example, Cominco hired women to replace male workers gone to war, but committed to rehire ex-servicemen on their return, recognizing their war service as accumulated seniority, a scheme which ensured the displacement of almost all the women hired during the war.[31] Furthermore, the province's intensive program of post-war economic development — the building of highways and mammoth hydroelectric dams — offered well-paid work for men. Where women have been employed in "male" industries in the province, they have tended to work in sex-segregated, low-paid areas of the industries, as for example in the shorework sector (assembly-line canning) of British Columbia's fisheries.[32]

By the 1960s and 1970s some women began to appear — as they had in the early part of the century — in the public sphere of electoral politics. Most of these elected officials were white, although one of the province's leading political figures has been Rosemary Brown, a Jamaican immigrant who served as a member of the British Columbia legislature from 1972 to 1983. In 1975 she ran for the leadership of the federal New Democratic Party, offering a distinctly socialist-feminist platform. Although she did not win that leadership drive, her work paved the way to party leadership for two NDP women who followed her, Audrey

McLaughlin (1989)[33] and Alexa McDonough (1995). In general, however, from the 1960s to the end of the 1990s, women's success in electoral provincial politics followed the "law of increasing disproportion," by which is meant "the higher the fewer."[34] And while women of the last generation have been more accepted in the paid labour force, their wages remain systemically lower than men's, with many occupations still largely closed to them except through token participation.

By the 1970s, when the youngest generation of our storytellers was born, the second-wave feminist movement was underway in British Columbia. Women's centres, transition houses, women's advocacy and lobbying groups, sexual assault centres and community-based Status of Women Action groups were opening as early as 1972 and continue, albeit under attack and in shifting forms, into the present. University- and college-based Women's Studies programs appeared in the 1970s, as well as grassroots, women-centred training programs. Women's movement newspapers such as *The Pedestal* (1969), *Kinesis* (1971), *Images: West Kootenay Women's Paper* (1972) and *The Emily* (1982)[35] were created, and women's conferences, on a wide variety of political topics, proliferated and were well attended. Feminist publishing houses like Press Gang of Vancouver were formed as well as feminist bookstore collectives that sold women's publications.[36] Perhaps the most telling indication of women's growing independence was the plummeting birth rate and the growth of the women's health movement in the province, aided by the creation and embattled maintenance of such institutions as women-run abortion clinics.

Such important achievements are invariably marked by problems that both halt the advances and prepare for the next stages. A characteristic example of such a process can be seen in the debate about lesbianism in the early days of British Columbia's first umbrella organization of women's groups, the British Columbia Federation of Women (BCFW). Formed September 13–15, 1974, at a conference attended by 350 women from virtually every area of the province, it united seventy-two very diverse new women's groups.[37] Recognizing the diversity and fearful about destroying broad-based support, the BCFW did not create a lesbian policy in that first meeting. As Julia Creet argues, "most women could tolerate lesbianism as long as it was discreet, but [lesbians] demanding rights and recognition launched it from the private into the political sphere, and into the lives of all women in BCFW."[38] The formation of a lesbian caucus and direct confrontations about this issue resulted in the departure within the first year of the more timorous or homophobic members, but this was also the point, Creet asserts, at which feminists in the province began to see how important conflict was, "as a test for support and unity."[39] One concrete result of this struggle in British Columbia was the rise of a "theory of lesbian feminism and the incorporation of lesbianism within the feminist movement." The struggle also resulted in the publication of *Stepping Out of Line*, a workbook on the connections between lesbianism and feminism — the first of its kind in Canada.[40] This debate, like all others in feminism, shifts over time. An example of one such shift can be seen in our fourth story by Anonymous, a lesbian in her twenties struggling in the 1990s not with being "out" but with the debate and developing orthodoxies about butch-femme identities *within* lesbianism. We find discussions of these and other issues in lesbian periodicals like Vancouver's *Diversity: The Lesbian Rag*, and Victoria's *LesbiaNews* (lately renamed the *Lavender Rhinoceros*).

As we approach the end of the century, we note that women's lives from all classes and ethnicities still carry unjustly heavy burdens compared with those of their male counterparts within their groups. But in British Columbia, some old racial patterns persist; the most disadvantaged citizens are agricultural workers, 70 percent of whom are women, mainly Indian immigrants, but also Chinese, Vietnamese, Aboriginal and Hispanic women. These workers earn the lowest wages in Canada and have little economic, environmental or social protection. Of course, in pointing out that reality, it is important to note, too, how the same groups have organized political resistance to that discrimination, for example, the South Asian Women's Action Network, and the Progressive Intercultural Community Services that advocate for the workers and initiate programs to educate and protect them in their workplaces.[41] Furthermore, while minority women from all groups work within their own communities, they have also achieved national prominence in "mainstream" feminist organizations, as for example, the successful work of Vanouver's Sunera Thobani, the first woman of colour elected (1993) to head Canada's National Action Committee on the Status of Women (NAC).

There have always been many reasons for coming to British Columbia, but some immigrants have come as political refugees escaping certain

death in their own countries. Our final story narrates the struggle of
Ana Torres and her Guatemalan family who came to British Columbia
in 1982 after fleeing through four other countries before finding refuge
in Canada. Ana Torres's parents, political activists in the Guatemalan
resistance movement, were marked for assassination when their names
appeared on a death squad hit list operated by the Guatemalan police.
In other words, this is a family in which none of the informants is born
in British Columbia, and yet such a family now belongs here and re-
configures our social and political landscape just as surely as have all
previous immigrant groups. This narration explores the ways in which *all*
generations of the Torres family share the loss of cultural and linguistic
continuity, even as they struggle to remake themselves to "fit" into an
alien, and alienating, culture. Active in the political resistance in their
home country, they choose to remain part of that historic struggle even
as they work to (re)make British Columbia as their new home.[42]

A feature of British Columbia's changing landscape today has been
both an increased acceptance of, and resistance to, the diversity described
above — a contradiction articulated by many of the women interviewed
for our stories. Thus, even as the province officially promotes multiculturalism and antiracism, hate crimes remain unrecorded and on the rise. All
women, but in particular women of colour, First Nations women and
lesbians, face renewed attack.

Not surprising, then, to discover that the topic of feminism is a
preoccupation of five of the six older women and all of the younger
women who narrate our stories. At the time of writing these stories, all
the writers were students at the University of Victoria. Five were under-
graduates (three in Women's Studies, one in human geography, one in
sociology), while our sixty-five-year-old narrator was completing her
doctorate on the history of Japanese immigrants to Canada. All of the
youngest generation of women who speak, and several of the older, express
some ambivalence or painful alienation from traditional women's roles
and, in a few cases, even from the foremothers whose lives embodied
these roles. Most of the interviewers have felt some unease at the idea
of probing sensitive issues with women so close to the core of that pain.
All of the writers here spoke of being deeply moved by the disclosures
of their women subjects. Most found themselves weeping at times as
they took on the pain of the other women's stories, which often related

experiences of loneliness and lack of confidence resulting from women's multiple oppressions. One stated explicitly that before this project she had "cut off intimate ties with [her] mother." Then she added an observation shared by all of the interviewers: "Getting to interview my mother broke down those barriers, reforged a connection between us as adult women." Indeed, one of the hallmarks of this project was the experience of sharing with other family women experiences and perceptions that had never before been expressed among them.

Learning to listen with attentive ears to others' stories was not an easy task. The most sensitive issue, however, was the problem of disclosure. What were the family secrets that could not be told, least of all to a family member intent on publication? What were the dangerous stories that could not be given a family name, or in some cases even published, although shared orally in interview? How capable were the younger women of hearing the "meanings" of their foremothers' lives, particularly those whose preoccupations seemed so different? To what extent did the older generations understand the complexities of the younger women's experiences? Memory itself is a very unstable factor in the construction of narratives, and collective memories nourished within families may be even more problematic. And yet the way women frame their experiences, even to the point of creating myths that can carry contradictory meanings, tell us a great deal about the hopes, disappointments and strategies women create in order to survive and thrive in often hostile environments.

Finally, we discover in all the stories women in the act of making meaning of the challenges and struggles of their everyday lives. What follows is a collection of narratives offering a tiny sample of the ethnic, religious, economic, sexual and regional diversities of the women of British Columbia. A million and a half stories remain to be told.

SIX RAVENS

Roberta Kennedy

◄○►

I AM ROBERTA KENNEDY (née Bennett). I am a descendant of the Edenshaw family. I belong to the the Y'akw 'lanas, or Raven, clan. My unofficial Haida name is Kwege-ii-ones (Big Precious Cloud). My mother is Leslie Bennett (née Baker). Her mother is Audrey Baker (née Brown). Her mother is Beatrice Brown (née White). Beatrice (Bea) is my Naanii (grandmother), her sister is Lavina White. I have chosen to interview Naanii Lavina because my grandmother Audrey died when I was eight years old, and my Naanii Bea is now ninety-six and reliving her second youth. All these women I have mentioned are from the same Raven clan. Naanii Lavina is really my great-aunt but, because we are from the same clan, in the Haida way, she is also my grandmother.

Naanii Lavina has told me to keep my stories oral because that is the way we tell our history. I have done my best to respect this in my telling here.

My granny Audrey died in a car accident when she was only forty-two. I sometimes miss her terribly, but my people firmly believe in the continuation of our spirits in our children. I truly believe her spirit is alive in my daughter, Martin. I believe this because Martin used to tell me, "I was your mommy and I carried you in my belly. I used to sing you old Haida songs." When she was born I knew she was special. Even while a newborn, she had these wise old eyes. Her eyes would look into the depths of my soul. How I loved those old and terrifying eyes. (I wish I could write about her two wonderful brothers, Robbie and Joey, but I will save that for another story.) Naanii has said in the interview, "The most gratifying moments in my family are when I see my great-grandchildren and I know the Haida people will continue." I look into my daughter's eyes and I know my people will be here forever.

Through these interviews, I discovered that for both Naanii Lavina and my mother, their role models were their matriarchs. For Naanii it was her mother, for Mom it was her Naanii Bea. I did not know how important these women elders were. I remember how, in being interviewed myself for this story, my role model was not my mother. (In fact, I did not have a role model.) I went out of my way to be different from my mother. I saw my mother in a very negative way. Listening to my interview, I realized that I previously had quite a superior attitude towards my mother. I mistakenly thought my mother was being a martyr when she did not pursue her education. The truth, I now realize after interviewing her, was she did not have the opportunity to continue her education. Through my mom's interview I realize that she is very intelligent, strong and kind, and she has had a very difficult and lonely life. For example, I learned that when she was only sixteen she left home because her stepfather was so abusive. She moved in with Naanii Bea and Chinni (grandfather) Cecil on Haida Gwaii. (European Canadians call it the Queen Charlotte Islands.) Mom became really close to them because of this move. As I mentioned, Mom's role model is her Naanii. Mom says Naanii worked hard all her life and never seemed to get tired. She says, "Naanii was mother, grandmother, sister and friend. She was also a daughter until she was almost eighty years old. She is fluent in two languages, and she is still alive at ninety-six."

My mother has also worked hard all her life. And as she is only forty-six she has a lot of years left to continue working hard. When I was little, I remember that she worked at the cannery. She said, "It was hard work. You stood on a concrete floor all day. And it was very cold, because there were no doors." Now she works in the kitchen on the Canadian Forces Base. This work is very hard as well. She works ten days on, and four off.

Mom's most gratifying moments are watching her grandchildren grow. Her most frustrating times are the feelings of emptiness she has now that her last child has left home. This seems ironic because I always got the impression that she wanted us kids to grow up fast so she could be free from us. Maybe we never realize what we have until it is gone. Or maybe it was another thing I did not understand about her.

Naanii Lavina's role model was her mother. She said without hesitation, "My mother, [Emily White, née Edenshaw] was my role model.

As was her mother [Isabella]." She said the matriarch is always the role model. The eldest daughter always takes that role on. Her mother Emily was the matriarch until she passed away in 1972.

Naanii Lavina's most frustrating moments in life are when she realizes that the government put our First Nations people on reserves and left us with no economic base. The result of this policy is that our people, our relatives, live in poverty.

Naanii Lavina has seen most of the changes of women's roles in Haida society. Naanii and all her siblings were forced by the government to attend residential school. These schools were located hundreds of kilometers from home. She went to residential school from age ten to sixteen. She said, "I felt an immense loneliness for my family and my homeland while I was there. It is hard for me to think of that time." When she was eleven, she refused to do the Bible lessons. So the priests expelled her from school for a year. When she was forced to go back, the once-a-year treat, a show in town, was cancelled without an explanation. Naanii organized a "sit-in." She got all the girls to sit out on the lawn. They were not allowed there. She was threatened with being expelled again. But they realized that was what she really wanted and kept her in school. She was twelve years old. Her political career started young. Naanii said she really did not learn much at the boarding school: "My mother taught me everything I know. At school, all I learned was a little English." She spent one half of the day cleaning and cooking for the nuns and priests. And the other half she had some lessons in arithmetic, reading and writing.

But there was one other thing she learned at residential school and that was racism. As soon as she entered the school, her brother was whisked away from her and she was never allowed to speak to him again. This hurt her more than anything and to this day she feels terrible when she talks about it. My mother also experienced racism, but in her case this only happened in the city schools she attended in Vancouver. The most important thing I remember about racism was when I was six years old. My Grade One teacher singled me out with the Haida kids so we could sing a Haida song. I was devastated. I went home, crying to my mom, "How could I be a Haida?" I asked her. She laughed sweetly at me and said I was Haida. I thought I was just like the majority in my class: white. Of course I was devastated. I had been bombarded (with) cowboy shows where the cowboys were always the good guys and the "Indians" were always the bad guys who spoke in broken English.

Naanii has always been politically active. Decades ago, she started participating in meetings for National Indian Brotherhood. She said when she started going to these meetings she was the only woman there. The men were uncomfortable with her participating at these meetings. One man came up to her and told her to go home and raise her children. She said, "My children are grown up now, and I am finished my mothering." He did not have a response. After a time she was accepted into this male-dominated group. She has been accepted by the First Nations people all over the world, as she travels, lecturing about traditional ways and First Nations politics. With her own Haida people, things have not gone so well. She recently lost an election for president for Council of the Haida Nation. She was the only woman running, and the men made it clear that her place was not in this political race.

I was really proud when I learned that Mom refused to get a status card. This is an identification card issued by the Canadian government under the *Indian Act* that "proves" that one is a First Nations person. She said, "I don't need the government to tell me who I am." She said she has always known that she is a First Nations woman, even when she lost her status through government fiat upon her marriage to my father, Wilfred Bennett, who was a non-status Haida because his family lived off the reserve. When I was born two months before my parents' marriage, I inherited my mother's status. Then after the marriage when my mother lost her status, I also lost mine. In my high school years I grew proud of my heritage, and I felt like half a person without my status. It wasn't until I was eighteen, in 1985, that the government changed the law and "granted" status back to all Native women.

Mom and I have very different views on religion. She really believes in the Anglican religion and in the Bible. I used to, but have since realized the pain and destruction this religion has caused my people. Now I firmly believe in the spirituality of my own people. Our people traditionally believed that our church was the earth, our bodies, the air around us, the sky. Everything had a spirit. And we prayed all the time. Not like the religions of today, but through our songs, dances and stories. Naanii used to go to church, but she, too, saw the destruction religion had caused our people, and she also believes in Native spirituality.

I have graduated from university. This is a big deal. Not very many of my people have graduated from high school. I feel I have had a lot of opportunities to pursue my education, because funding has been made available to me through sponsorship from my Band Council. And I have had a good support system from my loving husband, Kevin. Mom got her high school equivalency through night classes, many years after she left school. But her educational opportunities are still limited due to the isolation of her location. Naanii said that at boarding school, "they passed everyone at the Grade Eight level. If someone was sixteen, it did not matter what level she or he was at, they graduated you." When Naanii turned sixteen, she was finished school and was sent home. She was the happiest person in the world, because she missed her family and homeland so much.

Within the last week, even as I was writing this, my Naanii Bea died at ninety-six. It happened all of a sudden. Her sister, Naanii Lavina, expected her to get well, but she did not. Naanii Bea had a rich and happy life. She had nine children and one hundred grandchildren, great-grandchildren and great-great-grandchildren. She was a strong and happy woman. My Naanii Bea has really been gone for the last three years because she only recognized the people who looked after her. She did not know me at all. I am trying to remember her when she did know me. Like the day she gave me my button robe, a special cape with a family crest sewn onto the back of it. I had graduated from high school and she put it on me at the graduation ceremony.

I wore my robe to my university graduation ten years after that day. I still felt proud because my Naanii made it just for me. It is an heirloom, now, and will be passed down through my family with the wonderful memories of Naanii.

DOING THE TELLING

Nancy Pang

-◄o►-

I AM A FIFTH GENERATION Chinese-Indonesian of mixed heritage born on the island of West Java, Indonesia, and given the name Anggriani Dewi Pangsaredja. My mother, father and I left for Canada when I was three , and I've been in British Columbia for the last twenty-five years of my life. When I came to Canada people had difficulties pronouncing my name. I was thus given the name Nancy Pang. My first name is western, my surname is Chinese. I speak Indonesian fluently and locate myself as a Southeast-Asian-Canadian woman, a group numbering almost 27,000 in this province. This multiple identity raises many complex issues and requires intense introspection. I struggle not only to understand myself, and other women, but also the broader influences of history, cultural heritage and society. Who am I as an Asian? Who am I as an Asian-Canadian? Who am I as an Asian-Canadian woman? This introspection led me to explore the stories of three Chinese Canadian women of the same family. Since the grandmother speaks little English, the passage of translation from her Chinese dialect was done through her daughter, Xiao-fa.

Many stories about women are beginning to be told, but stories of the hundred thousand Chinese-Canadian women in British Columbia have only quietly and very recently been present in Canadian historical texts. *interrelated* Out of this silence arises these three individual but <u>interrelated</u> stories. All are of women born in Victoria, British Columbia — grandmother, mother and daughter.

The grandmother, whom we will call Kwei-yun (Precious Cloud), was born in Victoria in 1908. She was the first of three children. Kwei-yun was forced to deal with the burden and pain of sexism, poverty and racism in a white and male-dominated society, all without the language skills that would encourage interaction with the larger community. The new host country demanded many sacrifices, and the sense of family took on greater significance. Kwei-yun describes her experience:

...the females were treated as slaves and the males were the slave drivers. My brothers went to China to get married, had their children there, [and] I stayed in Canada because I was female, mother would not let me go with them. I was married [to an older man] while they [my mother and brothers] were in China. I had a baby boy in early days of the Depression. He died at six months — no food to feed him ... Time passed, I was given a baby girl to raise because the mother had nine children so she gave away most of the girls. She kept two girls and two boys. It was tough going. My husband was a wood cutter. He worked in the forest all day long ... not much money coming in. We lived in a little hut with a well, [a] fifteen-minute walk from the hut. I had to walk to the well five or six times a day to fill the water barrel ... Times were hard ... My husband died when my second son was three months old, there was no money to bury him. I went from door to door to collect money from people who could and were willing to help; most couldn't help me because they also didn't have extra money. After my husband died, my mother and my brothers came back to Canada. They had to leave their wives behind because Chinese women were not allowed into the country; the Canadians did not want the families to get together and have babies of the Chinese origin. If the men insisted, they had to pay a head tax of $500 for their wives [before the *Exclusion Act* of 1923]. Children were not welcome here either. It was only in 1950–5) after the law changed when my younger sister-in-law entered Victoria with two of her own children and a niece ... Because my English is limited, I stayed at home to take care of my mother. She passed away very young.

As Kwei-yun was thrust into an environment without the familiar networks of support, her daughter had to adopt her mother's resilient nature in order to survive in the places she should have been able to call "home" — her family and her country. This isolating experience streamed down to the next generation. Kwei-yun's daughter, Xiao-fa (Little Flower), discloses how vulnerable she was to discrimination and hardship while growing up in Canada:

My original family consisted of my mother and a very cruel and sadistic stepfather and one half brother and one half sister. I helped the family with the money I made by working two or three jobs at a time, banking during the day, salad or kitchen work three nights a week, baby-sitting the rest of the time ... I grew up without radios, electrical appliances and telephone. We shared what we had with other [Chinese neighbours]; if our house had no butter or jam, we would go to another house to see what they had. If they had the butter and jam then we traded, bread for a bit of jam and butter. There was no help from the western society ... racial put downs were [prevalent]. I was not allowed to talk to any "white" boys and the "whites" were not allowed near us ... I have experienced unfair treatment when I was working in the bank. The accountant did not like us. He kept the three Chinese girls (including me) until six p.m. every day licking stamps and envelopes.

In 1923, the Head Tax was replaced with the *Exclusion Act*, which ended all immigration of Chinese to Canada. This institutionalized racism created a hierarchy of oppression that permeated the Chinese-Canadian family. The abused became the abuser. Xiao-fa continues her story as she reveals the abuse with indignation:

... if I didn't bring a certain amount of money home, I would not be able to eat. I had to wash the dishes but no food was given to me. Mom was scared of her second husband so when she was hit, I would try to get in between the two, so I would get the blows instead of Mom. I still carry scars from those beatings ... Most of us growing up in the mid '50s to the early part of the '60s all had stepfathers. Two decades of exclusion meant that many of the younger women coming to Canada married men who were twenty to thirty years older, thus there were many widows with children and remarrying was the means to survive.

Xiao-fa's daughter, Michelle, was born in 1960. Her experiences growing up in Victoria were dramatically different from those of her mother and grandmother. Michelle's strong sense of respect for her extended family and admiration for the two important women in her life are heard through her voice:

✳ When I was growing up, my mother and father each had their own [different] responsibilities within the household ... As for us kids (older brother, younger brother and myself), we were quite spoiled; we did not have to do any of the household chores ... I am very close to my relatives on my mother's side. My maternal grandmother took care of me and my brothers when we were young. Whenever I had an argument with my parents and threatened to run away from home, I would run to my grandmother's place where I would seek consoling and a delicious home-cooked meal ... When I was young, I don't think I had a role model. If I had to choose, I guess it would be my grandmother ... she was always there for me. I now have three role models. I admire my grandmother for her kindness, my mother for her inner strength and my uncle for his positive attitude towards life ... Comparing my life with my grandmother's and my mother's, I have had an easy life. Also I feel fortunate that I have a lot more options in my life. I can have goals and can make them a reality.

The interaction with the larger community has made a significant impact on the hopes and dreams of these women as they lived in an environment of racism, class discrimination, segregation and sexism. The whole interconnecting question of self image, cultural identity and social roles is thus explored by all three women.

Kwei-yun had very limited access to an education because she was Chinese. She was a woman defined by Canadian law and custom as being the "other," the "alien." Kwei-yun remembers the bitterness and anguish:

We were not allowed into the elementary school system until the law changed. When I was fourteen, I went for two years then left to take care of Mom. I had six years of Chinese schooling and two years of English. I did not like the English school because they built two wooden huts and put us there ... It was cold and damp. The area was a forest then ... No choices were given to the Chinese race ... [B]eing Chinese, and being picked on by the whites like in South Africa, had an impact on my life. Made me very shy and unsure of myself when I was young. Still am ... Being widowed two times, loss of Mother and Dad in my early years and bringing up five kids on my own has changed my life. When I look back in my life, the one social change affecting me in my lifetime was being able to ride the street cars or buses. We [Chinese heritage men and women] were not allowed to until after World War Two. My life was hard. Had to fight for racial rights, my daughters were the same, granddaughters' lives are free because their mothers are well educated and did not keep their daughters home to work for them; granddaughters are free to travel, and so on My English is limited so I can't say much to my niece and nephews, but the important relationships are to my grandchildren. I hope that they think a lot about me.

Xiao-fa completed her high school, but then had to work so that her two siblings would have a chance to attend university. She also speaks about her changing attitudes concerning women's roles, her role as a working woman and a mother:

My own capabilities changed over time. Since I started working for the school board, I became a translator. That surprised me! I translated for parents and teachers during report-card time. The rest of the time I worked in the office of the school. I didn't think I was smart enough. I think these women who do volunteer work or many hours of unpaid work to their families and communities are never acknowledged publicly. It's sad because these women are very dedicated in what they do. I'm quite happy doing what I'm doing now ... But the most important personal change I've gone through in my life is to be able to talk back to people, especially my husband, mom-in-law and fellow workers ... As a mother, what I did was to go back into the workforce and get the money to give to my children what I did not do or get when I was young. I gave them a chance to see the world as soon as each one of them [my three kids] graduated from university, to see China, Japan and Hong Kong ... I think I did the right thing, because I gave them space and independence and [the opportunity] to expand their knowledge more. In this action I freed them from being tied to me. The most gratifying element of family life is that all my children respect me. They are more like friends than children to me ... As for my mother, she was my role model. She was always there when I needed her. And I would still choose the same role model now because she is a very stable person even though her life was not a very happy one.

Michelle expresses her thoughts on self-image, cultural identity and the tension between obligations and personal choices:

> As a child, I did not know the value of learning about the different Chinese customs; now I realize that this is part of my identity. During the time I was sixteen, life was quite difficult for I lacked self-confidence and peer pressure was the greatest [problem]. Through the years ... I have lost a lot of the insecurities that made life as a teenager miserable. I feel that I am just an average Canadian woman ... I don't think of myself as part of any particular community ... The place and community where I live has never pressured me to learn more about my cultural background. Traveling to Asia has affected my life considerably. I have a bachelor's degree in linguistics, and have studied in Japan for several years. My attitude towards my own capabilities has changed considerably ... I had set several goals for myself. One of them was to speak Japanese fluently. Since achieving this goal, I have more confidence in myself and in how I perceive my future. As for my relationships, compared with my mother's generation, I feel that women have more control in their relationships. My parents disagree with interracial relationships; they believe that their children should date and marry only Chinese-Canadians. I think that to some extent their disapproval of interracial relationships has affected the way I perceive my relationships. There is a part of me that wants to please my parents, and a part of me that wants to make my own choices.

She then goes on about racial discrimination that still exists in its various forms. Like her mother and grandmother, Michelle is not free from these constraints as she speaks about her experience:

> I have worked for a local major hotel, for a local community college [in Canada] and for a prefectural government office in Japan. When I was working in the hotel, one year, the position of head-room clerk was available. Despite having many years of experience at the front desk, I was not considered for this position. I believe that I was not chosen because of my race and my gender.

Our identity as Asian-Canadian women is strongly influenced by how others see us, but of more importance is how we see ourselves. Kwei-yun's, Xiao-fa's and Michelle's stories paint individual portraits on a common canvas. Each stroke of their brush shifts and reshapes the image as a whole. The self-silencing has been conducive to maintaining the pattern of prejudice. So what matters here is who is doing the telling. They speak in hopes of breaking the silence, of naming the stereotypes and of transforming the representations drawn by the larger society. Now they have constructed their experience through their own eyes by expressing the pain and struggle of their foremothers, and they speak of their resolve to make their daughters' lives easier. Their lives as marginalized individuals have shaped and reshaped their definition of themselves not only in the context of being Asian, Asian-Canadian or Asian-Canadian women but more specifically in the context of the inseparability of these identities. The trajectory of these experiences leaves imprints on our minds, our hearts and our being. These women come from a people with a long history and distinctive grace. They are Canadians. Chinese-Canadian women.

trajectory
弾道, (すい星, 惑星の) 軌道

money, absolutely no money. There were no jobs, you couldn't get a job for anything. I did do housework, ten dollars a month — I'm not saying a day, a month. Of course you can't save much on that. I did that all through high school to get all my books. I finished my high school and that was the last of the education in the Kootenays, [though] I feel I learned a lot being in my hometown in lots of other ways. I just about had enough money to go [to nursing] and then, of course, [Grandpa] was transferred up here and he was lonesome, so I just said, "Oh well, we'll just go for that then." He lived in a bunkhouse for three months and that was enough of that for him. He wanted somebody to look after him. I wouldn't want [my daughter] to get married that young. I don't feel that was a good idea really. You miss a lot of youth. It's not that I feel I made a mistake, it's just that I feel that I've missed something.

The traditional female responsibilities have shaped my grandmother's life, though she has not felt as constrained as her mother was. My grandmother said, "Grandpa was very considerate. He did a lot of the gardening, but I felt kind of guilty if he did the dishes. I always felt that it wasn't part of his chores. In my day women were more chattels than they are now. Men thought that they could rule the roost. They made all the decisions. [In my parents' relationship it was] very much so, more so than in mine." My grandmother has rarely worked for pay, though she has done much in the home and in volunteering in the community, for friends and for organizations. She did paid work for the census and also once at a laundry, but she felt her family did not approve.

In many ways, my grandmother's life has been defined by family. Recently widowed, her life has undergone even greater changes. She explains:

First of all I was one of seven with my dad and mother, and then I came to this town as a bride and became two people and I was very, very lonely for my brothers and sisters. Then I had two children and that made my life more rounded and I didn't miss my family as much. And now I've lost my husband and several of my brothers. I have become one person and that's kind of a different world altogether. I didn't think it could be that different. You get more freedom but you have to do all your own thinking.

Having lived in one area, in one community with a shared history and workplace, has provided Grandma with a great sense of security. She told me:

My father worked for the company and to have [my husband] working for the company was security and a steady income. We knew where we were going from one day to the next. We knew how to plan our lives. We knew what our children could do. As far as being in my hometown is concerned, at one time, until just very recently, we all belonged to Cominco and that put us all in one category. There wasn't any distinctions to speak of between miners or farmers or ditch diggers, they were all Cominco employees and once they got the job we were all equal. [Management] was a little separate. We weren't in that class, that's for sure, but then we didn't feel we had that education. We don't feel that we can discuss things with them, do you know what I mean?

My mother also believes her life has been more fulfilling through the stability, security and sense of shared history present in family:

I felt there was a need when I was younger to be married because that was sort of the expectation at that time. I knew that I would be a mother. I had to be a mother even if it meant adopting children. And I wanted to do all the motherly things. And again it was expected to go out and get a job and that fit me, too. I had no quarrel with the role at all. The most gratifying part of my life right now is still my children. They play a very, very big part in my life, outside of my husband. And I'm very fortunate that my marriage has hung together for twenty-five years and we've got a large history and we've got lots of family that also we have all intact.

My mother has inherited the sense of what is a woman's duty as reflected in my grandmother's life. But she also feels her life breaks away from the more rigidly defined woman's role. She said:

My life is very different from my mother's because my mother always believed that she had to [fulfill her duties]. I think even when my father said she didn't have to fit a certain role model, she felt obligated to. For instance, it was expected that if she worked she wouldn't work for money and I think they suffered because of that.

I think my father could've accepted it, but she wouldn't allow herself to do that. And I think I have a sense of duty, but I don't feel that it's that restricted. I feel that I can discuss it. I still feel I have a duty in that, for instance, when [my husband] wanted to move I felt [I had to] even though I didn't want to move at all. But I think I would've felt that even if my partner had been another woman or even just a real good friend. I think again that's part of being family and you can't just be thinking of yourself all the time.

Though she feels women now have more opportunities, older women have been an inspiration to my mother in her life choices. "[I have enjoyed] belonging to a woman's church group and finding out that this age group has such a marvellous [viewpoint]. Older women have such a marvellous [perspective] of what life is and should be, whereas younger women are so challenged and so fast-lane that they haven't got time to have their philosophies. [It's] the calmness and the serenity again, that's really been a major force in my life."

The growing participation of women in public life combined with the relative security afforded the white lower-middle-class in resource towns have given my mother greater freedom. She did university training to become a teacher and has, in later years, pursued a degree by correspondence. In the intervening years she has worked in a variety of capacities: "When I was first graduated I was of the age where we became a nurse, a secretary or a teacher and I was definitely steered away from what I probably would have been best at and that was engineering, maths. I think [now] I put on a show of being very confident, very capable even if it means that I have to be a workaholic to prove my capability. [My job is] very important, not at a social level, but at a respect level, it's very, very important to me."

Growing up in and spending a majority of her life in small towns has also helped provide stability in my mother's life. She has liked both the physical space available and the warm sense of support. She told me: "I think that very populated is very stressful to me. I feel there is a great feeling of comfort, of safety, in a small town because people know each other and they all look out for each other. [Living in the North] could have given me a lot more respect for all people in all walks of life because when you know these people you find that they're just as lovable as in any other walk of life." My mother feels her life has been deeply affected by the growth of this increased recognition of women and other oppressed peoples. She feels strongly this is about "enjoying the diversity rather than resenting diversity. I think that's coming and some people are really totally accepting of this. I think a lot because of Sesame Street and Star Trek. And others just cannot accept it, they haven't come any distance at all. But I think that the trend is total and it's going to come." Despite this, my mother admitted to being mistrustful of the women's movement of the 1970s, which rejected the traditional women's roles that have provided an anchor for so many women's lives. She feels society's expectations for women have changed. She said, "[The] big difference between me and my daughter is that I feel it's really important to meet society's expectations a lot, because I find if you make people happy that the rewards come back to you."

In many ways my life has been a continuation of the patterns of my grandmother and mother, though I have struggled with this. I was also raised in resource-based communities and grew up imbued with traditional gender roles. I observed these roles in my own family in the division of labour. I also spent the first part of my life caught between my mother's standards of "proper behaviour for girls" and what I see now as a need to prove my own heterosexuality to myself. For the most part I felt very asexual and that didn't fit with what I saw around me. I tried hard for a long time to find what I would see in the movies and in books about love, and of course it was all heterosexual images in that time and place. Even the word "lesbian" did not exist in my adolescent imagination. It was only as a result of my first contact with the gay community in university that I began to understand my earlier experiences. Coming out was a big change in my life. I think my mother hoped that I would be happy, and in her ideas, being happy means having a stable life. In other words getting married, being normal.

Most recently the struggle within me, between myself, society and my family has manifested itself in my lesbian identity. As a lesbian I have had few role models in the world around me. I am torn by a desire to remain faithful to both my family and myself. The deep commitment to family that I have grown up with and a sense of duty have often put me at odds with the feminism of other women. I have felt torn by the politics and protection of family and the desire to find women's empowerment. It has been in making a home, making dinner and providing care that I have finally struck a balance between home and work. It's very different from my original family home in the sense that both of us are women but in some ways it's very similar, in terms of one person doing one set of jobs and the other person doing others.

It is important to me that I have an extended family, with close ties, but it is also painful, as it is in my family relationships I have felt the most fear of homophobia. The question of how I'm going to deal with the rest of my extended family has haunted me. Everything is so marriage and family based. It is an issue not solved through any simple feminist theory. Family, with its sense of duty and shared history, seems to evade the often cut-and-dried politics of "women's liberation." I also don't believe butch and femme — the lesbian masculine and feminine genders — have been fully accepted by the lesbian community of today. I'm not sure what they mean to me, but I do know that in them I can find some sense of what my family role models teach me to find security in.

I feel I have had more opportunities than my foremothers. I have had the space to go to university and explore my interests. My parents' encouragement has helped me to fulfill this but I think I also wanted to go to university to escape. Now I would like to go back to small towns and the North. I feel torn between having access to things down here, feeling safe in the lesbian community, and wanting to live in a small place up North. I see now it would not be so utopian, as any kind of minority, to live there. The home I have counted on is simply no longer there.

I currently feel very settled down in some ways, but not settled that I am doing the right thing in other ways. My various selves have drawn me in different directions and with different judgements. Correct politics and what is right have little meaning and provide little guidance in a world of shifting and conflicting roles: my duty as a feminist, my duty as a daughter, my duty as a granddaughter, my duty as a partner. I am still struggling to discover what is my duty to myself.

WITHIN THE MOUNTAINS

Stacy Morrison

—◄◦►—

THE FAMILY STORY BELOW blends four generations of white women of British descent. Their stories are drawn from both sides of my family. It is also the story of three small villages in British Columbia and includes knowledge about them that I uncovered in the course of preparing this family narrative.

Elizabeth Scholes was my great-grandmother. The daughter of a headmaster in Britain, she was a teacher by profession. In 1920 she quit teaching in England and moved with her husband to Orizaba, Mexico, where her husband opened a cotton mill, part of Britain's expansion into Mexico. They spent the next seven years there. The first of their three children, Joan Inez Markwick, my grandmother, was born in May of 1921. In her recollections of her Mexican childhood, Joan comments on her family's privileged social position, as well as the class and cultural chasms:

> As a little girl in Mexico the rebels would come down out of the hills, march through the town. We had all the windows and doors barred in those days ... The houses were built with a courtyard in the centre and all the rooms around the outside, and you would stay in your little courtyards ... Even as a child I had a personal maid ... I remember going out onto the street and I used to think that it was fun to eat some of the food they would sell on the streets because at home you would never get anything like that ... We ate our own [British] food.

The death of the family's second child, at the age of one and a half from meningitis, prompted the family to move from Mexico to Canada. They travelled across the Mexican border, through the United

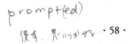

States and into Canada — "all the way by train."

With the money earned in Mexico, they purchased a plot of farm-land in the Arrow Lakes, in the interior of British Columbia. Their new home was Graham's Landing, located on the west side of the Upper Arrow Lakes, twenty-one miles south of Nakusp. The journey to Graham's Landing took several days by train through the Fraser Canyon, an area dotted with tiny hamlets and mining communities that, like the train line, have subsequently disappeared. When they arrived at Arrow Park, the last leg of their journey, they travelled by steam paddler to the village of Graham's Landing.

The decision to move to this isolated place stemmed from the family's desire to provide an environment for their children that was physically healthier than the city. This choice of village lifestyle has persisted into my own generation.

Most of the property in Graham's Landing was farmland owned and run by approximately twelve families. My grandmother remembers: "There was nothing. Some farms and a mill and a one-room school. There was a store at Arrow Park, which you could go to but it was four miles away ... We just bought a farm. My mother didn't know beans about farming. It wasn't a big farm, just enough to keep us. We had chickens and a couple of horses ... It was a healthy life for youngsters."

The family moved to Port Arthur, just outside Vancouver, in 1941, because Joan's father, my great-grandfather, wanted to help with the war effort: "My dad sold the farm on the lake and they moved to Vancouver so he could work in the shipyards as he had in World War One."

The village where the family lived and farmed is gone. From 1967 to 1974 three hydro electric dams were built on the Arrow Lakes and the adjoining Columbia River. The Arrow Lakes were flooded and the entire farming region, including Graham's Landing, disappeared.

While living in Graham's Landing my great-grandmother, Elizabeth, worked on the farm with her husband and raised her daughter and newborn son. This was a huge change from her genteel pre-Canadian past. Yet Joan, her daughter, remembers her as being "quite happy at home. She sang and played the music beautifully on the piano. She had a beautiful voice."

My grandmother, Joan, was six years old when the family arrived in Graham's Landing. She began school in that one-room school the same year she arrived. "When I went to school the first year, the kids used to tease me and call me the 'little Mexican devil.' I would get mad and they would say, 'Oh, the little Mexican is getting mad.' That would make it even worse. I was brown of course from the sun. I would start talking to them in English and then I'd get mad and fly off in Spanish. I took that for a couple of years until I got over it. It was a little rough." Despite her childhood experiences she still struggles, at age seventy-five, to maintain her Spanish vocabulary.

She finished elementary school and chose to continue her education. This choice was not made easily because the only high school on the Upper Arrow Lakes was in Nakusp, twenty-one miles down the lake. The steam paddler was the only form of transportation, and it ran in just one direction on the lake each day. Thus a student wishing to attend high school in Nakusp had to pay room and board during the school week. At the insistence of her mother, my grandmother, who was only thirteen years old, decided that she would go to high school. But the decision to attend high school required that she pay her way by working at the Pine Lodge boarding house. She points out that this was unusual: "Many of the students from my elementary school didn't go to high school. They just went out to work." After completing high school, my grandmother decided to attend the University of British Columbia (UBC) in Vancouver:

> You could be a nurse, a teacher or a secretary. These were the things that were open. They were the things you became if you didn't want to do menial work or get married. I didn't even give it a thought about how I would go, I just naturally wanted to go to school. I went to UBC from a little high school; I went to Vancouver on the train. I had written and gotten a place from UBC. In those days a lot of people boarded and so I had this address [for a rooming house]. I got on the boat and went to Arrow Head and got on the train and went to Revelstoke, got on the main line and went to Vancouver, got off, got on a streetcar. I didn't know where it ended. I was so green. This guy helped me get off in the right place and showed me how to find this address.

After completing her first year at UBC, she continued her post-secondary education at the Victoria Normal School in Victoria. In

1942, after completing a full year of study, two full semesters of summer session and two full years of student teaching, my grandmother became a certified teacher. Her two "teacherages," or student teaching positions, were very fortunate. She remembers one especially: "All the other girls at all the little places were in teacherages by themselves. They were 'batching it' and listening to the howling of the wolves at night. Here I was in a lodge in Longworth. A hunting lodge with running water, indoor plumbing, beautiful meals and even a post office. I was so lucky." In 1943 she quit teaching full time and married my grandfather. My father was born in 1948.

My mother was raised in Nelson, in a wealthy family. Her mother, Margaret (Burns) Shrieves, was a nurse by profession and a shareholder in her husband's ready-mix and gravel company. When pregnant with the first of her five children, she quit working as a nurse, but continued to be a shareholder in her husband's company, which meant that she still received a paycheque of her own every two weeks.

My mother was her first child, born in July of 1950. She attended one of the small elementary schools in Nelson, then transferred to the junior high school in Grade Seven. She remembers transferring schools because "it was the first time I had ridden the city bus. We were just a big group of kids. We did everything together." My mother was also a member of Job's Daughters, a social club formed for the daughters of establishment businessmen in the Masonic Temple. ⑦

After finishing junior high school, my mother attended the senior high school and graduated in 1969. Her parents, she says, had strongly encouraged her to attend a university after high school: "It was to be done, everyone did it. [My parents] always encouraged us to go. They always wanted everyone to go to school and for us to know that money was no problem." Although Notre Dame, the only university in the interior of BC, was located in Nelson, my mother chose to attend the University of Victoria (UVIC). She left Nelson in September of 1969 for UVIC, but, missing Nelson, she returned to attend Notre Dame University in October. While attending Notre Dame, she continued dating her high school boyfriend. She became pregnant but finished her first year of university before having me in July of 1970. She entered the paid workforce as a school library worker at age thirty-five when her third child entered school.

I was born in Nelson. My parents and I moved to a small community named New Denver ninety miles north of Nelson when I was a year old. My father, like his mother Joan, his great-grandmother Elizabeth, and his great-great-grandfather, was hired as a teacher. New Denver had been a small mining community and an internment camp for Japanese-Canadians during the Second World War. The community of approximately six hundred had, and still has, one school for students from kindergarten to Grade Twelve. The students are separated by classroom but share the gymnasium and the library. The small class sizes (eighteen in my graduating class) and the variety of ages within the building require close relations between all students and teachers.

＊ New Denver[43] was a town that had different populations, but crossing the political lines of each group was difficult. One group consisted of a few Japanese-Canadians who chose to stay after their release from internment; another were the draft evaders of the Vietnam war from the United States; the third, hippies searching out alternative lifestyles; the fourth were mining and logging resource workers and the town service people. As educators, my parents did not belong easily to any of these groups, nor did I. Over my lifetime I have experienced growing hostility in the community over environmental issues. This makes it difficult for me to return to the small town after defining myself as a feminist and an environmentalist.

I left New Denver after graduating from high school to attend the University of Victoria. Like my grandmother and mother, I was "supposed to" go to a university after completing high school. For every year I have attended UVIC, I have taken a year off to travel or to work. At the age of twenty-five I am now finishing my degree. Unlike my foremothers, my education has mortgaged my life for the next ten years as I struggle to pay off my student debt. I cannot afford to be unemployed. The financial instability that I face causes me to question the value of a university education. However, my grandmother, Joan, sums up the expectation for members of my family to attend university, in a statement that encompasses their values and my own:

＊ I wanted my children to get an education and get out and see the world. I say it doesn't matter if you get a job or not: your outlook on life with every subject you take is widened. If you live in a small place, a small town, you don't see these things. Education is really important. Maybe not to get a job anymore, but it's an education just to go to university. Isn't it?

This expectation, which is directly linked to class position, is also a result of raising families in isolated communities. The remote geographical location of each community limited the influences of the outside world. For example, while growing up in New Denver, I had access to three television stations and two radio stations, and fashion came through the Sears Catalogue. While I attended high school, there were only three Japanese-Canadian students and there were no students with obvious physical or mental challenges. The community offered a very insulating and limited view of the world; post-secondary education was and is an escape from this buffer.

Just as the surrounding mountains enclose the town, the community of New Denver can limit the lives of its young adults. All of the nine women in my graduating class left New Denver. None has returned. The mountain-surrounded valley where I grew up left me feeling smothered. My self-identity was always defined by the community. As I finish my degree at UVIC, I again feel smothered — by other people's expectations and political labels. Ironically, I find my escape from these constraints in the mountains. Rock climbing forces me to combine my mind, my body and my spirit. Without the proper combination, I run the risk of losing myself and free falling into the void.

ENTENDER / COMMUNICAR[44]

to understand.   to communicate.

Ana Torres

—◦—

WHEN I WAS FOUR years old, my parents were coming home from work at the National Centre of Workers in Guatemala when they noticed that a van was following them. The van tried to push my parents' car off the highway and finally succeeded. Both my parents were hurt. They found out later that the vehicle belonged to the Minister of the Interior, which controls the police. My mom was conscious when a group of men came and tried to force them into their car, saying that they wanted to take them to the hospital. My mom started screaming her name and where she worked and asked for help. She asked all of the people who were there to recognize that the people in the car were *los querian desaparecer.*[45] This is the way that the military in Guatemala terrorizes people; in this case terror was used against the labour sector. My mom screamed until the people milling around the sight of the accident refused to let anyone take my parents.

Usually, my mom would have picked up my sisters and me from my grandparents' place before heading onto the highway. My grandmother often took care of us when my mom was traveling or was very busy. But the day earlier, my grandmother had cut her finger, so when she had to get stitches my mom decided that the children would stay at home. That is how I and my sisters escaped that attempt on my parents' lives.

Approximately a year later, when my mom had just given birth to my sister, Andrea, a death squad published a list of the people they were going to kill. My mom and dad were on that list. My mom had to go into hiding because she was still too ill after the birth for a long trip, and she did not have documents for the baby to travel. My grandmother took care of us then. A month later my mother piled all of the four girls into a car and drove into Mexico. We did not know that we would never return to Guatemala. I remember that when we said good-bye to my grandmother, she cried. I did not really know why.

Over four years, we lived in four different countries. In 1982 we were granted refuge in Canada. In 1992, my grandparents were granted refuge as well. Ever since my mother had left, my grandparents had been receiving death threats and their son was kidnapped, interrogated and tortured. He also came to Canada.

My grandparents' desperate situation escalated when my mother, who is a member of RUOG (Representatives of Guatemala's Exiled Opposition), returned to Guatemala, in 1992, with international support. In my grandmother's words:

> The threats became much stronger. In June [1992], some individuals entered our home. They were armed to the teeth and were threatening us with death. They put the guns to our heads and they were asking us questions about Marta Gloria and Rigoberta and in reality we could not answer anything. There were around three of them and more outside in cars without license plates (we know this because people who saw them told us later). They were threatening Mario with a knife at his throat, plus the guns they had at our heads. I think what saved us is that some people came to visit. That is why they did not [kill] us. Because of all of those threats we had to leave, because the next time they wouldn't have forgiven us.

My grandmother's name is Maria Dora Gill De La Vega. I remember that my grandmother used to be almost like a mother. We nicknamed her Mamadorita. Mama means mom, Dorita is a diminutive version of my grandmother's name. She was born on July 3, 1929, in Guatemala City. My grandmother is *Mestizo* (of both Spanish and Indigenous origin) like the rest of my family and most Latin Americans. Married at age seventeen, my grandmother did not complete high school. She began working when she was fourteen years old and worked her whole life in various jobs. She worked at a bank for thirty-six years and helped her husband with his printing press. She did not tell me what she did at the bank, nor at the printing press. My grandmother had three children; my mother is her eldest child.

My mother's name is Marta Gloria De La Vega. As a young woman in Guatemala she went to university and became a lawyer. My mom

had wanted to be a doctor but she missed the entrance exams. As a lawyer, *persecuted*
she worked on behalf of unions and because of this was persecuted. For
her, education is a responsibility: "I think that university education carries
a responsibility not only at a personal level but also at a social level. I
felt that the knowledge that I gained was to be used to serve the more
oppressed persons in the country."

My mother continues to work for human rights because she does
not want anyone to go through the pain that she suffered. Each person
needs to be free. My mom has sacrificed and is still sacrificing her own
personal goals for her dream of a free Guatemala: "I would like to be
able to practice traditional Guatemalan and 'Canadian' medicine ... but
it is not possible because I would have to leave what is very important
to me, which is the work of human rights. By human rights I include
women and myself."

I learned a lot from both my grandmother and my mother. My
mother is a very strong woman who has spent her life fighting for her
rights and the rights of others. Because I was not able to spend much
time with my grandmother, most of what I learned from her was from
the stories my mother told me about her life. My grandmother has always
worked very hard; she still works hard today. My mother and her parents
have a very special and close relationship. Both my grandmother and
mother believe that families are precious and should be the focus of
one's life. I agree that families are precious and I recognize that my family
has given me lots of strength and courage. I discovered this after I left
home at age eighteen to go to the University of Victoria, where I have
not had many connections with other *Latinos* or Guatemalans.

My grandmother, mother and myself all believe in fighting for
women's rights. But when my mom first became politically active, her
struggle was not women's rights. However, my mother has been influenced by strong women and her role model was her grandmother. She
says, "The central figure of my family was my grandmother. She was like
a column and everything revolved around her. She was alone because her
husband had died. She had raised her children and worked making
food for others." Yet even though my mom's grandmother was a central
figure, the men in the family occupied the most "important" roles. My
mom always disagreed with the fact that her grandmother felt that she
had to serve her husband or other masculine figures. This situation

continued into my grandmother's generation, as my mother observed: "I used to see my mother coming home after eight to ten hours of work. She would be tired. But she also had to do all of the work in the home. My father is a good person, but like the majority of Guatemalan men, he did not do housework. My mother would come home from her job and had to work at home as well." It is interesting to note that my grandmother did not explicitly mention the fact that she was responsible for the domestic tasks and that when asked about the distribution of domestic tasks in her home, my mother answered that she, like her mother, was responsible for most of the domestic tasks in her immediate family.

Lately, my mom has begun to focus on the struggle over gender inequality. I think that it is because she has seen the hypocrisy that exists when men say that they are fighting for human rights but refuse to respect the rights of their wives and daughters. A catalyst for my mother's involvement in the women's rights movement has been the end of her marriage. According to my mother, part of the reason her marriage ended approximately five years ago is because she felt that her relationship was not fair and that domestic tasks, family responsibility and political participation should be divided equally. This separation has been very difficult for all of the family. My mother's relationship with my father was the only romantic relationship that she has had. She was in love with my father and worked hard to ensure that the relationship continued on a different basis, but it was not possible.

One of the more touching aspects of the interview process was when I asked my grandmother who her role models or heroes are, she said: "My children. They are all heroes, because what haven't they achieved with their families and what haven't they done to help others? Especially my oldest daughter. Even though her life is in jeopardy she still continues to work for the people of Guatemala." My grandmother sees a change in the way that women's roles are defined in Guatemala and in Canada. She says that women in Canada and the United States have more opportunities than she had when she was growing up. For example, my grandmother had wanted to complete her diploma in accounting but, "because her last classes were in the evenings, she could not complete them. In Guatemala in that age, it was very improper for women to be around in the evenings." Yet even though my grandmother

seemed very happy about the changes that have been occurring, which
have facilitated a change in gender roles, she also feels very worried
about the environment in which we are living.

*emancipa-
tion.*

In both of the interviews my grandmother and mother spoke a lot
about the fact that they believed in the emancipation of women. I was
surprised because I have always considered them to be accepting of
their gender roles. I do wonder, though, if their emphasis on women's
rights is because they think that I am an "ultra radical feminist," and
they thought that is what I wanted to hear.

My mother says that she would not try to influence any of her
daughters or younger female friends about their romantic lives or in
any other aspect of their lives, except if they were involved in abusive
relationships: "If I saw that my daughter was abused, either physically
or in any other way, yes, I would act. I could not stay quiet because I
would feel that someone who is very special to me is being destroyed."
From the stories my grandmother told me, I learned that she has also
helped other women in abusive relationships. My mom feels that there
are changes occurring in the male–female romantic relationships, but
that these changes are occurring too slowly.

My mom's closest friend is her sister. "It might sound strange because
she is a family member but she is very important to me. Because of the
level of communication that we have, the level of confidence, it is a
privilege that she is not only my sister but as well my friend. And we can
both count on each other." The family is very important to her. She has
always tried not to burden her children with any political or financial
problems.

I had spent my life, until I was nine years old, moving from place
to place. Moving to Canada was a move into physical safety but also a
move into another kind of social, economic and cultural danger. Our
standard of living was very low as compared with all of the other kids
in our school. This was the opposite of what it had been when we were
living in Latin America, when we were of middle class. As well, I had to
learn a completely different language and culture. This affected me in a
negative way. I was in a very small school in Vancouver and we were the
only kids who did not know how to speak English. I remember that
one of the teachers tried to have an English as a Second Language class
just for me and my sisters. I hated it because we were treated as if we

did not understand anything. I specifically remember her speaking very slowly as if we were stupid. The kids in school were not much better. At first we were a novelty and were interesting, but later they would refuse to speak to us unless we spoke perfect accentless English. So I refused to speak. My sense of feeling inferior to my school peers, of being from the wrong class and culture led me to hide my former animation. I hated being treated as dumb, which led me to become somewhat "obsessed" with school, until I gained a reputation for being a "brain." But I hardly spoke. It has taken a long time for me to feel secure enough to speak. Although, sometimes, when I am nervous or insecure, I believe *que nadie me puede entender. Que puedo commincar con nadie.*[46]

My teen years then, were full of insecurities. People were not supposed to have more than one or two siblings; I had four. People's parents were supposed to speak perfect English; my parents spoke with accents. People were supposed to be rich; we were not. So I alienated myself from both my family and my community. I started working at a restaurant when I was fifteen so that I would be able to buy clothes. I remained alienated from my family until I left home just after I turned eighteen. In the last few years, living here in Victoria, I have come to gain some pride in my life as a Guatemalan woman. I have come to appreciate the sacrifices that my mother and grandmother made for me. I have come to recognize their courage and strength and, like Mamadorita, to admire my mother's heroism. Although we fight and are not able to communicate about a variety of issues, I am quite certain that I have their support.

Part of the process of getting to know the identity that I hid was helped by the fact that my grandmother moved to Canada. I have enjoyed getting to know her better and listening to her stories and tales about Guatemala. I have realized that there have been a lot of changes in my life, most of which I have had little or no choice about. Some of these changes have been harmful and others have helped me grow.

When I asked my mother if she would be part of this project, she agreed, saying that she saw the project as an opportunity for her and me to become closer and to become friends. This goal was achieved. However the process of writing this piece has been difficult. The interviews were conducted in Spanish, translated into English. I had difficulties with excluding the lives of my other sisters (Gaby, Maria and Andrea) and my dad (Enrique), my brother (Mario) and my grandfather (Chato).

Our whole family has been touched by the events which led up to us moving to Canada; each member has had to develop their own ways of dealing with the situation; each deserves to be heard. My mom says that each of us are linked to one another in our slow, painful and beautiful generational journey towards love, justice and real peace for all. In hearing the voices of three of the family members, our family is represented.

Notes

We are grateful to Annalee Golz, Lynne Marks, Katie Tucker and Beth McAuley for their helpful suggestions and editorial expertise. The mistakes remain our own.

1. These statistics are problematic in that before the 1981 census, each individual had a single ethnicity in the census polls, and this, in a remnant of patriarchal social organization, was determined by the father's ethnicity. In 1981 multiple ethnic origins were allowed, then divided into the various groupings. Jean Barman, *The West Beyond the West: A History of British Columbia* (Toronto: University of Toronto Press, 1991), 363.

2. Barman, *The West Beyond the West,* 369.

3. Adele Perry, "'Oh I'm Just Sick of the Faces of Men': Gender Imbalance, Race, Sexuality, and Sociability in Nineteenth-Century British Columbia," Annalee Golz and Lynne Marks, eds., *B.C. Studies: A Special Double Issue on Women's History and Gender Studies* 105/106 (Spring/Summer 1995), 27.

4. Barman, *The West Beyond the West,* 350.

5. Ibid., 14.

6. Census of Canada (Ottawa: Statistics Canada, 1991. Tables 1, 1A, 1B, 2. Catalogue 93–310). For a recent examination of the effects on Aboriginal children at one BC residential school, see the film *Kuper Island: Return to the Healing Circle,* producers and directors Christine Welsh and Peter C. Campbell, 1997.

7. Barman, *The West Beyond the West,* 145.

8. Mahinder Doman, "A Note on Asian Indian Women in British Columbia, 1900–1935," Barbara K. Latham and Roberta J. Pazdro, eds., *Not Just Pin Money: Selected Essays on the History of Women's Work in British Columbia* (Victoria: Camosun College, 1984), 102.

9. Yuen-Fong Woon, *The Excluded Wife* (Montreal: McGill-Queen's University Press, 1998), ix.

10. Pseudonyms have been given to these women at their request.

11. Audrey Kobayashi, "For the Sake of the Children: Japanese/Canadian Wives/ Mothers," in Audrey Kobayashi, ed., *Women, Work and Place* (Montreal: McGill-Queen's University Press, 1994), 45–72, quoted in Michiko (Midge) Ayukawa, "Good Wives and Wise Mothers: Japanese Picture Brides in Early Twentieth Century British Columbia," in Golz and Marks, eds., *B.C. Studies: A Special Double Issue,* 108.

12. In 1996, Michiko (Midge) Ayukawa completed her PhD dissertation at the University of Victoria entitled, "Creating and Recreating Community: Hiroshima and Canada 1891–1941."

13. Barman, *The West Beyond the West,* 148.

14. Alexander Freund and Laura Qualici, "Exploring Myths in Women's Narratives: Italian and German Immigrant Women in Vancouver, 1947–1961," Golz and Marks, eds., *B.C. Studies: A Special Double Issue*, 163, 168, 181.

15. Barman, *The West Beyond the West*, 143.

16. Gillian Creese and Veronica Strong-Boag, eds., "Introduction," *British Columbia Reconsidered: Essays on Women* (Vancouver: Press Gang, 1992), 6.

17. Michael H. Cramer, "Public and Political: Documents of Woman's Suffrage Campaign in British Columbia, 1871–1917: The View from Victoria," in Creese and Strong-Boag, eds., *British Columbia Reconsidered*, 55–59.

18. Ibid., 59.

19. Margaret Hillyard Little, "Claiming a Unique Place: The Introduction of Mothers' Pensions in B.C.," in Golz and Marks, eds., *B.C. Studies: A Special Double Issue*, 93.

20. Ibid., 91.

21. Angus McLaren and Arlene Tigar McLaren, *The Bedroom and the State: The Changing Practices and Politics of Contraception and Abortion in Canada, 1880–1980* (Toronto: McClelland and Stewart, 1986), 58.

22. Ibid., 60.

23. Ibid., 67.

24. Ibid., 84. For a more detailed study of this phenomenon, see Angus McLaren, *Our Own Master Race: Eugenics in Canada, 1885–1945* (Toronto: McClelland and Stewart, 1990).

25. Gillian Creese, "The Politics of Dependence: Women, Work and Unemployment in the Vancouver Labour Movement Before World War II," Creese and Strong-Boag, eds., *British Columbia Reconsidered*, 365–366.

26. Irene Howard, "The Mothers' Council of Vancouver: Holding the Fort for the Unemployed, 1935–38," *B.C. Studies* 69/70 (Spring/Summer 1986), 249–287.

27. Creese, "The Politics of Dependence," 369.

28. Mary Patricia Powell, "A Response to the Depression: The Local Council of Women of Vancouver," Barbara Latham and Cathy Kess, eds., *In Her Own Right: Selected Essays on Women's History in B.C.* (Victoria: Camosun College, 1980), 255–278.

29. Ruth Roach Pierson, *They're Still Women After All: The Second World War and Canadian Womanhood* (Toronto: McClelland and Stewart, 1986), 12.

30. Ibid., 13.

31. Elsie G. Turnbull, "Women at Cominco During the Second World War," Latham and Pazdro, eds., *Not Just Pin Money*, 429–432.

32. Jill Stainsby, "It's the Smell of Money: Women Shoreworkers of British Columbia," *B.C. Studies* 103 (Fall 1994), 59–81.

33. Marjorie Griffin Cohen, "The Canadian Women's Movement," in Ruth Roach Pierson, Marjorie Griffin Cohen, Paula Bourne, and Philinda Masters, eds., *Canadian Women's Issues: Twenty-Five Years of Women's Activism in English Canada*, Volume I,

Strong Voices (Toronto: James Lorimer and Company, Publishers, 1993), 25, 94–95. See also the autobiographical study, Rosemary Brown, *Being Brown: A Very Public Life* (Toronto: Random House, 1989).

34. Lynda Erickson, "Political Women in a Partisan World: Women Party Activists in British Columbia in the 1980s," in Creese and Strong-Boag, eds., *British Columbia Reconsidered*, 100.

35. *The Emily*, published by women students of the University of Victoria, is Canada's longest-lived student newspaper, and can be found in the archives of the National Library in Ottawa.

36. The struggle of Little Sisters Bookstore in Vancouver, charged with contravening the pornography laws with its imported lesbian erotica, offers one of Canada's most remarkable examples of the struggle against state-imposed censorship. See Janine Fuller and Stuart Blackley, *Restricted Entry: Censorship on Trial* (Vancouver: Press Gang Publishers, 1996).

37. M. Julia Creet, "A Test of Unity: Lesbian Visibility in the British Columbia Federation of Women," Sharon Dale Stone, ed., *Lesbians in Canada* (Toronto: Between the Lines, 1990), 186–187.

38. Ibid., 189–190.

39. Ibid., 195.

40. Nym Hughes, Yvonne Johnson, and Yvette Perrault, *Stepping Out of Line: A Workbook on Lesbianism and Feminism* (Vancouver: Press Gang, 1984).

41. For discussion of the situation and the resistance work, see Gurcharn S. Basran, Charan Gill, and Brian D. MacLean, *Farmworkers and Their Children* (Vancouver: Collective Press, 1995); and Sylvia Bardon, Prince Jusu Nallo, Josie Schofield, and Angela Heck, "The Exploitation and Marginalization of Women Farm Workers in British Columbia" (paper available from offices of VIPIRG, University of Victoria, and the Victoria Status of Women's Action Group, 1995).

42. For discussions of issues important to Latin American women, see *Aquelarre: The Latin American Women's Magazine*, published in Vancouver.

43. The one-hundred-bed tuberculosis sanitorium that was built in New Denver during the war for the incarcerated Japanese-Canadians was used during 1953–1959 as a residential school, where the government kept the children apprehended from the dissident Sons of Freedom sect of the BC Doukhobors. The children were kept behind a high-wire fence, leaving only when bussed to the local school. The aged and infirm Japanese-Canadians still living in New Denver took pity on the children and brought them treats and extended their love. In the spring of 1987, when a group of Japanese-Canadians made an Internment Camp Bus Tour through the Slocan Valley, grateful Doukhobors feted them at Rose's Restaurant in Crescent Valley. — Midge Ayukawa

44. *Entender/Communicar:* To understand/to communicate.

45. *Los querian desaparecer:* Wanted to make them disappear. Making political dissadents "disappear," through kidnapping or extermination, is a form of state intimidation and control.

46. *Que nadie me puede entender. Que puedo commincar con nadie*: No one can understand me. I can communicate with no one.

Study Questions

1. How did the various women in the six stories react to being asked to narrate their own lives? Can you determine the reactions of the six authors to the stories they were hearing? What problems or barriers might the authors encounter in their task of interpreting the narrated stories?

2. This chapter chooses to gather stories of different ethnic groups in order to give, in these few pages, as broad a picture as possible of life in the province. Comparing the different family stories here, examine the ways each family's different background and position in British Columbian society created both oppressions and opportunities for the women.

3. What do you know of your own family's history and the effects on your family of their economic, ethnic and geographic locations over the last several generations? How do the gender roles vary within each generation and across generations? How would you go about discovering this information if you were unable to use the tool of oral history employed by these six authors?

4. What are some of the ethical challenges facing the interviewers in these stories and how do they resolve them? How would you have responded to these challenges?

5. In the past, the mainstream women's movement has not been inclusive of diversity, and this is an issue that many women are currently struggling with as they attempt to create a more diverse and representative political movement. What are the specific commonalities and what are the significant differences in the life experiences of the women interviewed for these stories? How would we need to take account of both commonalities and differences if we are to create effective coalitions?

ALBERTA

St. Albert
Edmonton
Red Deer
Jasper
Lake Louise
Calgary
Okotoks

High River

Bassano
Lethbridge
Redcliff

Brooks
Medicine Hat

• Saskatoon, Saskatchewan

• Regina, Saskatchewan

• Winnipeg, Manitoba

• Moncton, New Brunswick
• Halifax, Nova Scotia

"OUR SKY"

Eliane Silverman

◄○►

ALBERTA IS A PROVINCE whose geography cannot be ignored. Land and sky have combined to create the backdrop for its history. The people of Alberta are always conscious of the natural environment. The view from here is first the sky; it is immense, intensely blue much of the time, its clouds always dramatic. The climate is dramatic, too, piercingly cold and windy in winter, dry and scorching in summers that are punctuated by violent lightning storms and pounding hail. Women in Alberta — Native and non-Native alike — have been influenced by the natural world, not desiring to control or master it but allowing themselves to be formed by its sounds and its forms.

Women of the First Nations knew the land first. The dense brush and forest of the north, the windswept prairies of the south, and the towering mountains of the west have provided Native women the settings to do their work. Native peoples included the Blackfoot, the Blood and the Peigan of the Plains Indians, and the Chipewyan, Slavey and Beaver of the Woodland tribes. Up north they trapped and fished the profuse land and lakes; the buffalo in the south gave them an economy of plenty. Native women lived with their communities in the mountains only until the seventeenth century, but the mountains continue to serve as spiritual homes for Native peoples and as a setting for their legends. In their communities, young women were taught the important tasks of cooking, skinning, tanning and making clothing. Women provided healthcare, childcare and aesthetic needs. In addition to looking after the needs of children and men, Native women held important political and spiritual roles in their societies — a status they lost with European contact. When some Native women assimilated into white European society, brought by men who were trappers and traders in the nineteenth century, their roles as care givers and providers in the private sphere were reinforced.[1] For thousands of years, Native women inhabited the land and created cultures of women. But in the 1800s, these cultures were severely damaged by European contact and settlement of the West. Government policies pushed Native culture to the margins of the newly forming white society, restricting their lives and existence to the boundaries of reserves. Native women continued to play key roles in the preservation and revitalization of their societies. In their communities of the late twentieth century, Native women are reclaiming their social status and participating in the reconstruction of their culture.

European women who arrived here as settlers found it difficult to inhabit the land. Alberta was the site of the last land rush in North America. In the 1800s, the Canadian federal government offered free homesteads to settlers in exchange for making improvements to the land: breaking sod and clearing the bush, building cabins and putting in fencing. Through homesteading, economic and psychological opportunities became available for Europeans who were both pushed out of their countries of origin and pulled across the ocean. Freedom beckoned to men, and usually their daughters and wives accompanied them, but some women came on their own, seeking adventure or desperate to leave their old lives behind. Government and railroad advertisements described an abundant future for the settlers they longed to attract to populate the West, provide markets for eastern products, and supply wheat and cattle the railroads would carry to other areas of Canada and the US. Women's roles were clear in this new society: they would bear children to provide the labour necessary in a growing economy and they would provide their own labour on farms, in paid workplaces and in households to shape the future province. But they also had to contend with the geography.

By 1885, women settlers began to arrive in rural areas and small towns. They came by wagons drawn by oxen and in horse-drawn carts, but mostly they came by the railroad, "to the end of the steel," as they said, as far as the tracks had been laid. They came from Western Europe and from Ukraine, from the United States and from Eastern Canada. White women and Black women. Jews and Christians. They came from China to join their husbands who worked on the railroads. They worked along with their husbands and community to establish wheat and cattle ranches in the southern prairies. They supplied labour to the forest industry and coal mines of the mountains and the foothills, and to the growing industries of the expanding cities.[2]

Alberta's population grew from 78,000 in 1900 to nearly ten times that in 1929, at the beginning of the Great Depression. The incoming settlers little knew what they would need in the new world. Some women brought as much of their old lives as they could — pianos, feather beds, cooking utensils to perpetuate old culinary arts and familiar cultures. Others came with very little, sometimes thriving as the years went by, sometimes sinking into depression, anxiety and despair. The migrations continue today, over a hundred years later, with newcomers arriving from Latin American countries, from the Caribbean, from India and Hong Kong. They come alone or with relatives, even with whole villages, pushed from their places of origin to the unknown. They continue to arrive for the same kinds of reasons — to escape hunger, deprivation or tyranny, in search of prosperity and with hope for something better. And they continue to bring new languages, new ways of farming or of doing business, different modes of child rearing, hopes for better healthcare and better educational systems for their own and other people's children. Alberta continues to change, but the geography remains the same.

Perhaps the geography created the sense of isolation that the women settlers experienced, or maybe the sky intensified their loneliness. Those who came with a community of people from their homeland were able to join others whose ways they knew; they could feel more connected. Their language might separate them from the region, but they had a community, a Norwegian community, say, or an Italian or a Chilean one. Other women, who came alone or with only an immediate family, began to create the institutions which would make the new environment feel more like a society. They began to alter the experience of frontier isolation, turning their loneliness and their need for connections into the beginnings of a culture with clubs, schools, healthcare facilities, public places for recreation and churches. Alberta's women settlers involved themselves in creating all these and more, in an ongoing attempt to create a culture in which to locate and ground themselves, an attempt to feel the loss of departure less keenly. They were looking for organization, for institutions, for human society — for a social order that would counteract the unpredictability of the land and the sky.

Women settlers from all backgrounds began to form groups and make a place for themselves in the new society. They needed to be able to live here and feel at home. The isolation that almost all settlers experienced had to be overcome; women had to connect with other women. auxiliaries The United Farm Women of Alberta, women's auxiliaries of political parties, literary societies and chapters of the National Council of Women, the YWCA, cultural associations, the Women's Institutes — all these attracted rural and urban women.[3] They came together for reasons of community, especially for community with women, but they soon agitate began to agitate for social and political change. As women joined with one another, they began to comment on what was not working well, be it the paucity of schools, or women's lack of access to university education, paucity or the absence of social halls where people of the community could meet. Furthermore, they recognized that women's and children's daily linoleum needs for things even as basic as indoor plumbing and linoleum on the floors would continue to take second place as men's money was spent on men's things: machines and tractors and expensive bulls.

By the 1920s, Alberta's women had become influenced by the American and English suffragists. They began to think about the limitations of their sex. They began to see that their labour and intelligence was being taken for granted and that they had no political voice. Some women decided to find a way to play a role in the political development of the province. The frontier demanded women's active involvement in making a new society. Women were more confident, perhaps, than in other regions of Canada because their roles were integral to the growth of Alberta's economy. They farmed with their fathers and husbands. They worked in chocolate factories in Calgary and at Great Western Garment in Edmonton. They made altar cloths for churches and paid for and furnished church buildings so that ministers could live there permanently. They delivered each other's babies, sewed for their families and cooked huge meals for threshing crews at harvest time.

Now, their husbands' and fathers' labours were beginning to show some results. Sod houses were replaced by clapboard structures. Wooden sidewalks were laid over the muddy streets of villages and towns. Men laid in place the institutional accoutrements of society — governments, schools, courts. They were becoming richer. And as some of them turned from farming to industry and to business and professions, they became rich enough to want their wives not to work for pay. The middle class was born, and middle-class women began to take on new roles as they relinquished economic productivity. They became the guardians of children and did the emotional homework of their households even as they did all its physical unpaid labour. They were responsible for creating the homes that by the early twentieth century were increasingly represented as refuges from the competition of the growing frontier. The worlds of women and men — the private and public spheres — came to resemble each other less and less; men and women came to seem more like different kinds of people. Men were raised to be aggressive, competitive and individualistic; women were supposed to be obedient, compassionate and nurturing. The "lady" was born.

Alberta's middle-class women of various European and North American backgrounds began to understand themselves as different in particular ways from men. As they gained greater control within their own households, they began to realize that their world could expand, and that just as they were responsible for the emotional climate of domestic life, so could they play a similar role in the public sphere. There was little doubt in their minds that the influence of women in the public sphere would benefit society. This was the thought that motivated some Alberta women to enter the temperance movement for the prohibition of alcohol. They saw that drunken men behaved very badly, especially by being violent towards women and children; they would reform men with their benign influence. Women could, in short, uplift men and improve public life.[4]

One of the most important and direct ways that some women could express their desire to engage in public life was through the women's suffrage movement, which demanded the most visible symbol of democratic citizenship for women — the vote.[5] The provincial vote for women was achieved in 1916 by a concerted strategic campaign waged by some very smart and energetic activists of first-wave feminism. Not all women were included in this struggle, however. Many farm women had the opinion that winning political reform would have little effect on their lives. Their paid and unpaid labour would continue unchanged, they felt, even though suffragists also campaigned for better wages for women. While groups like the United Farm Women of Alberta ultimately supported the vote for women, most of their members were not very enthusiastic, one way or the other. In a sense, they felt it was the campaign of "ladies," not of themselves. And perhaps it was; this remains a question to debate. Did suffragists intend to include only people like themselves as voters, or did they envision a truly inclusive, democratic society?

How interesting to see that in this first women's movement, the divisions among Alberta's women were connected to perceptions of class and power — who had it? who didn't? If women could see themselves as activists, they were able to conceive of having domestic or public power. Power and influence would belong to them, they tended to think, based on their unique and probably innate perceptions of social injustice; they would act on their perceptions out of their uniquely moral knowledge. But other women did not see themselves as players in the political arena — unless they belonged to women's organizations whose platforms put women squarely into political work. And then their involvement was more at the local/municipal level of politics. Farm women were in this category, so were women who worked for pay in the industries of Calgary and Edmonton, the province's largest cities. In the 1910s, a few women began thinking about the role of city or provincial governments in regulating workplaces. Some women, by the 1920s, entered labour union activism, others entered municipal politics and yet others created or joined new political parties, such as the Communist Party and local socialist parties, that advocated for people at the margins. Teachers joined together in the Alberta Teachers Alliance in 1917, and two years later they went on strike for a week in Edmonton — that was the first teachers' strike in Canada. Edmonton waitresses became union members and succeeded in cutting their work week and raising their wages, not great material advances since their work remained ill-paid and demanding, but a sign nonetheless of growing political consciousness among women.[6] Throughout all of these political activities, the ongoing question that would remain for Alberta women was, How does one best exercise power?

The struggle for the vote, even though it did not actively engage all women, nonetheless lives on as an important symbol and its success survives as a turning point for women in Canada. The struggle began in 1914, when the Edmonton Equal Franchise League and the Calgary

Local Council of Women presented a petition with twelve thousand signatures to the provincial government, demanding the vote for women. When Alberta women won the vote in 1916, the politicians were persuaded that the "ladies" would help keep them in power. Willing to use any ploy to gain political recognition, suffragists active in the campaign did not disabuse male leaders of this thought, even though they intended to apply their independent minds and capacity to learn for their own means. The initial victory was not universal suffrage for all women but was limited to women of English descent and to those related to servicemen; universal suffrage came later. The stage was set for defining women's political action as radical resistance or maintenance of traditional gender arrangements. However, it was often men with power who defined those actions, rewarding one, not rewarding the other, hoping to make alliances with "ladies" and to silence potentially radical women.

Fortunately, most women interested in making social, political and economic changes were unwilling to be labelled or manipulated. For example, Emily Murphy, Nellie McClung, Louise McKinney, Irene Parlby and Henrietta Muir Edwards petitioned for women's right to sit in the Senate. The Supreme Court ruled that they could not, as they were not "fit and qualified persons." Known as the Famous Five, these women took their case to the Privy Council in England, who on October 18, 1929, designated women as persons.[7] Were these women radical in hoping to extend women's rights as citizens? Did they represent the centre and not the margins? Did they simply reinforce the positions of power of white middle-class women who might actually aspire to serving in the Senate? Do labels applied to women activists separate them from other women?

Let us consider a more contemporary example of such questions. In Calgary there is a group of women who are incorporated as the Famous Five Foundation. This group of women worked ardently between 1995 and 1999 to raise money for two sculptures to commemorate the seventieth anniversary of the Persons Case, celebrated on October 18, 1999. To honour the five women's achievement, a sculpture is to be raised in Calgary in 1999 and another statue of the five is to be installed in Ottawa in 2000 — they are the only women besides Queen Victoria represented in public statuary on Parliament Hill. The Foundation women who made this happen are well-established public people

and could be thought of as mainstream women. However, the programs
they have instituted in connection with the anniversary have included
programs heavily funded by women who could afford them: luncheons
to which young high-school women are invited as guests; scholarship
programs; women's history programs in the schools; and an international conference on the rights of persons. The Foundation board
members have also been active, over the last thirty years, in abortion
law reform, divorce law changes, advocacy against women's and children's
poverty, improved women's healthcare, *Indian Act* reform, establishing
women's advisory councils inside governments, media monitoring,
campaigns for women's advancement in industry, immigrant women's
centres and improved childcare. Are they radical women? Are they not?
They are obviously hard to label; indeed, should we be so quick to want
to do so? Are we only adopting definitions used by the opponents of
people who advocate, noisily, intelligently and, yes, stridently for improvements to the status of all women of all classes and races?

In Alberta, it has been almost customary and far too easy to dichot-
omize or polarize women into good women and bad, into supporters of
the status quo and radicals, into feminine women and feminist women.
While the word "feminist" only came into common usage here in 1970,
despite its much earlier origins, the sentiments arrayed against the idea
of women's potential for autonomy, independence and wholeness have
been long-standing and potent. Alberta's economy, religion and politics
have lent themselves to leaving women out and deriding women who
have sought power. Until recently, Alberta's economy has been called
resource-based, which means that coal and oil have dominated its prosperity, supplemented by the cattle and wheat ranches. These industries
have traditionally been male preserves, their need to exclude women
buttressed by frontier myths of male superiority and male bonding;
women were not even allowed into the lunch clubs where men talked
business. Only in the 1990s did women start entering senior management
ranks, many of them fully aware of the barriers they needed to break.
But these barriers continue to be in place, even in the new technological
and financial sectors taking hold in cities like Calgary. One can only hope
that women who reach senior positions in these industries will agitate
for improved working conditions for all women.

Alberta's religious history has also created impediments to changes in the status of women. Fundamentalist and evangelical Protestantism are both a religious and a political force that women must contend with. Their male leaders often enter the political arena, as they did during the Great Depression of the 1930s when the Social Credit government began its thirty-year reign. The Social Credit party was clearly dedicated to preservation of its own power, and embedded in Social Credit pater-nalism was a vision of the right kind of family, headed by a man who, even while he might be gentle and kindly, must be obeyed by his wife, his subsidiary and auxiliary, his helpmeet, as they said. Both parents must be obeyed by their children. It was a pyramidic or hierarchic arrangement that replicated church organization, with God at the top, ministers below and members of the congregation below that. These kinds of relationships still persist as the ideal in Alberta's fundamentalist churches.

While the majority of Albertans probably do not adhere to such a rigid patriarchal configuration of families, the fundamentalist presence in politics has created difficulties for women who want to make diverse social changes. For women who are not necessarily political activists, views of marriage — the very necessity, indeed, of heterosexual marriage — as the appropriate adult goal have often gone unquestioned. As we will see, even the youngest generation represented in this chapter expects some day to marry. These are women who certainly hope to make a living for themselves; they are unlikely to need husbands to do so for them. They speak about financial independence as a goal, their income deriving from interesting careers. And yet, traditional configurations of families are the norm. It is possible, however, that their exposure to their contemporaries and to Canadian and international changes in the status of women may change their views on marriage and the family.

The Irene Murdoch divorce case of 1973 shocked Canadian women into recognizing how tenuous their position was within marriage and family property law. When Murdoch sued for divorce in 1968, she claimed a share of the family ranch, which she had worked for twenty-five years. The judge denied her anything, saying she had only done what any farm wife was expected to do. After five years of appeals, Murdoch was granted a lump-sum maintenance payment, but received no entitlements to the property or to economic benefits from the ranch to which she had contributed. The Murdoch case was truly a monumental turning point in the self-consciousness of Alberta's women.

They had learned that women would have to fight for their economic entitlements.[8]

Certainly, women today are surrounded by dramatic events, many of which originated as a result of second-wave feminism. The second wave probably began in Calgary in 1970 with the founding of the Calgary Abortion Information Centre. From this small group of seven volunteer feminists in their twenties and thirties grew many other feminist groups dedicated to cultural, legal and political change. Rape crisis centres, distress hotlines and battered women's shelters came out of a recognition of the social problems women face daily. Volunteers working for reproductive choice set a model for other feminists to follow. They took the information they were gathering from their experiences with women clients, friends and each other into the public eye: to governments, to high schools, to newspapers, to hospitals. They learned how to work with the police, school administrators, lawyers and doctors — and most importantly, with women themselves. In the reproductive choice movement, activists saw that women no longer wanted advice, they wanted information about their bodies — information they could easily understand and assess. Women wanted to weigh their alternatives and make decisions about their own lives. From reproductive to legal rights, feminist activists fought for official recognition at provincial and municipal levels. The Calgary Status of Women Action Committee and the Alberta Status of Women Action Committee were established in 1980, and the Alberta branch of the Women's Education and Legal Defence Fund (LEAF) in 1985. Lesbians established the Lesbian Mothers' Defence Fund, which by the 1990s had grown into a drop-in centre. Feminist psychologists started co-operative therapy clinics. The list could go on and on. The developments of the 1970s and 1980s were dramatic examples of a feminist rebirth.

These activities did not go unnoticed by the provincial government, which responded to public pressure. The government funded women's conferences within the province, in which rural and urban women met one another, shared observations and created provincial networks. In 1985, after years of feminist pressure, the government established the Alberta Women's Secretariat and hired a staff of women to run it. The Secretariat's budget enabled them to research workplace, childcare and household issues. But the organization was not empowered to lobby the government on behalf of women. Despite its best intentions, it often lacked credibility within the impatient women's communities, while at the same time the government gave it little credence. By the 1990s, however, the Conservative agenda began to implement its fiscal and political restraints and the government shut it down. Today, the vast majority of Tory politicians pay women's issues little attention — funding for many women's initiatives have been and continue to be drastically cut. In a conservative, even retrograde, political climate, women's needs have been redefined as families' needs — as if women existed only as heterosexual wives and mothers. Women's rights are threatened and feminist activists are reviled. Most reviled are lesbian rights activists. Lesbians are deeply suspect, even to the extent that their right to be foster parents is being questioned, same-sex marriage is not sanctioned and homosexuality is not protected under the *Alberta Human Rights Protection Act*. Obviously, diverging from veneration of the white, Christian, old-fashioned ways is not a good thing here! And yet Alberta women continue to be adamant in their quest for autonomy, economic possibilities and political and legal rights.[9]

Over the years, philosophies have changed, strategies have expanded, some feminists have grown old and died, and younger women from unions, churches, universities or no particular affiliation have entered feminist organizations. New organizations have grown: Native women's groups, high-school women's organizations, ever more battered women's shelters, the Women of Colour Collective. Women's Studies in the universities has blossomed and feminists continue to write and publish. But many of the same questions persist: Should we work inside power structures? Do we remain purer outside them? Who should our constituencies be? When and how shall we make coalitions? Which issues are most meaningful to women of colour? working women? women with children? lesbians? Are we effective? No matter the answers, not one Alberta feminist has ceased to be a feminist. Not one has recanted; not one has written she had been wrong. Feminism in Alberta can be an incredibly strong bond among women because of the political, social and economic climate that surrounds us: icy glares must be warmed by passion — and by friendship and trust. Overall, Alberta's feminists get along well with one another, perhaps better than elsewhere in the country, because whether blue collar or pink collar, professional or unemployed, straight or lesbian, and no matter our cultural/racial background, we need one another in a hostile political and social climate.

Women are changing Alberta. Women of colour, women with disabilities, married women and single mothers, new immigrants, farm women — we are all overcoming the isolation of the prairies. We are working together to plan strategies and finding ways of implementing them in the political arena, in the boardrooms, courts and schools of our society. We are tapping into our energy and our ideals so we can bring the prospect of a more generous society to fruition.

Young women, like the four undergraduate students who collected the interviews for this chapter, stand at a junction in Alberta's history. They can face forward and combat racism, sexism and homophobia in concert with other women born here and elsewhere. They can join the political struggles of equality-seeking people and fight for expanded daycare, higher minimum wages, justice for Native peoples and for gay and lesbian rights. Or they can face backward towards the mainstream tradition that has perpetuated the power of a few white men. We cannot know now which direction they will go in the future.

The women's stories in this chapter give us a glimpse of the many changes that women in Alberta have experienced, a glimpse into their lives and the directions they have chosen. These stories were gathered by Kelly Anderson, Leita Blasetti, Kathy Cardinal and Christine Forner — four students in Women's Studies at the University of Calgary. They each interviewed their grandmothers and mothers and then interviewed each other. They are women of Alberta who have experienced many of the social and political themes we have just discussed. As they are a random group of women, they should not be understood as representative of Alberta's women. Their stories, however, are part of the generational fabric of the province, unique to time and place and yet part of a collective voice that we must hear.

We begin with the generation of the grandmothers, and will talk about each woman in order of her date of birth. The four women of this generation were all born during or after first-wave feminism. Their dates of birth span twenty-six years, and so they were influenced by different local and international events. While they may say that they were largely untouched by the social politics of first-wave feminism, they nonetheless saw its effects on their personal lives.

Grandmothers: Boundaries

Katherine Addy was born in New Brunswick in 1912. Most of her childhood was spent there; she married there in 1931. She and her husband came west to Winnipeg, where Katherine raised two children. There she volunteered extensively with the United Church, becoming president of the United Church Women; she volunteered in hospitals, too. In 1989, ten years after her husband's death, she moved out of their home and into an apartment. She now has the freedom, she says, to travel around the world. She began a new phase of her life in 1993 by moving to Alberta, to Jasper in the Rocky Mountains, to be near her daughter.

Katherine has seen both of the feminist movements of this century and is not much taken with their benefits. She fears that women over the course of the century have become "more aggressive," especially in their relations with men — clearly not a good thing; yet she believes that "it is a wise young man and woman who know their way around a kitchen." Domestic skills are practical for both sexes, but she does not care for women's taking men's places in public, entering what she believes to be the realm of men. The sight of "a lady in the pulpit" does not please her, and "if women want to play ball, they should form their own teams and not play on men's."

It may be that Katherine's choices about her own life and her opinions about the lives of others were affected by her generation's expectation that women would marry. When doing so they learned a certain helplessness, probably intensified by limited control over finances, especially in the cases of women who did not work for pay. Both she and her husband were raised, Katherine Addy said, to know their sex roles — he did what was "manly." In her own childhood, in the 1920s, girls learned their lessons well. Her father went to work and her mother took care of "the castle." All of this has become badly confused, she fears. The women's movement, she says, reflecting both on what the women's magazines of the 1950s advised and what antifeminist articles at present describe, has simply turned women into complainers. "A woman should not complain to a man when he comes home from work. Don't meet him at the door with your complaints." Katherine clearly believes that the polarities which were men's realms and women's

· 89 ·

realms must for the moment be perpetuated. And yet she does not entirely close the door on change: "Women should not be impatient because change takes time," she concludes.

Madge McAdam was born in 1917, in England. Her family emigrated to Alberta, starting with farming and then moving to the city. Madge fulfilled her dream to become a nurse, and worked in a tuberculosis sanatorium in Calgary, which was considered the kind of dry climate beneficial for people with the disease. She married during the Second World War and had three children. They grew up in the house where she still resides. Madge stayed at home until her children were in high school, then for financial reasons went to work in a bookstore. Eventually, she took a retraining course in nursing and worked as a nurse and an administrator until her retirement. She currently volunteers at the Rocky View Hospital and has received a national award for her work.

She looks back at the socialization of women in her earlier years; clearly she has observed great changes in sex roles over the course of her life. The contemporary women's movement has affected them, she says, "women and men are closer now, and boys and girls can talk more easily." She has more to say about heterosexual relations. "In my generation, you knew where your place was. You were the wife. As for me, besides being a nurse, I wanted to marry, have children, and have a nice home, and I wanted to have frilly curtains on every window. You were supposed to stay at home and be a housewife." Having children forced her to challenge herself, getting involved in her children's education, thereby developing organizational skills and learning perseverance. The more she became involved, the more confidence she developed. "Had I not had children I doubt I would have done that. I would have been a 'yes' person." After their husbands' deaths, women had to rely more on themselves, doing things like writing cheques which their husbands had done before. She herself took her nursing refresher course when her children were grown and returned to the paid labour force. Madge never relinquished her dream of being a nurse, and returned to it when she was at liberty to do so, bringing to her profession the skills and the self-confidence she had developed over the years.

Madge has experienced the effects of both first-wave and second-wave feminism on the choices she has been able to make in her personal life. She does not recognize its benefits as a political movement or a social movement, however, and expresses ambivalence about the effects she sees in public life. "I am just now beginning not to expect a man to hold the door open for me, and I think that women are missing something when we let that go." She is not expressing profound antifeminism here, but rather a fear for the loss of civility as she understands it, marked by her social and life experiences. "It was nice to get attention from men." And yet, "Women have got to stand up to males, have got to be equal. I hope that women are not always being put down by men." She affirms her growing sense of self, released a bit more, perhaps, from heterosexual obligations: "I think I have more confidence now than I had fifty years ago. I hope I have."

Jenny Niznik was born to Ukrainian immigrant parents in a small Alberta town in 1923. She met her husband in Cassils, when she was in high school, and they married in 1941 when she was eighteen. They settled on family land 20 kilometres from the farming community of Brooks. Over thirteen years, Jenny gave birth to four boys and a girl. She still resides in the house she and her husband built when they married. The domestic and childcare work was, without a doubt, her own. Cooking and cleaning were only the work of women, as was "keeping peace in the home." She learned her gender lessons early, when she had to look after the younger children; her brother, a year and a half younger, did none of the childcare. Nonetheless, she never found her childhood and youth isolating or restrictive. Frontier girls had more liberties than urban girls, being able to range over more open countryside, having to go further afield for their schooling and their friendships.

The world of women had its attractions. Particularly in a frontier society in a farming community, the connections among women became life-sustaining. Jenny found other women a source of support and companionship. Neighbours, one of whom was a midwife, or her mother or mother-in-law came to help her with her children and her daily chores when the children were born. "Women should work together," she said. "We used to get together and do big meals around Christmas and brandings. We used to do pancake breakfasts." She did not feel lonely in those years.

However, when her children finished school, she felt cut off from town life, since her children had "told me about the happenings of the town." She was particularly lonely after her daughter grew up and left home. Her children were her true connection to contemporary life. After her husband died, Jenny seemed not to seek out women's company, but rather visited with her family or did things alone. "The winters are harder. Being by yourself kind of gets to you." She now does many things by herself that would have made her very self-conscious before, like going out for dinner. She, too, never knew how to write cheques before her husband's death. Despite having learned some independence, she worries that feminism simply means more "boldness," more freedom of thought, and she fears that it will go too far. "The women's movement sometimes gets carried away," she says, but unfortunately does not clarify what she means. Can it be that she is simply responding to antifeminist propaganda? Like Katherine Addy, Jenny Niznik's personal mobility has expanded over her lifetime, but she does not connect that with new possibilities offered women by second-wave feminism.

Elisabeth Sharfe is the youngest of the generation of grandmothers, born in 1938 in Germany. She and her husband emigrated to Canada in 1963. They came first to one small town in the southern part of the province, later buying a farm just outside of Brooks, where they did mixed farming. Elisabeth had been trained as a kindergarten teacher in Germany, but in having to upgrade her education, she completed a degree in education and now teaches near Brooks. She has four children, two girls and two boys.

Elisabeth has experienced first-hand some of the restrictions on women's lives. As a young woman, she had wanted to become a home economics teacher, but "Dad said that was a lot of time in school. If I got married, then the education was a waste both in terms of his money and my time." She insists on having some financial control in her household; she has her own bank account so that she does not have to "worry about my husband's side of the spending." Despite her earning power and her decision to proclaim a degree of financial independence from her husband, she also maintains the small-town tradition of connections among women. Upon her arrival in Canada, women in her rural community offered her help, and when she became more established she in turn sought to help other women. "There were garden bazaars, afternoon teas for new people moving into the community. Neighbours were logical for friendship." Social activism grew out of those friendships.

"Should we provide daycare? Transportation for disabled people? School playground upgrading? In retrospect, it was the women's groups that were the social support for the community. Oftentimes the work is just expected, but I don't think that women would be happy if they weren't allowed to do it."

None of this work, though, was undertaken in the name of feminism. Nor has Elisabeth thought highly of the women's movement. Her own work experiences notwithstanding, she believes that "you can't carry on a full-time job and be a full-time mother." Despite saying that, she does not question "mothers' centrality to the family," nor does she seem prepared to reconsider sex roles. Feminism's emphasis on women is misplaced, she thinks. "I do not agree with feminism. It is much broader than that, standing up for women's rights and everybody's rights. I wouldn't exclude men. I don't have to go out and be militant about it. When working with children, for example, one can't only deal with girls." Her "humanism" may be for her the most workable response to a farming community which, as her daughter Kathy Cardinal recalls, "discriminated against anyone that was different. Also it was very sexist: an oil community, a working man's community, and women were very much verbally abused. The working man was the ideal."

Growing up here will also have influenced Kathy, as we will see when we listen to the next generation's stories. Feminist sentiments will have a hard time making their way in a region of masculinity unleashed and glorified. The kinds of social change that Elisabeth participates in with other women cannot, apparently, be undertaken in the name of women. Yet even so, Elisabeth yearns for some of feminism's benefits — time alone, time for herself, even silence. She would like to take a computer course, and she loves the peace and quiet of being alone. She will never forget her first time alone away from home. "I was away sitting by myself with a book and thinking, 'I don't have to eat when someone else wants to or I could sit and read the book if I wanted or I could go to bed.'" However, like the other grandmothers, she is not able to make the connection between her own need for independence and how feminism has addressed that need. Asking outright for independence may be too scary, for now.

MOTHERS: TENTATIVE STEPS

Let us move on now to the next generation — the daughters of the four grandmothers. In their lives, they are mothers. *Linda Anderson* is Katherine Addy's daughter. She was born in New Brunswick, in 1947, moving to Winnipeg as a child, where she later attended nursing school. In 1969, she travelled to the Rocky Mountains in Alberta. She met her husband there and they moved together to Calgary, where she had two daughters. She lives now in Jasper, volunteering as the pastoral care co-ordinator for the local hospital. In her youth, she says, she was directed only to train for nursing or teaching. "I honestly don't know what else I could have been. I was never encouraged to think about it." While her working life took place in the female-dominated profession of nursing, she did not connect with women politically either through the nurses' union, which is strong and organized in Alberta, or through the contemporary women's movement. And yet, there are hints of a vision of the profession as an expansive setting for women. She observed, "I had two aunts who were held up as role models because of their careers as nurses. Really they were 'spinsters' and my father admired their independence." A curious comment: her career choice was influenced by her family. Did her father not expect that women must marry? If so, he would have been unusual for his period and class; even more necessary than a nursing career was marriage.

Linda Blasetti, Madge McAdams's daughter, was born in 1947 in Regina, though she grew up in Calgary. Of Scottish and English heritage, she represents the dominant cultural majority of the province during her early years here. She characterized her childhood as "probably very typical of middle-class fifties upbringing." It was probably typical only of an Anglo-Saxon upbringing, and not typical of a middle-class youth from a different racial heritage. Linda clearly says that at no time did she feel excluded. It is unlikely that a member of the majority population would experience discrimination.

She went to university in Edmonton to study nursing, in time-honoured fashion, and in similarly time-honoured fashion married a man in the army after her education was completed. His army career moved them around the country. Their first child was born in Halifax. They returned to Alberta where she had two more daughters while living in a small town surrounded by farms, south of Calgary. While her children were young, Linda did not work for pay, but returned to the paid workforce in the late 1980s as the volunteer co-ordinator for the town of Okotoks. She suggests that she worked out of necessity. By the time her children were in their adolescent years, "it was evident that women were going to have to be working. Two incomes would be required to support families." Her comment was directed at her daughters as much as at herself.

She is right, of course. Single women clearly must work; women in a household with two adults are likely to need to work, too, since the concept of a family wage — usually the male head of the family making enough money to support a family — has virtually disappeared. Increasing numbers of women over the course of the century have worked for pay. Everybody is paid less now. The nostalgic public rhetoric about "the Alberta family," which hopes to re-create an imaginary world in which men took care of finances and women looked after the emotions, is a contemporary reprise of the "frontier family" theme, replete with strong men and doting women. Public constructions of ideal family life are one thing, personal and economic realities quite another. The middle generation, the mothers, even as they worked for pay, still thought it was their duty to give the illusion of not being workers, of being supportive of their husbands' ambitions and quiet about their own.

Oddly enough, *Fiona Forner*, the third woman of this generation, was also a nurse. Perhaps it is not so odd: these women are from a generation whose educational opportunities by and large extended to nursing, teaching and clerical work. Fiona Forner is the daughter of Jenny Niznik. She was born in 1943 and lived on her parents' farm until she finished high school. Sex roles were rigidly observed, she said. Women were in the house and men were outside. Her brothers never helped with indoor work, while she never did farm work. "When I was looking for a career, women were either a nurse or secretary or teacher." She began her career as a nurse in Medicine Hat, where she met and married her husband in 1964. The couple and their three daughters lived throughout the western provinces; Fiona worked as a nurse during her entire marriage. Despite her financial contribution, and despite managing the daily expenses of their household, she says that she felt very little control over the family's finances. She managed daily expenses but did not control major financial decisions and was informed of them only when her husband chose to tell her. Her daughter added, probably referring to Fiona's experience, that women are often left ignorant of the "financial working of the world," leaving them with feelings of naiveté and powerlessness.

Thus far, the mothers here seem to express little affiliation with the contemporary women's movement, very little more, indeed, than their mothers. Fiona says, "Feminism is defending the rights of women. The feminist movement is a good thing. I don't think it necessarily has to be called feminism. What feminism wants for women should be made available to men or women. It's the rights of a human being, that's what it is." The mothers agree that women should have the same rights as men, but find, as the grandmothers did, that change is happening too quickly and express their fear that a backlash will result. Yet they mitigate any possible accusations of feminism by saying that, really, all people need to be treated equally.

The fourth member of this generation, *Kathy Cardinal,* the daughter of Elisabeth Sharfe, is frankly a feminist. She was born in 1959 and may not fit chronologically with this middle generation of mothers. There she is, however, both a daughter and a mother. She serves as a transition to the generation of daughters. As we have seen, the middle generation, three of them born in the 1940s, is more like than unlike the grandmother generation. Considerably younger, Kathy's experiences and thoughts reflect the influence of the contemporary women's movement. She was born in Germany, and immigrated with her parents to Brooks at the age of four. Arriving without speaking English, she found that she was "treated very meanly and rudely," a target of the ethnocentricity of too many Canadian children. In 1980 she moved to Red Deer, a small city midway between Calgary and Edmonton, to study art at the college there, eventually taking science courses. She divorced her husband in 1991, and Kathy moved to Calgary with her three children, where she attended university. She majored in microbiology with a minor in Women's Studies, and is now about to complete medical school.

Feminism for her is quite simply "empowering women." She believes women can control their lives, although it is certainly not easy. "I had always thought that the government would never support a single parent with three children through university, let alone support my studies to become a doctor. I suddenly realized that none of this was true and that it was just a myth to make sure that I stayed where I was." Perhaps she had an early start in thinking about the politics of everyday life by modelling herself on her grandmother. "She was active politically long before women were commonly in public roles and she didn't do much housework. I admired her because she was the head of the household and because material possessions didn't mean much to her. She was more concerned that the family down the street had enough to eat."

Kathy explores the conflicts in her life — studying, raising children, working for pay. "Sometimes I feel like I am swinging back and forth. I am putting too much energy in at home and then I have to put more in at work and then there isn't enough left for home and so on and so on and so on." She has had to do all this on her own since her divorce.

At that time, in her twenties, she met a group of women who, she says, "rescued" her after her divorce, saving her sense of self and helping her re-create a rich life for herself and her children. Together, they explored myths constraining women, "the whole media image of a heterosexual family with two children as the ideal to strive for." She is distressed by many myths about women and families including "the disproportionate glorification of single fatherhood in the media right now." The myth that affects her most is that "parents' divorce supposedly predestines children to low marks." She shakes her head: her daughter's teacher expressed his surprise that the honours student came from a single-parent home.

Kathy finds a safe place in her connections with women. "My communities have invariably been communities of women. Men seem to drift in and out of my life but my community of women is ever present and ever expanding." Her circle of friends arrived at the perfect moment. "I'm not sure why we developed the friendships because they are all very educated and at the time I was not. They are all politically and socially active. We used to sit together for hours drinking tea, nursing babies and arguing about politics, parenthood and other social issues." Despite her close friendships she, like the other mothers and grandmothers, seems to assume heterosexuality as unquestionably the norm; she hopes her daughter will marry and have children, as well as an education, a career and financial security. While the economic roles of women of her age have changed, domestic arrangements are not much different than in the past — at least for the time being. Still, female friendship will undoubtedly sustain her throughout her life.

DAUGHTERS: BEGINNINGS

In her overt admiration for women who are whole, strong and political, Kathy Cardinal shares more with the third generation, the daughters, than with her own generation. In fact, she is their contemporary in a very significant way: she is a student, as are all the daughters, and she calls herself a feminist. The daughters have been influenced by the women's movement in Alberta, by the feminist writings that surround them and by participation in Women's Studies at the university. Kelly Anderson is Linda Anderson's daughter and Katherine Addy's grand-daughter. She was born in 1972, and after moving around the province, she settled in Jasper with her family until she went to the University of Calgary. She majored in psychology, minoring in Women's Studies. During the summers, she works for pay in Jasper and volunteers for the Seminar on the UN and with children with learning disabilities.

She says that she is a feminist. For her, feminism means "empower-ment to women, giving them the power to be the people they want to be in a society that often condemns that." By empowerment, then, she does not suggest joining in political activism with other women. Rather, her notion of empowerment means less political power than it means individual possibilities for individual women. She does, however, feel that the counselling in AIDS awareness she does is aimed at political reform, and that in that setting she treasures her work with women. She also announces that her closest friends are women and that her role model is her mother. Still, when she thinks about her future life, she describes its conflicts as individual, the conflict so many women face "balancing a family and a career. I want to have a family, but I also want the fulfillment of succeeding in something of my own. It will be difficult but I will expect help from a future husband to make it happen." Fulfilling paid work and female friendships have been added to a vision of life not unlike her mother's, although the "feminist" word may cause her to keep questioning.

Her contemporary, *Christine Forner,* was born in 1969. She is a Women's Studies major, Fiona Forner's daughter and the granddaughter of Jennie Niznik. She lives in a small town east of Calgary with the man she married at the age of twenty-four. Despite her outspoken feminism, her configuration of intimate relations includes marriage, not only now for herself but for future generations. Christine hopes that the daughters she anticipates one day having will be able to be independent, "to have a good work ethic and to be responsible for themselves before they get married."

Christine has volunteered for eight years both at the Distress Centre, a facility that provides emergency help for many social and personal crises, and at the sexual assault centre. Feminism, she says, "is everything. It is a lifestyle, it is a political affiliation, it means that women are trying to gain the respect they deserve." Feminism as an ideology and a political movement made sense of her life: "I now have an understanding of why certain aspects of my life made me feel bad about being a woman." Guilt is what she means, and she is no longer a practising Catholic because she did not feel "that women in the church were treated very well." Instead, she has "taken to the religions of the Goddess and I believe in a spirituality that encompasses all things."

Feminism provides her with the analysis she needs to make her paid job as a cocktail waitress bearable. Feminism also guides her in the way she wants to be in the world, both in her volunteer work and in her relationships. She is emphatic on the importance of affiliations with women, especially those who share her thoughts and feelings about feminism like her two closest friends. Friends, sisters, her mother, her grandmother — all these provide her, she says, companionship and support. They aid each other in the knowledge that women must get more support in their political activism than they do now.

Leita Blasetti does not speak much of feminism. In this she probably resembles her grandmother, Madge McAdam, more than she does her contemporaries in the daughter generation. In fact, her grandmother is her role model "because she worked. She seemed so open. She was always doing different things for different groups, and she seemed so caring." Leita was born in 1971 on the East Coast; two years later her family moved to Alberta. She lived in Okotoks, where her mother Linda Blasetti still lives, until she moved to Calgary to finish high school and then to go to the community college for a diploma in recreation therapy. She now works in that field in Lethbridge, a small Alberta city, and is studying for a degree in community rehabilitation.

segregated She is not, however, unaware of the culture's influence on growing up gendered. She saw rigidly segregated sex roles while she was growing up, differences between the sexes being normalized down to every last detail. "Girls had baths and boys had showers. Mom knitted and sewed; Dad built things." Influenced by social changes in the years since her childhood, she believes today that women should be equal to men; clearly, men are still the norm in her scheme.

Chelsea Cardinal, the daughter of Kathy Cardinal and the grand-daughter of Elisabeth Sharfe, is only thirteen and in junior high school. She is much involved in school activities and very interested in the sciences and in art in which she achieves honour grades. Her mother, she said, is her role model, "because she always wanted to be a doctor and now she's going for it." For Chelsea, feminism is, "well, not exactly favouring women, but supporting females more than males!" She may be the only person of these three generations, because of her age and her own mother's strength and independence, to take for granted a sort of public feminism, an assumption that women will be entitled to make their way in the world. She is heir not only to the political developments of the last hundred years but also to the exuberance, the limitless possibilities of the Alberta frontier now becoming available to women.

CONCLUSION: POSSIBILITIES

The question for these young women is whether they will only desire the future possibilities for themselves or whether they will join together to make the political changes necessary to ensure women's continuing autonomy. All three generations of Alberta women have been influenced by the first- and second-waves of the women's movement. While many of them did not claim to believe in feminism, they saw its effects on their personal lives. First- and second-wave feminism have caused women to think about their desires for themselves. The women interviewed for this

chapter share a hope to find out what they can do on their own. They
want their daughters and granddaughters to be whole and independent;
they anticipate that women may have more choices about their education.

Many of them have not had a great many choices about the shape
of their lives. Some have told us that career choices were clearly
prescribed, if they were to have careers at all. Others have told us that
household finances were not theirs to control and that they had little
knowledge about their families' economic positions. Many of the women
saw restricted and dichotomized sex roles, with clear prescriptions for
what women could do and what they could not do or be, as their appropriate path. As a result, they almost all assume that women must have
men in their lives to be complete. They still assume that women
should marry well for financial and emotional security, little knowing
that women's own education may translate into economic self-sufficiency.
Most of them, while they have enjoyed the company of women, even   validate
needed it, still tend to believe that men's approval validates them. As a
result, they fear that the women's movement will somehow render
women less "feminine," and hence less appealing to "manly" men. Furthermore, working with women in women's traditional fields has not
translated into political action side by side with women, to advance
the causes of women and children. Most of the women speaking here
do not identify themselves as feminists, even though their own lives
have benefited from the changes that women's struggles have wrought
in the twentieth century. And yet, each woman expressed desire for a
strong sense of self, and for a place in the culture.

The daughters of the third generation are heir to the frontier tradition   heir
that shaped the bold women of the early twentieth century. They are exposed to feminism through their reading, their education and the example
of the varieties of feminist women who are making changes in Alberta's
society. They are seeing how women benefit from women's shelters, anti-
rape legislation, lesbian activism and Women's Studies programs. They
have greater occupational access to non-traditional careers. They may
know men who participate in child raising and they may witness a
greater acceptance of different forms of family. And they have grown up
during a time when greater numbers of women lead successful careers in
politics. These daughters combine their awareness of these political and
social developments with a frontier tradition of women's connecting with

women. They have all learned from their mothers and grandmothers about women working and socializing together — on the farms and in the cities. Finding their place under the enormous sky that is Alberta, women have been, and continue to be, a part of Alberta's history. They will continue to seek power for themselves and for one other. Working together to build community and breaking isolation.

Notes

1. There is a growing body of literature in which Native scholars and activists are critically analysing Native women's roles within their traditional societies and the devastating effects that colonization had on these roles. See, for example, Kim Anderson, *A Recognition of Being: Reconstructing Native Womanhood* (Toronto: Second Story Press, forthcoming 2000); Christine Miller and Patricia Chuchryk, eds., *Women of the First Nations: Power, Wisdom and Strength* (Winnipeg: University of Manitoba Press, 1996); Laura F. Klein and Lillian Ackerman, eds., *Women and Power in Native North America* (Norman, OK: University of Oklahoma Press, 1995).

2. Eliane Leslau Silverman, rev. ed., *The Last Best West: Women on the Alberta Frontier, 1880-1930* (Calgary: Fifth House Press, 1998).

3. Catherine Cavanaugh and Randi Warne, eds., *Standing on New Ground: Women in Alberta* (Edmonton: University of Alberta, 1993).

4. Veronica Strong-Boag, "'Setting the Stage': National Organization and the Women's Movement in the Late Nineteenth Century," in Susan Mann Trofimenkoff and Alison Prentice, eds., *The Neglected Majority: Essays in Canadian Women's History* (Toronto: McClelland and Stewart, 1985), 87–103; Alison Prentice, Paula Bourne, Gail Cuthbert Brandt, Beth Light, Wendy Mitchinson, and Naomi Black, *Canadian Women: A History* (Toronto: Harcourt Canada, 1996).

5. See Catherine L. Cleverdon, *The Woman Suffrage Movement in Canada: The Start of Liberation* (Toronto: University of Toronto Press, 1978).

6. Cavanaugh and Warne, eds., *Standing on New Ground.*

7. Nancy Millar, *The Famous Five* (Cochrane: Western Heritage Centre, 1999).

8. Paula Bourne, "Women, Law and the Justice System," in Ruth Roach Pierson, Marjorie Griffin Cohen, Paula Bourne, and Philinda Masters, eds., *Canadian Women's Issues*, Volume I, *Strong Voices* (Toronto: James Lorimer and Company, 1993), 339–340, 373–376.

9. Kay Sanderson, *200 Remarkable Alberta Women* (Cochrane: Western Heritage Centre, 1999).

Study Questions

1. In what ways was first-wave feminism in Alberta similar to first-wave feminism in Ontario? In British Columbia? In what ways did it differ?

2. In what ways were the women of the grandmother generation influenced by the first women's movement in Alberta?

3. All people must live within the constraints of their society, and yet some people rebel against them and sometimes create change, as their rebellion

turns to political action. By reading the stories of the Alberta women, what conditions do you think might cause a women to resist the limitations of her society?

4. Many books about feminism classify the women's movement with adjectives like radical or liberal. Do you think such labels are appropriate to attach to the women in this chapter? What about antifeminism?

5. The lives of the women in this chapter span about ninety years. Do you think the generations are more like each other or unlike each other?

6. What aspects of Alberta women's lives are influenced by the frontier heritage of the province?

7. One of the first anthologies about women in Canada was called *Women Unite!* Would that title appropriately describe women's feminist activism in Alberta?

8. Do you think that the experience of the particular women interviewed for this chapter is unique to them as white women? Are the immigrants among them different in any ways from those born in Canada?

9. How does the geography of a place influence its women's history?

10. Why are the Persons Case and the Murdoch Case considered to be major turning points in Alberta history?

MANITOBA, NORTHWEST TERRITORIES & NUNAVUT

Southampton
Coral Harbour
Baker Lake
Rankin Inlet
Hudsons Bay
Arivat
St. Albert, Alberta
Saskatoon, Saskatchewan
Vancouver Island, British Columbia
Regina, Saskatchewan
Churchill
St. Boniface
Steinbach
Winnipeg
Elm Creek
Roblin
Wawanesa
Melita Brandon
Spanish, Ontario
Montréal, Québec
Ottawa, Ontario
Napanee, Ontario

PURPOSEFUL MOVEMENT

Keith Louise Fulton

◄o►

"I'VE GOT MY MOTHER'S EYES, see the world as she did."[1] These lines by
Manitoba songwriter Deborah Romeyn affirm the sense of our continuity
with women before us, a continuity that has been nurtured by the
women's movement. In the last thirty years, we have focused on linking
the concerns of women across the divisions of time, place and culture,
identifying the shared issues and conditions, organizing for change and,
more recently, unpacking our participation in the relations of power
that create difference.[2] The discovery that women could learn about the
world by taking ourselves seriously was articulated in 1977 by the poet
Adrienne Rich: "No one ever told us we had to study our lives,/make of
our lives a study ..."[3] In this collective and global movement of women
making sense of our lives and the world, metaphors of vision emphasize
the significance of what has been (made) invisible, not noticed, just as
metaphors of voice stress what has been left unsaid and who is yet to be
heard. The silences of unheard voices are about women as speakers and
writers, as authorities in our lives and on our lives. Margaret Laurence
explores discrediting women's voices in *The Diviners*, when she has her
writer-protagonist Morag respond to her husband's critical questioning
of whether Morag's character is expressing anything "we" haven't known
before. Morag says, "No. She doesn't. But she says it. That is what is
different."[4] When we listen to women speak for ourselves as women, it
opens up opportunities for us to realize the differences among us and
the challenges we face in working together to make collective change.
The making of meaning through our own voices and based on our own
perceptions is profoundly important not just in understanding women
and the world, but in making decisions for ourselves as persons and citizens. Each of the women writing in this section has learned about her

own authority, a word that refers both to the work of a writer and the empowered knowledge of an expert. Like Margaret Laurence in her memoirs, we discovered that we had both known and not known how our mothers saw their lives. When we connected our interviews to our own lives, we recognized new knowledge and old — ours and theirs. Laurence writes: "I had three mothers. I have countless foremothers. I never saw my mothers dancing. But now I know their dance."[5] To the metaphors of vision and voice, we add dance, that purposeful movement which is both beautiful and political.

There have been hundreds — even thousands — of women's conferences, workshops and meetings of this century that attest to women's purposeful movements for change. Among these, the Canadian Women's Music and Cultural Festival, held for three years (1986–1988) in Winnipeg, exemplifies the vision of the women's movement from those years. Organized by a collective of volunteers, this Festival brought together women activists and artists from North to South and from East to West with the message "*our time is now.*" The sense of possibility was everywhere as arts activists worked with feminist organizers, and refugees from Central America mixed with refugees from living rooms. Women were challenging the politics of public and private spaces. The Festival explored alternatives in the cultural diversity of performers, the inclusion of French and Aboriginal languages and material, the provision of childcare and festival activities for children, the provision of accessibility to women with disabilities, and the signing of voices to go into the worlds of the hearing impaired who cannot choose to come into the world of the hearing. In spite of these progressive preparations, the inclusion of *all* women was more symbolic than real; greater numbers of women have never heard of this festival than have attended it. Yet activities such as these that celebrate women's voices and the women's movement, even though our organizing only partially accomplishes our vision, have formed a lens that helps focus what we mean by *women.* As users of glasses, microscopes and telescopes, we know that lenses enhance visibility within specific boundaries of focus; in each case, knowing what the lens is doing is critical to realizing distance and maintaining relative perspective. A good way to think about theory (whether critical theory or feminist theory) is that through it, writers attempt to describe our lenses and discuss the differences they make in what we know and do. Culture and society contribute to a huge lens, a way of seeing. When we get so used to it that it feels "natural," it is called ideology. Feminism tries to change the lens.

There is a theoretical perspective, then, to the stories in this chapter, which use a feminist lens to focus on women's visions, voices and movements. Culture is the site where values are (re)produced, just as society is the site where social power is (re)produced. When we change the ways we live our values and see our lives, we contribute to the growth of social movements, just as we do when we participate in organized changes to the social institutions of government, work, family and education. Of course, cultural values can be manipulated by social power, as we can see in the mainstream use of resources to produce "culture." But as women and other oppressed peoples know, we can be creative in reproducing the values we care about. A feminist perspective can help us to recognize what women have insisted on reproducing or have refused to let go, our work of resistance and our creativity in living despite changes not of our choosing.

Manitoba, the Northwest Territories and Nunavut are big. On the map, these look like a tree with Manitoba as the trunk and its spreading canopy of branches reaching across the North to the Northwest Territories (NWT) on the left and to Nunavut on the right, opening to the morning sun. We need poetry to live here, to belong in these communities, shaped by people and by spaces of wind, earth and water.[6] And because we need one another as well as our environment, we need politics, that official, and also unofficial, system of communication and determination that organizes power in our lives. By power, I mean the resources of energy that are both personal and public — the land, forests and water, the creatures and the bodies and spirits of women, children and men. But I also mean ideology, the ideas of what is possible and probable, and through the use of power will be made to happen. Voice is crucial to power — how do you ask for what you need or want and get it? The "we" I use is a good introduction to the issue of voice, for with it I acknowledge my belonging to community as well as my ability to speak of that community and, in a sense, for it. With "we" I am both poetic and political, imagining a community and engaging in one. In the history books and even the books of literature in the first decade of the twentieth century, when the oldest of the women in these stories were born, there was almost no "we" spoken by women's voice. By the 1970s, when my daughter Emily was born, things were changing. Over those seventy years, women gained the right to vote in provincial and federal elections (1916 for non-Aboriginal women, 1952 for Aboriginal women, and 1960 for *all* women), and the right to be legal "persons" and to hold office (1929). Yet these official rights to a public voice are only a small part of the struggle of women to speak for ourselves and about ourselves, to participate in the poetry and politics of where we live.[7]

As women we are still discovering and creating who we are in the world, and writing our herstories is a critical step. To the women in our writing group, the 1995 United Nations Conference on Women in Beijing was important symbolically, for it offered the opportunity to speak to women from places we didn't know and whose lives we could barely imagine and gave us a reason to take up seriously the everyday, but difficult, task of speaking to the women in our lives. Even harder was the work of sorting out from the stories we heard through our interviews, what we would be able to write for others to read. For behind the issues of voice and breaking the silence are those issues women have felt and experienced as personal and have only since the 1970s begun to name as political. These issues are many and are witness to the multidimensional reality of our lives: pregnancy, abortion, mental illness and depression, sexual abuse, incest, violence against women and children, eating disorders, unpaid and underpaid labour, unemployment, poverty, financial dependence and independence, stealing, isolation, privacy for the body and for the mind, alcoholism and addiction, prostitution, sexuality and compulsory heterosexuality, love and desire, ambition, marriage and non-marriage (or not-marriage), polygamy, family, the responsibilities of caring for children (and the old and the sick), women's roles and experiences in ethnic and religious heritages and in politics, and the racism, sexism and classism diffused throughout almost every facet of our society. But not every one can speak them, for these experiences are still surrounded by shame and blame. Through silence and misnaming, women get the message that we are lesser for these experiences and that these situations are our fault. We often hear, "If you had been a 'good girl' and stayed in your place, these things wouldn't happen." The feminist insistence on re-establishing context for women's lives and choices and the resolute refusal to participate in a misogyny that "blames the victim" (or even assumes victimization) helps us find the voices to break that silence and to name our knowledge. Even so, for each of the women in our group there were omissions.

 n·省略, 脱落, 急慢

THE WOMEN IN OUR GROUP AND OUR RESEARCH

The interest and commitment of the women in our group were rooted in their personal histories and their motivation to discover more about their lives and the lives of their foremothers. Our project was to interview the women in our families across three generations of grandmothers, mothers and daughters, and to explore the changes in their lives. Some of us were keenly aware of differences between our lives and the lives of our mothers; all of us were seeking feminist changes to improve our lives and those of our daughters and sons. Speaking with other family members is an approach that uncovers the often contradictory knowledge women try to pass on or withhold from other generations. The approach to the project also explores a methodology open to every woman. We came together as a group when Greta Hofmann Nemiroff invited six feminist scholars into this project from across Canada. We formed the core working group and in turn recruited participants to form the six regional groups. Our regional group was responsible for Manitoba, the Northwest Territories and Nunavut. In our group, we worked as feminists, speaking in turn around the circle, developing consensus as well as our own voices and perspectives. This way of doing our research engages the interdisciplinarity and multidisciplinarity of Women's Studies, which begins not with the disciplines and their methods and rules for evidence, but by situating women in the centre of inquiry. In Women's Studies we have learned to seek out women's questions and perspectives and to value women's agency in determining what constitutes knowledge. Nevertheless, we have also learned from the disciplines, even those we criticize as feminists. Each of us in our regional group is involved in writing, teaching or theatre, and those disciplinary traditions of literature, drama and education inform our ways of asking questions and interpreting answers. These last two decades in the millennium may be the first in history where young people learn in Canadian schools that there are women authors.

None of us in our group would have read many women writers in school, and each of us has been part of that change.

The daily pressures in women's lives quickly reduced the number in our working group from ten to six. All six of us are in the middle years of our lives: Miriam, Yvette and Lora are in their early thirties; and Linda, Irene and myself (Keith) are in our forties and fifties. Miriam Toews, a novelist and mother of two, grew up in the Mennonite community of Steinbach. She is the author of two novels: *Summer of My Amazing Luck* and *A Boy of Good Breeding*.[8] I first met her in the 1980s when she was a student in my English and then my Women's Studies classes. That is also where I met Yvette Nolan, a playwright, director and performer who lives in Manitoba, the North, and the rest of Canada. In addition to writing and directing such plays as "Annie Mae's Movement" and "Six Women," she is the executive director of the Playwrights' Union of Canada. Lora Schroeder is a performer who was writing a play for children about eating disorders when I met her in 1990. In the last month of the project she gave birth to her first child and dropped out of the project; though her story is not here, her passionate honesty enriched our process. Irene Heaman is a writer, the mother of two grown daughters, and a farm woman from the sandy soil of the Parklands near the Saskatchewan border and the richer clay of southern Manitoba. Linda Pemik is a writer, mother and teacher from Arviat; she wrote from her home (then in Rankin Inlet), connected to our group through her friendship with Yvette, our phone calls and the tapes of the meetings where we worked through our interviews, discoveries and drafts. I am Keith Louise Fulton, a mother, professor of Women's Studies and English, writer and lesbian, loving where I live in Winnipeg. While these writers have some formal links to Women's Studies, the group is primarily connected through a feminist and activist network that sprawls across the borders of academic, cultural and political institutions. Networks like these have fostered Women's Studies to create a knowledge that is by, for and about women.

These stories are not representative accounts of women who live within an already understood framework of history; instead, the framework is developed from the accounts, according to the questions we ask and the issues they present. Because our lens has been ground in Women's Studies scholarship and in the cultural politics and feminist theory of the women's movement, we look for answers to questions about family and relationships, the dreams and growth found in religion and education, work in all forms inside and outside the family, and political participation. The initial research design of using daughters' interviews of mothers and grandmothers to explore how three generations of women have experienced change, revealed certain unwarranted assumptions about us as researchers and about our families and the women who nurtured us and whom we nurtured. Of the five writers here, only Miriam was a daughter who interviewed a biological mother and grandmother. Yvette interviewed her mother and a chosen grandmother. Irene interviewed her mother and one of her adult daughters. Linda interviewed her adult daughter and her Inuit friend. And I interviewed my daughter and my partner, partly because my own mother and grandmothers have died, and partly to make visible my chosen family as a lesbian. That research modification allows for the consideration of how contemporary lesbians form families from models which our mothers both did not live and yet, in their values of autonomy, in some ways did. Our approach throws into relief various forms of family; all five of the stories here tell of families created by combining patriarchal, biological and chosen families. If we had stayed with the first design, we would not have the stories here from Yvette, Linda and Keith, and the realities of not-marriage, women's friendship and lesbian relationship would be part of the silence.

In all the stories there is a theme of resistance to the power imbalances of the conventional patriarchal family and community and a struggle to speak about what has been kept quiet. The group supported that struggle, much as consciousness-raising groups have supported women in speaking about the personal and discovering the political. The experiences from the interviews coming into words were often raw with regret and unreleased pain. Surprisingly, there was also unreleased joy. Speaking through tears, we also exploded in laughter. The feminist recognition that voices empower other voices, and the writer's knowledge that stories bring about other stories, are both important to this section, for we are interpreting not just information and meanings, but feelings as well. The stories we have told each other would make ten books in place of these five short accounts, but they make these accounts possible.

Almost any group of women will uncover diversity among themselves, though it may be masked by an apparent ("assimilated") sameness. That we even appear the same is largely the work of ideology, the term for those invisible explanations and accounts that shape our daily lives. The pressure to conform to a "mainstream" closets languages and histories as well as sexualities. Exploring our own stories challenges those assumptions of sameness as well as many of the stereotypes of difference. The ethnic backgrounds in our group include Mennonite, German, Aboriginal, Scottish, English, Inuit and American, which reflects only some of the ethnic and cultural diversity of Manitoba, the Northwest Territories and Nunavut. Many families now are from a mix of these ethnicities, as we see in the stories of Yvette, Linda and Keith. In the last century there were waves of immigrants, sometimes enticed by opportunity, and often attempting to escape hardship, persecution or starvation elsewhere. The majority of recent immigrants to Canada come from countries outside Europe.[9] The 1991 figures indicate that 9 percent of all women in Canada are visible minority, and 79 percent of those are immigrants. These women continue to experience discrimination and oppression in Canadian immigration law and policies, in the licensing of professions and trades, in employment, in language policy and training, and more.[10]

According to 1991 census figures, there are some 588,000 women in Manitoba and the Northwest Territories (including Nunavut, which was formed in April of 1999). The 560,600 women in Manitoba make up 50.4 percent of the province's population, and the 27,600 women in the old Northwest Territories are 47 percent of that population. While gender breakdown of the population begins to provide context for women's stories, the additional information on ethnicity, immigration, rural/urban and race/language/culture also provides awareness of broader social patterns within which women experience our lives. In Manitoba, 11 percent of women are Aboriginal, while in the old Territories, 63 percent are Aboriginal. There are a number of problems with these figures for Aboriginal peoples, for the numbers are determined by shifting politi- cal definitions and not by self-identification.[11] Over half of the women in Manitoba (296,500 of the 560,600) live in Winnipeg. In fact, the majority of the population of Manitoba is urban, not rural as many imagine.[12] In Canada as a whole, women with Inuit or Aboriginal origins only were more likely to live in rural than in urban areas. Rural areas are also home to 79 percent of women with Inuit origins only, 54 percent of those with multiple Aboriginal origins, and 51 percent of those with North American Indian origins only.[13] In the Northwest Territories and Nunavut, the majority of non-Aboriginal women live in the five bigger communities of Yellowknife, Iqaluit, Hay River, Fort Smith and Inuvik, while the majority of Aboriginal women live in the smaller fifty-five communities, including Rankin Inlet. Data such as these from Statistics Canada can provoke intriguing questions and approaches: What social policies encourage migration to the city or support the existence of small and rural communities? What are some of the experiences of women, like those in the stories of Miriam, Yvette and Irene, who live in rural areas or who move to the city?

Land, language and colonization provide enormously powerful contexts for these stories. The vast areas of land and water, into which we are born or to which we have migrated, are marked by long severe winters and short intense summers, and just as profoundly marked by political histories and ideologies. Known as the land of 100,000 lakes, the "Prairie" province of Manitoba covers 650,087 square kilometres, of which 101,592 square kilometres are water. To the north, Manitoba shares the border at the 60th parallel of latitude with Nunavut, which used to be the eastern half of the Northwest Territories. On April 1, 1999, after some thirty years of political struggle, and four years after the interviews for these stories, Nunavut became a territory that includes some two million square kilometres and spans three time zones. The names Manitoba and Nunavut are important because they are part of the languages and histories of Aboriginal peoples who have inhabited these lands for thousands of years. "Nunavut" is Inuktitut for "Our Land," and, while the origin and exact meaning of "Manitoba" is uncertain, there are as many as eighteen variations of the word in the Cree, Saulteaux and Assiniboine languages.[14] The formation of Nunavut came about through the Nunavut Land Claim Agreement between the Canadian government and the Inuit, who make up about 85 percent of the 25,000 people there. The government in Iqaluit is the first Aboriginal self-government in Canada, and Inuktitut is now an official language there, along with French and English.

The name "Manitoba" was insisted on by Louis Riel, whose Provisional Government negotiated the confederation of Canada's fifth province in 1870. Manitoba then was just a "postage stamp," less than 160 kilometres on a side and only about 4 percent of the present province; it had a population of about 12,000, almost three-quarters of whom were French speaking and Roman Catholic.[15] The 1870 Census on the population of Manitoba shows that 87 percent of the 11,963 were Aboriginal — listed as Francophone Métis, Anglophone Métis and Indian.[16] Land, religion, language and education were all issues in those negotiations; while Riel's government secured provincial status and control of education, they were forced to give up control of their natural resources.[17] Even though there were to be other negotiations before Manitoba reached its present boundaries, lingering resentment against Central Canada may stem in part from this discrimination. But it is also related to the colonial mentality and the racism that sparked the raising of a thousand troops in Ontario, which under the leadership of Colonel Ernest Wolseley advanced in 1870 on the undefended Fort Garry to punish the Métis and their leader Riel and to occupy the colony militarily. While there was an attempt to create a province where English and French languages were balanced, which is still visible in many French communities and small towns, the English language has dominated. With even casual conversation today, you can find people who speak Cree, French, Michif, German, Ukrainian, Polish and many other languages, and you can also uncover not just systemic bias but also emotional resentment against any language except English.

Racism and colonialism mark the histories of Manitoba, the Northwest Territories and Nunavut. Much of their historical documentation comes from the records of colonizing ventures in the fur trade, in the settlement of Assiniboia and in the exploits of agriculture, trade, industry and mining. The political records are those of governments and owners, both private and corporate. While oral histories continue their living record in bodies and memories outside our institutions, even they are affected by being excluded, consigned to the "past." But the discrimination and exclusion are present and are part of our knowledge structures and institutions today. The historical accounts of the Aboriginal peoples and their cultures, their world views and understandings, are still largely excluded from what Canadians recognize as knowledge. In the last hundred and fifty years, schooling, education and research have all been conducted from the perspectives of those groups who hold most power politically. Only in the last twenty years or so have some universities and schools included any possibility of studying Aboriginal languages and the living cultures of which they are a part. The contradictions of incorporating subjected knowledges and peoples within our academic institutions are difficult: the very academic standards and degrees have been part of the colonialization through which they have been excluded and subjected.

Women, too, those teachers of the mother tongues, have been until recently largely excluded from the institutions where knowledge is formulated and passed on. While we can surmise the work of women *surmise* in teaching children language, living skills and values, what they have taught has been captured and reshaped by social institutions of government, church, education, law, industry and medicine. Family and marriage are also social institutions, controlled by law and economic and social policy as well as by custom. Even in the dominant groups, women have been confined to gender roles that continue to shape and limit their participation in culture and society. The arts, too, have been dominated by certain classes of men, whose perspectives and values shape what is regarded as beautiful and valuable. Racism, sexism, classism all work together and are interrelated: each form of discrimination contributes both to the power of the dominant and to the social structure that validates and sustains the dominance. *Validate*

The women's movement, in the last thirty years, has been characterized by resisting the power structure or at least the roles that women are assigned in it. The resistance takes different forms, from attempts to gain the privilege of some men to efforts to transform the structure to make it more fair to *all* (though it usually turns out to be for some) women. At its most radical, feminism seeks to transform patriarchy — the whole historical system of dominance in which men have held the positions of authority over women and children, the earth and other men. That authority does not just mean political power, but moral and intellectual power — the right to speak and to be heard as truthful, right. And the right to speak for others.

Perhaps the most famous organized resistance of women in Manitoba was the struggle for the vote for women, which in January 1916 made Manitoba the first province to extend the right to vote to some non-Aboriginal women citizens (not *all* women). There are many issues woven into the fabric of this organized effort as there are woven into the equally organized backlash: the draft of the First World War, pacifism, class power, sexism and racism. One reason the vote is so famous is that it represents the effort of women to claim a place in the structure of a newly formed democratic society, a goal clearly defined within and by the existing patriarchal powers of the press, law and government. But like the confederation of Manitoba, and possibly even the forming of Nunavut, that struggle was a complex negotiation in which some things were gained while much of the existing and discriminatory conditions were maintained and even strengthened. For example, in 1906, the First National Conference of the Canadian Women's Press Club was held in Winnipeg. This group that transformed lady journalists into presswomen was formed in the same year that the Manitoba legislature removed the municipal voting rights of married women property owners, though they didn't get away with it.[18]

Symbolically, the vote had enormous power to evoke the will and longing of women for a voice in public and private affairs, which continue to be expressed in women's organizations of this century. Voice of Women, the Canadian organization of pacifist feminists, had a strong chapter in Winnipeg in the 1970s and 1980s, which focussed the antiwar efforts of women and mothers to be heard in their opposition to the militarism of patriarchy. There are still women in Manitoba who are part of this organization, working largely outside the structures of political representation in the legislature and parliament. In the 1980s, in particular, women in Canada were successful in gaining the support of federal and provincial governments for the organizations that supported their citizen involvement in creating equality. In 1980 women had become involved in the struggle to enshrine women's equality rights within the Charter of Rights and Freedoms, and for a decade or so, their arguments were heard.[19] In the 1990s, however, many groups like the Manitoba Action Committee on the Status of Women, which had been so effective in developing the citizen participation of women, became starved for funds as the Canadian government closed down the Canadian Women's Advisory Council and changed funding policies to support specific projects and not organizations.

The women's movement is full of women choosing sometimes to work through recognized political parties and sometimes through women's groups, citizens' groups or through coalitions.[20] In her 1918 autobiographical novel, *Aleta Dey*, Francis Marion Beynon describes the interconnections among personal and political aspirations and experiences in the protagonist, who is a pacifist presswoman.[21] The autobiographical novel tells more than Beynon sought to tell, however, in the romanticized figure of the "hero" lover, who we today would recognize as abusive. Just as significant is the death given to the heroine; though Beynon was forced by the unpopularity of her pacifist views to leave her job in journalism and her life in Winnipeg, she does go on living in New York and she does write the novel. Only recently have adventurous female protagonists not been punished by their fictional deaths and allowed to live. Yet, in some symbolic ways, Beynon's political and personal voice in Winnipeg does die with Aleta. How would we write this novel today, and what would our choices reveal about our insights and hopes?

The forms that women's voices take as writers and speakers are shaped by the societies and cultures in which women learn language and what is allowed to their voices. Miriam writes about her grandmother who hints of what she might say in church, even though she has never been asked; her expression is a silent look into the distance. Even when we resist our roles, even when we organize to transform social structures, we do so partly within the ways we have learned to speak and write. Education continues to be a site of struggle. The language of instruction validates and sustains particular cultures and ethnicities, and the absence of that language in the school contributes to the erasure of that culture, whether it is English, French, Michif, Cree, Ojibway, Inuktitut, Japanese or German.

Miriam's story about her father's mother Anne, her mother Elvira, and herself is situated in the historical context of Mennonite immigration to Manitoba in the 1870s, the 1920s and the 1940s. And those immigrations are embedded in the conditions of Czarist Russia, in Russia after the Revolution, and in Germany after the Second World War that prompted Mennonites from Russia and Germany to seek new homes. They are also embedded in the profound ideology of a predominantly English Canada that saw the Prairies and the North as unsettled territory, disregarding the Aboriginal peoples who were already there — the Inuit, Dene, Cree, Saulteaux, Ojibwa, Dakota and Métis.[22] People didn't just "come," however. Though the majority of settlers between 1870 and the end of the First World War were English-speaking and from Eastern Canada (with some French-Canadians among them), large numbers of settlers responded to opportunities which were politically constructed. The "settlement" policies of the Dominion government, for example, created reserves of land to attract immigration of particular religious or ethnic groups. While these groups included the Swedes, Scottish crofters, Hungarians, French, Ukrainian and Icelandic, the Mennonite settlement was larger and more successful partly because their social organization provided economic support and co-operation.[23]

Katherine Martens observes that while Mennonites believe in the fellowship of all believers, "in practice, the equality seems to be reserved for male church members. Their patriarchy is not different from patriarchy in other groups."[24] And so, Miriam writes, "My grandma does not believe in women and men having equal rights." Nevertheless, the most important social change in her life (1906-1998) "occurred when men and women were allowed to sit together in church instead of on opposite sides like they had been doing for, well, forever." The political struggle of women to gain the vote in provincial and federal elections is not even mentioned, perhaps because it made no impact on her life. Yet these political and legal changes brought cultural changes in some opportunities to be educated and to earn an independent living that were critical to Miriam's mother Elvira. While she had already discovered humour as the great resource for personal happiness, she had to fashion her own faith in herself from a restrictive Mennonite tradition that had affected her childhood. In that tradition, "sex before marriage was sin, and, in marriage, refusing to have sex with one's husband was sin."[25] Thus, many families were large. Elvira was the last of thirteen children, six of whom died in infancy. Her mother died when Elvira was fifteen. The most important change in her life was to learn to listen to herself and to trust herself. Miriam's own journey through university, to Europe and through the self-hatred of a Mennonite girl, has as its context both her mother's positive model and also the realities of discrimination within the Mennonite communities and against them. During the Second World War, the children from these homes were forbidden to speak their mother tongue of Plautdietsch or German outside the home, and they learned both fear and shame. Miriam's writing takes back the "word" from the religious authority of church fathers and from the social authority of an ethnocentric and misogynous English mainstream and fashions stories that are both funny and true.

Yvette, too, is a writer with a sense of humour and a passionate politics. Her work in theatre and her stories in this chapter of herself, her mother, Helen Thundercloud, and her chosen grandmother, Marj Jamieson, reveal and resist complicated patriarchal and colonial conditions. While Helen became an educated teacher and activist, the theme in her life was that no one, neither parents nor teachers, "ever expected her to achieve anything more than Grade Seven or Eight and having a brood of kids; rather all the figures of authority in her life have stood as impediments to her education and fulfillment." The facts of leaving her Québec reserve at age seven for a tuberculosis sanatorium, and from there to a residential school, and then back to care for three younger siblings when her mother and grandmother struggled with alcoholism, before she was able to run away *to* an Indian residential school could be the facts in the lives of many children who are trapped by social barriers and blamed for them. The only ways out offered to her were to become a nun or to marry, which she did in a "fairy-tale" wedding to a good Christian man who moved her to Winnipeg. There, university (which she attended in secret) and women's liberation changed her life. Millie Lamb's Nellie McClung Theatre Group gave her a community of women. While Millie started it with the feminist, socialist and communist ideals of the 1960s, it continued the Manitoba tradition of women acting out skits for women's equality that had been part of women's gaining the vote. Women wrote and performed for social and political occasions — strikes and demonstrations and festivals — and still do, although Millie herself died in 1997. Yvette writes that both Helen and her chosen grandmother, Marj, empowered her "to choose not-marriage" and to believe she could achieve anything she desired. The "not-marriage" category, like lesbian, is not part of Statistics Canada classifications and reminds us of the many ways women live that are still officially invisible.

The struggle to take oneself seriously and to provide for one's own safety and security is a theme across all five of these accounts and indicates how much even contemporary conditions discourage and confine women. Education has been key to each in learning about the world and in gaining the confidence and training to make other choices for themselves. While financial independence and security is critical to the freedom these women have sought, it is not a matter simply of hard work nor of education.[26] Like Miriam and Helen Thundercloud, Irene Heaman too came to Winnipeg, where about 56 percent of the Manitoba population lives. Here, poverty is a problem, particularly for children and women. Called the child poverty capital of Canada, Manitoba has one in four children living below the poverty line, and poverty is a working condition for many people. While the minimum wage was raised in 1999 to $6.00 an hour, a single parent with one child and working full-time would have to earn almost twice that to get *up* to the poverty line. About 15 percent of the children living in poverty come from families where one or both parents work.[27] Poverty is the major factor behind the death rate for Aboriginal children and teens; First Nations children are more than four times as likely to die as non-Aboriginal children of the same age, and teens are over three times.[28] And where there are poor children, there are poor women. Women in Canada earned in 1994 on average $0.72 for every $1.00 that men earned; in the Northwest Territories in 1992, that figure was $0.63.[29]

While the possibility of paid employment means that some women can live on their own, the threat of poverty still keeps many more within the patriarchal family. There, women's unpaid work in the home and in the community supplements the family income and provides for some comfort, though frequently at considerable cost to the women themselves. For women, homes continue to be more dangerous than the streets. Violence there takes many forms and at different ages in our lives: emotional, mental and sexual abuse; assault; neglect; harassment; battery; rape; stalking; and intimidation. Prostitution, forced marriage and forced pregnancy, compulsory heterosexuality, and sexual abuse often shape our lives before we are old enough to make choices. And just as early in our lives, many of us learn to forget, or drink, or take drugs — even as we struggle to create our lives and to be daughters, mothers, grandmothers and friends. Women are still defined by personal relationships even though the majority of women now work in paid (and underpaid) employment. In the early 1950s, only 11 percent of married women in Canada were employed. Now women represent 45 percent of the total labour force. Even though the majority of women have paid employment, they still spend at least two hours more per day looking after families and homes than employed men.[30] In Manitoba in

1991, 71 percent of women working had children at home; in the NWT, over half the women working had children under six.[31] Women who manage jobs, housework, childcare and care of the ill and elderly must accommodate the conflicts among these roles and expectations by ourselves. Increasingly, cuts to health services mean that more women are now caring for the ill and elderly in the home. We are still waiting for universal and accessible childcare.

Neither the vote for women nor the guarantee of equality in the Charter of Rights and Freedoms has yet delivered equal treatment to women. In the area of marriage, although "theoretically, the 1968 and 1986 federal Divorce Acts treat both sexes equally, the effects of divorce on women, especially those with custody of children, are frequently economically disastrous."[32] Mona Brown, who founded the Manitoba Association for Women and the Law, notes that, in the 1970s, "Canadian women reeled in disbelief when the Supreme Court of Canada told Irene Murdoch that she wasn't entitled to a share in the family ranch after years of unbelievable hard work and an abusive relationship."[33] In her recent book, *A Partnership of Equals*, Berenice Sisler recounts the struggle for reform of family law in Manitoba, concluding that "a great deal still remains to be done."[34]

Irene Heaman's stories of her mother Wilma's work on their farm and her own experience leaving a farm wife's "career" after marriage separation explore different dimensions of working poverty. Irene notes that "small towns and rural life are still based on free work given by women in churches, in communities, on farms, in the home. The paid work a woman might find in these communities is still service work based on this premise, and the wages are low." While Irene now has a home of her own in Winnipeg, for ten years she worked at minimum or near minimum wage while taking herself to university, "having constantly to reclaim my right to this education." Her struggles to obtain an education also contributed to the collective struggle of women inside and outside the university to get a Women's Studies program. In 1986 she signed a petition that was presented in the fight at the University of Winnipeg to get a Bachelor of Arts program with a major in Women's Studies; the Senate passed that proposal in 1987, the year that I took up the position of the first Prairie Regional Joint Chair in Women's Studies at the University of Manitoba and the University of Winnipeg, later renamed the Margaret Laurence Chair in Women's Studies.[35] This Endowed Chair was part of the Secretary of State Endowment Assistance Program in Women's Studies that was announced in 1985 as part of Canada's self-assessment before the UN Conference for Women in Nairobi. Manitoba's two Winnipeg universities made a successful proposal in this competition largely because of the work of community women's groups and because three women (June Menzies, Mavis Turner and Elaine Adams) volunteered to do fundraising to match the Secretary of State grant of $500,000.[36] Working to change her own life, Irene has contributed to the changes in the lives of others.

Linda Pemik writes that her decision to move North in 1968 at the age of twenty-one, "first to Churchill and then Arviat, was about wanting to change." As a social worker in the isolated community of Arviat, she "found that people were not valued for their possessions or level of education or class" and she learned from the elders to "understand that people are always growing and changing as their *ihuma* develops." Reversing in her own life the colonial process, Linda learned Christianity from her friend Emiline, whom she met first in 1968. This strong friendship, like the friends Irene Heaman refers to, is central to her life. While admiring of the Inuit heritage where the "survival of all" depended on the mutual respect built in relationships, Linda recognizes the impact of "colonization and social turmoil." When Emiline was young, the priests had more authority than the elders and could force young people to marry. They also forced her father to choose to live with only one of his wives, leaving the young Emiline and her mother Tagalik on their own. Emiline's vulnerability as a girl child was heightened by her mother's tuberculosis and the violence against women in the small community of Coral Harbour: "men going around chasing women ... If they raped somebody, it wasn't considered rape. It was the men's right." She had "some bad experiences that I haven't talked about ... that really ruled my life, I guess, for the rest of my life." Now, like many women in the 1990s, Emiline and Linda both juggle their commitment as wives, mothers and workers. Their dream for Nunavut is for "a society where men and women work together in harmony." The social problems relating to poverty, colonization and upheaval are challenging, however. The average income in 1999 in Nunavut is only $11,000, with prices about twice those in southern Canada. Suicide is six times the Canadian average, and the birthrate is more than twice the national average. About 9,500 of the population of 25,000 is under the age of fifteen.[37] Some of these may be the hope of this new land, however. Born in 1975, Linda's daughter, Tagalik Kathleen Pemik, is fluent in Inuktitut and "seems to have the heart and soul of her Inuit ancestors."

In all of these stories, at least two of the three generations are actively seeking new models for changes in their lives, personal relationships, work and political governance. Feminist organizations, friendships and writing have offered political and cultural contexts for these searches. For Sally and Keith, both lesbian feminists, making a home means combining the personal and political communities and relationships. While Sally's work has addressed violence against women and Keith's has focused on Women's Studies, there has been considerable overlap where we have worked together, such as the building of the December 6th Women's Grove Memorial Garden on the grounds of the Manitoba legislature. A collective political activity piloted by ten women over ten years as a public education project, this Garden is a site now for the vigils when a woman is killed in violence against women, a place for healing and a place for concerted dedication to the struggle. There, carved in stone, are the words in Cree, French and English: "a living commitment to end violence against women" and "a living commitment to the lives of Manitoba women."[38] Now at the end of this millennium, young women and men are taking up that commitment. My daughter Emily points out changes that she sees in her high school, but she recognizes that "it's one thing to hold a belief, it's another actually to put yourself on the line and speak it."

Women have been organizing, learning from our experiences, but we are also demanding as individuals the freedoms for ourselves that we fight for collectively. What we put in these stories is the woman-by-woman creativity, courage and strength to claim our lives through changes we didn't ask for and through changes we demand, and the courage to speak of them — not abstractly, but in detail to those we love. The difficulty we had in our group to find ways of asking questions and of understanding the responses or non-responses has helped us to recognize how the historical records of women's voices could omit so much. We have also been alerted to the silences that continue to be maintained, for we have felt the ambivalence between wanting to be truthful and also longing to believe and protect these women and ourselves. What we have written reflects what we see as well as what they said. Together these words come with the gift of surprise at our purposeful movement.

I AM NOT GERTRUDE STEIN

Miriam Toews

-◄o►-

ANNE KROEKER, MY GRANDMOTHER, has always done the right thing according to Mennonite tradition. As a child she obeyed and revered her mother and father. When her parents died, both at a young age, she left school and went to work in their general store. At twenty-one she married her first husband, Henry, a kind, gentle man who worked in a feed mill for $70 a month. My grandma has lived in Steinbach, Manitoba, all her life. She is eighty-eight years old.

Henry died of stomach cancer in his sixties, and seven years later Anne married another Henry, the first Henry's first cousin. I asked Anne if she would describe either of her marriages as romantic, and she smiled and shook her head, "No ... no."

My grandma does not believe in women and men having equal rights. For her, a woman's role is in the home, taking care of children and doing the housework, and the man should be the breadwinner. She can't remember ever arguing with either Henry. In the church, she believes that women should not try to outdo the menfolk. There is no reason *menfolk.* for women to get up to speak. However, Anne said, that if SHE was asked, and was able to, she would get up and say a thing or two. Like what? I ask. She smiles so much her eyes almost disappear and she smooths out her skirt. She looks out, way out the window past Friesen Avenue and Brandt Road, past my parents' house, and out towards Abe's Hill, and doesn't answer the question.

Anne wants her children and her grandchildren to be happy. She wants for them "the best that is in life, whatever that is, whatever is best for them." She would not try to tell them what to do, who to marry or what to think. Not anymore anyway. Her oldest son's wife, Elvira, my mother, has always (except for when her kids were very little) worked outside the home, is university-educated, is outspoken and has stopped attending church because she cannot honestly adhere to most of its beliefs. Yet my grandma believes my mother is perfect for my dad (her son, who, until his heart attack, had never missed Sunday morning church in his life), because, well ... "Melvin, sometimes he doesn't see the bright side of life and your mother always does. I'm very pleased with her."

I asked my grandma what it is to be a Mennonite. She said she didn't know. She's always been one, that will never change. Whatever you are, you are, she said. Then she added, "They have their own beliefs. Certain things are wrong according to the Bible. Whatever is wrong is wrong and whatever is right is right. No Mennonite can change that." (Then it was my turn to smile and stare out past the town of Steinbach towards the big city, and say nothing.)

I asked my grandma what she thought about spirituality. She said it was tied into religion and the church. She had joined the same church her parents were members of, back in Russia, and their parents were members of, and it had always been very good to her and very important. The most important social change in her life occurred when men and women were allowed to sit together in church instead of on opposite sides like they had been doing for, well, forever. How did it feel? "Nice," she said, "very nice." Spirituality, she said, is a belief in The Church and its ways.

My mother, Elvira, was the thirteenth and last child born to Helen and Cornelius Loewen. Elvira's mom was quiet, gentle and religious. Throughout her married life, she was pregnant or nursing a baby. Six of her children died in infancy.

Elvira's father was the wealthiest businessman in town. They kept a bear as a pet and used their dining-room table for playing ping-pong with an old pair of Elvira's stockings tied across for a net. From the age of thirteen, Elvira was allowed to use the car whenever she needed it. It was generally believed that her father let his kids do as they pleased. He encouraged them to have fun.

When Elvira was fifteen, her mother died. Elvira describes the year of her mother's death as "cataclysmic." Shortly after her mother's death, her father had a debilitating stroke, and Elvira was sent, by her busy and well-meaning older brothers, to a Mennonite boarding school in

cataclysmic   debilitating

· 128 ·

Winnipeg. She had a reputation there as a rebel, as wild and funny and independent. It was the loneliest year of her life.

My mother often speaks lovingly of her mother and tells me, "I know that my mother, to know what my thinking about God is now, would have been disturbed by it. I also know that she would have wanted me to have a secure, happy life and would have loved me regardless of our different spiritual parameters. My mother would have wanted to have kept me from all pain. But she would have liked who I am."

When I was a kid my mom would embarrass me regularly by laughing in church. She made no sound, but her shaking sent a tremor down the entire pew. Grandma Anne, in her big square hat, would turn and frown/smile at my mom. She did say she appreciated my mom's bright side, didn't she?

Years later, when I was about ten, I was old enough to sit with my friend Julie Reimer, a few rows in front of my parents. Julie and I played a wicked game called Panties. We'd cross out certain words in the Bible and substitute them with the word Panties. "No sooner can a wealthy man enter the Panties of heaven," or "Give us this day our daily Panties." One Sunday, unable to contain our laughter, we exploded during Silent Prayer. My mother, horrified, marched us both out of the church, past a stunned congregation, and onto the sidewalk outside. She muttered, "Keep walking," until we were out of sight and earshot of the church. She sat down on the steps in front of the post office and, tears streaming down her face, began to laugh. She sat there in her flowery Sunday dress, legs splayed across the concrete, and laughed and cried until Julie and I asked if we could go home. My mother's faith in a loving and forgiving God is very strong. But she worships laughter.

I asked my mom what she thought was THE most important personal change in her life. Her response was, for me, both an answer and a challenge. "I have learned to listen to myself, and to trust myself."

This summer my mom turns sixty. She's a family therapist and works in her home, in a small bedroom that was once mine. It's where I plotted my escape, smoked my first cigarette, raged at the world, cried my eyes out over a boy or two, and laughed and talked, sometimes till two in the morning, with my mom. The little bed and white dresser are gone from the room, of course, but I like to think that the spirit of my innocence remains, and that when my mom enters the room to do her work, it greets her like an old friend.

My mother does her best to keep me from all pain. And I love who she is.

My name is Miriam Helen Toews. As a Mennonite, I guess I've committed just about every sin in the book. The other day my mother told me, "There's nothing new under the sun." She added, "That's from Ecclesiastes. Don't you remember?" I said, "Yeah I know about it, I just don't believe it." She laughed, naturally.

Just like my grandma and my mom, I grew up in Steinbach. My childhood, like my mother's, was idyllic, carefree and fun. The entire town was my playground. The siren at the firehall rang out all over town at six and nine p.m. so every kid knew when to go in for supper and when to go in for bed.

My sister is six years older than me. I used to love lying in bed and watching her get dressed for school. She'd start off in ordinary cotton underwear and silly-looking baby dolls. But then, whoosh, whoosh (I loved the sounds) on came the long men's dress shirt, usually green or orange, with the wide lapel (no bra underneath), the black velvet choker with the blue bead in the middle, the flared Lee jeans with the paint stains and the platform shoes. Long hair, combed a million times straight down around her head, no bangs, and tons of eye makeup, no lipstick.

Before she moved away to go to university she decided we should have the talk. She asked me just one question. Did I know what a hard-on was? Of course, I answered. Good, she said, and left for the city. I knew that if she could transform herself from Small-Town Mennonite girl into Woman of the World, so could I.

The day I graduated from high school, I cashed in the trust fund my grandfather had set aside for me and left Steinbach for good. I will never forget the force of my mother's embrace on that day. The next ten years I flitted around in some sort of accelerated program of my own, trying to make up for what I saw as lost time. First I went to northern Québec to study French, then to Belfast with my boyfriend because we thought Ireland was the most magical place to be, then all over Europe. We lived on a beach in Crete and picked olives to stay alive. I called myself an atheist and made up exotic stories about my background. I was ashamed of being a Mennonite from a small prairie town. I wanted to be Gertrude Stein. Back to Winnipeg, to university for a while, to Montreal to wait tables and live, to new boyfriends, back to Europe, back to Canada, to wait more tables, to New York City to be cool. Back to Winnipeg and whoops, I'm pregnant. Great, another experience! At twenty-two, I had a baby. I finished my degree, broke up with my son's father, met another man, had a baby with him, moved to Nova Scotia, finished another useless degree, returned to Winnipeg, and then ... I stopped.

I was tired. Was I a Woman of the World yet? I don't think so. And now I don't care. I'm thirty years old. I am becoming a mother to my mother. That means going to Steinbach a lot. My own children want to know the truth about my life, not some exotic lie. And I think I'm ready to tell it. I think I'm safe.

I'm not Gertrude Stein. I don't even know much about her. I'm not an atheist either. How could I be? I'm the granddaughter of Anne Kroeker and the daughter of Elvira Toews. We all grew up in a small Mennonite prairie town called Steinbach.

SHALL I BRAID US AS WE DO SWEETGRASS?

Yvette Nolan

-◦-

HOW AM I TO TELL the stories of we three very different women? Marj Jamieson, whom I have known for twenty years, fills the role of surrogate grandmother in my story. Helen Thundercloud is my mother, who left her Native reservation in Québec as a child and never went back, choosing instead to re-root in the Prairies, where she raised me. I am Yvette Nolan, a prairie woman through and through, who falls asleep to the sound of trains in the night and gets claustrophobic within the sight of mountains. How do I weave us together? The playwright in me searches for a metaphor. Shall I braid us as we do sweetgrass we take from the earth, the way we braid our hair, in three sections, with this prayer, "body mind spirit body mind spirit body mind spirit"? If so, then Marj is body, I am mind, my mother spirit.

Before I can interview Marj, we have to eat. Marj and Wilma lay out a spread of cold cuts and potato salad, strawberries and ice cream. In another young woman's writing, Marj and Wilma are thanked "for feeding me physically and spiritually." In all the years that I have been coming to Marj and Wilma's, I have never once not been fed. And although Marj is not a mother, never a wife — and the stories in this book have tended to be about women and their mothers and daughters and granddaughters — a score of young women have passed through Marj and Wilma's doors, been fed and nourished and gone on to succeed at things they chose to do.

At lunch, I meet Angel, the most recent young woman to be delivered into Marj and Wilma's care, whose extended family in China has pooled its resources to send her to school in Canada. Before Angel there was Norma, who acknowledged Marj and Wilma in her thesis. Before Norma there was me and Sandra, and before us, Judy. "For you kids, it was just really wanting success for you, but we knew you were going to get it, we just knew, for Judy we knew, for you we knew, for Norma ... It's just so nice they haven't forgotten us."

Us is Marj and Wilma. It's impossible to talk about Marj without talking about Wilma, who was perhaps the first young woman adopted by Marj, although truly it was Marj's mother who did the adopting. Marj begins to explain how Wilma became a part of the family, but Wilma joins the discussion and soon they're finishing each other's sentences.

> *Marj:* She was very unhappy at home and finally she just moved in with us, it was just something that was done. Hang on, I gotta ask Wilma something. Wilma, I guess your main reason for moving in with us was you were just bloody miserable?
>
> *Wilma:* Yeah, that was it.
>
> *Marj:* She felt closer to ...
>
> *Wilma:* Mom and you guys ...
>
> *Marj:* ... than she ever did, you see, ...
>
> *Wilma:* ... to that other family.
>
> *Marj:* So that's when Wilma came in and when we came to the city, when Wilma helped me with Pete, putting him through school, and with Mom, so then there was some strength, then there were two. Our lives have always been connected, and I'm glad they have been because it's a close family member, it's a close friend, it's a business partner, it's everything, it's absolutely everything.

It was the strength of these three together —Marj and Wilma and their mother — that allowed them to buy a house together in Winnipeg in 1961, the first women in Winnipeg to receive a mortgage without having a man sign for them. They paid mightily for the privilege; they were offered 12 1/4 percent interest at a time when the going rate was 4 percent. "The house was a disaster, but it was all we could get because we were 'such a big risk.'" Marj learned carpentry and together they renovated the house, doubling their money in a few years.

Marj never married. "Maybe I wanted the freedom I didn't have when I was younger. Maybe I didn't want the responsibilities. I had everything else. I had the home, I'd had the kids in *the brothers*, thanks very much."

Marj's father worked "for the hydro," so she grew up in a series of small Manitoba towns: Elm Creek, Wawanesa, Brandon. When he died, Marj quit school to go to work "because it was more important that the boys finish school ... girls were judged by how many bales of hay you could move, not by your marks at school." She worked two or three jobs at a time to support them, and that caregiving has never quite ended. Over the years, Marj and Wilma have helped out both *the brothers* and *the brothers' kids*: "Old habits die hard, for them as well as for us. The strangest part is, I now have more than they ever had — I have more than the boys and they had the all-important beginning."

My mother, Helen Thundercloud, also missed out on that "all-important beginning." Her education began in traditional Aboriginal healing, under the tutelage of her grandmother, a medicine woman; that education was suspended when she contracted tuberculosis at age seven and was sent to the sanatorium to recover. There, impressed by the nurses, she decided that she too would be a nurse. From the sanatorium, she was "scooped," taken to an Indian residential school where she discovered both book learning and the fact that there were few expectations of a young Aboriginal woman.

This is a recurring theme in my mother's story. No one — not parents, not teachers — ever expected her to achieve anything more than Grade Seven or Eight and having a brood of kids; rather, all the figures of authority in her life have stood as impediments to her education and fulfillment.

Because her mother, my grandmother, was an alcoholic and struggled with that demon at various times in her life, my mother was recalled from residential school in Spanish, Ontario, to care for her three younger siblings. "I pretty well was playing mother, making meals, chopping the wood ... what I saw on *the rez* was girls who became pregnant. If they had Grade Seven, that would be as high as they went. I realized that I had to get away, so I went to the Indian agent's office, Monsieur LeClair. He came over to the counter and I told him that I wanted to go to school somewhere else, all *en français*. And he told me, 'You know what, you're a little Indian girl,' ... *une petite sauvagesse* ... 'and what you have to do is just accept that, and eventually what you're going to do is have a bunch of kids just like all the girls you see on the rez.' And I thought, oh my god, I am really stuck here, no one is going to help me."

She helped herself, approaching a woman who ran a fishing lodge for work, cleaning cabins to earn the $40 train fare to Kenora, Ontario. In the fall, she appeared at the door of St. Mary's residential school in Kenora with a cardboard box. "A kid who would run *away to* Indian residential school was really unique; most kids ran *away from* Indian residential schools."

At school, the world of learning opened up to her. She met my father, her high-school teacher, and he introduced her to, amongst other things, W.B. Yeats, Brendan Behan and the encyclopedia. As she learned about the world beyond the reservation, she learned also that that world was not intended for her. Sister Florence took the encyclopedia away from her, telling her to "leave those books alone." Still, she clung to her aspiration to be a nurse.

The summer my mother was seventeen, working at Hockey Haven cleaning cabins to send herself to the nursing school in St. Boniface, where she had been accepted, my father gave her an engagement ring. "The nuns gave me a fairy-tale wedding. They loved Kevin, because he was a good Catholic man. If you don't become a nun you might as well get married."

"We lived happily for many years," my mother says, moving around northwestern Ontario and northern Saskatchewan, and finally settling in Winnipeg, where my mother's life would once again change dramatically. Around the time of the birth of my brother Patrick, her third child, my mother discovered the women's movement. "I went to a meeting and I met Millie Lamb, who is the mother of women's liberation in Winnipeg, and I started to learn about the oppression of women and how there were other things we could be doing — that the business of homemaking could be very oppressive if one didn't have a choice — and that's when I decided that I wanted work for others not just myself ... Kevin became very depressed because we had gone into a very traditional marriage. I realized that I was two people; I behaved in a certain way with him — passive, traditional, respectful — and when I was out with women I had this power ... I became intoxicated with it and at some point came to the realization that I wanted that more than I wanted my other life ... but I felt the repetition of being on *the rez* and thinking there's no way out of here, I am really stuck."

My mother's liberation began quietly. She took a sociology course at university "on the sly," pretending that she was going elsewhere two nights a week. "One day someone said to Kevin, 'Helen had an exam today, how did it go?,' and he came home and he was absolutely furious. That was the beginning of the end." The disintegration of the marriage took seven or eight years, and the final act was bloody, as it usually is.

My mother's career is still in healing, in a way. She has worked her way through rape counselling, social programing and the federal human rights commission. Today, she is a cross-cultural educator, teaching diversity management, teaching fairness, justice and equity, trying to heal the world. In spite of all the changes she has seen, she doesn't think that women are much further ahead than when she was a teenager. "I worry that we've fallen right back to almost where I was before I discovered Millie Lamb ... it could be part of the backlash, that men are so afraid of the power women have [and] we women are [responding to] that — we so badly want to be accepted that we take steps backwards in order to be accepted by those who have power."

I know the backlash; in my work I write about the social issues that my mother addresses in her work. I write to try and change the world, to change people's minds. But I realize that the life she has led has made my choices easier. I grew up believing that education was my right and, in spite of my father's ten-dollar bet with me that I would be married by twenty-one, I have never married. And I realize now that it is Marj and my mother who have empowered me, who have given me the right to choose not-marriage, who have instilled in me the belief that I could achieve anything I desired, because *they* did. Marj, who chose not-marriage "and got away with it," who made it on her own terms, who always believed that I would succeed. My mother, whose life is a series of leavings, who refused to believe that because she was Aboriginal, she would amount to nothing.

What Marj and my mother have in common is that they have both succeeded far beyond any expectations ever imposed on them. I have the strength of these two behind me, within me. Together we are three, braided together, strong women with strong lives.

BETWEEN THE LIVES

Irene Heaman

-◄O►-

I FIND MY GRANDMOTHER'S LIFE fascinating, wanting to get to the big questions through her. The big questions of my life are separation, divorce and poverty, which my daughters and I know as me living on a terrifically reduced income as a separated person and all of us having to live on the incomes produced by working for minimum wage. A lot of the stigmas of women are experienced by us — by me having to go back into the work force in my late forties, having "given up my career" to work on the farm as a homemaker and helper, my children having to experience the desire to improve their lives by attending university and finding there is no money available for them to do so. I was able to finish university as a mature student, attending classes as my children were growing up, finding my life enriched by the information I received and having constantly to reclaim my right to this education.

The big questions include my struggle with depression, an illness common among many members of my family, and a lack of self-esteem, which comes from having to come to everything the hard way. You are loved. You are loveable. The big question that surrounds all of us is, How to find and give love easily in a hard society?

One richness I had when I was growing up was family. My extended family is the way I understand life and growth — not individually but in the common good. As one would understand the gang, "the family," the Mob. Maybe it is not possible to find out who you are out of context of the family. I have always thought in ways that are now called feminism. It is possible, though, that what I have thought of as feminism may be a Libran attachment to justice!

In 1932 my mother's family moved from Melita to the Parkland area, a hilly and treed region in northwestern Manitoba. My mother,

Wilma (known to her family as Bill), was nine years old. It was the height of the Depression, there was no rain on the Prairies; the light, sandy land of the Parklands dried out and blew away. There was no feed for the animals and the grasshoppers sometimes hid the sun. Conditions were different in the Parklands. There was less sugar value in the food so the animals did not prosper. The land they had settled on was light and hilly and even when better times came there was never a lot of income. My grandmother, taxed by poor living conditions and poverty and having just given birth to her sixth child one month earlier, had to return to southern Manitoba to a mental institution to receive treatment. This left the young family struggling to provide food and care in conditions of hardship that would try many adults. Some of my mother's sisters married young, even at age fifteen. (This was a role model for me. I knew if I married, even at age fifteen, this would not be viewed by others as a tragedy. I, on the other hand, believed it would be.) My mother was the fifth in a family of seven children. There were only two boys and one was the new baby, so the girls did the outside work as well as the keeping of the home. When I asked my mother how the work was shared she said, "The men were the boss of the outside and the women were the boss of the inside." But my mother has always done the outside work of the farm just as naturally as the work in the house.

Though my mother has done many of the kinds of work there are to be done on a farm, from milking and caring for cattle to hauling grain and running the machinery, she does not like seeing women in roles traditionally done by men. She sees women as "butting in," wanting to get in to a man's world whether the men want them there or not.

"Do you think it's for better pay?" I ask.

"No, I don't think so, women are not built for [doing the work traditionally done by men]. I think women who take on work, such as construction work, work as fireman or policework ... are asking for trouble. But in a lot of things, they do as good a job as the men and should be paid the same as the men ... if they're doing the same job."

For me, to be poor was to not have enough books to read. There was always enough food, though there was not always money for clothes or extras. But it is true that the things you don't have bother the parents more than the kids. They know what's missing — the kids don't know. There is no comparison now in the daily work that women did but it is not that women do less now than their mothers and grandmothers; their work is completely different. I think that the superwoman of today who has a career, raises children, and is involved in the community is the counterpart of the farm woman of yesterday.

Poverty for all of us has been reflected by lack of education. My mother was able to complete Grade Nine. "I guess I should have finished high school, but I would have had to go to [the next town]. You had to board, buy your clothes and books, but there was no money for clothes, never mind books ... I remember my mother taking apart old coats to make jumper dresses. There was very poor clothing and very poor boots. I never wore boots all summer because that wears them out," she says with a laugh.

My daughter, Shelley, dropped out of school at the beginning of her Grade Ten year. Peer pressure was just too crazy, along with her parents just going through a separation. "I'd [drop out] again," she said, "but I would go back to school and university more quickly." She has completed her high-school education at an adult learning centre and is planning to go to university.

After more than fifty years of marriage, my mother doesn't accept the concept of romantic love (except, for some reason, the books that we had to read as I was growing up were Harlequin romances and romance magazines!!). My mother feels a healthy relationship between a man and a woman is one based more on respect than on "love." Shelley says, "Fairy tales made me demented, in their depiction of a helpless damsel, when [I] knew [I] could handle anything. I was no helpless damsel and knew it." *damsel*

My mother speaks of women of her generation. "You always had little kids in the house; sometimes you'd take them to the barn or the field. The work was very influenced by the children; you did what you could do but you always [had to] think of their safety." There was a great feeling of satisfaction and togetherness for her in working with her sister who lived close by and in sharing the care of each other's children. "Mae and I worked so closely together [that] her kids were my kids and my kids were her kids," she says.

Shelley at times wants children and at others is not sure. "Will I be a good enough mother, will there be nuclear war, will we all be living like a Third World country?" She feels she is lucky that she has a partner who wants children. "Men are getting better," Shelley says. "They're taking care of children, they push strollers, they aren't afraid to change diapers, they will let a woman work and they will be housekeepers. It's not so stereotyped any more." The pressure for her is when to have kids. "I have so much yet to do," she says. "When I'm ready, may be too late for the other person ... I feel I have so much more to accomplish in today's society. There is so much you have to obtain to have security."

A lot of women have been taught to believe that other people's needs are more important than their own. We are trained by our culture to give up self, not to listen to our own needs, to do for others rather than ourselves or to do the same thing everyone else is doing. Our whole society is based on what women will provide for free — systems are set up for women to do caring work. Small towns and rural life are still based on free work given by women in churches, in communities, on farms, in the home. The paid work a woman might find in these communities is still service work based on this premise, and the wages are low. Well-paid jobs for women are almost non-existent except in the professions where the wages are still lower than those paid for comparable work in the cities. Men's work (truck-driving, construction work, farm-ing) is remunerated at a rate approximately three times what "women's work" is paid if women's work is paid at all.

Roles were quite defined for my mother, less rigid for me and less yet for my two daughters. What we do to be part of the community has changed. "The change is not necessarily a perceivable change within the life," says Keith, "but between the lives."

The true community, the sharing of basic assumptions, is visible in the friendships we share with others. My mother's friendships are based on couples that she and my father both enjoy, for fun and for sharing "in the deeper times of life." My deep friendships are with women and groups of women. This is where I find my centring and my energy and where I get support for my own observations and beliefs. Shelley finds that her friendships are with both women and men. "Sometimes men surprise me," she says. "Some say the nicest things, some say the most horrible things, some say human things. They're not just women, they're not just men, they're people."

Home is very important to each of us. "It is my whole life," says

Shelley, "where I live; where I can be myself without fear of being invaded; where I can be in nature; where I can hang my art; where I write or work with my hands; where there are animals; where there is privacy." For my mother, home is a place where people come, to sit around the kitchen table with coffee and sometimes chocolate cake, to swap stories and opinions of events and of people. For me home is still a thing I need, for it is a place I gave up when I left my husband, a place I yet hope to find, a place I long for and yet, for now, is an apartment in the city, indistinguishable from others, with a cat who sits on my desk or my pen or the paper I am trying to read.

IN THE SAME YEAR, FAR TO THE SOUTH

Linda Pemik

—◄o►—

THIS IS THE STORY of three women of Nunavut: Emiline Kowmuk, Linda Pemik and Tagalik Kathleen Pemik.

Emiline Kowmuk, Oodleak, was born in the early summer of 1947, at the northern tip of Southampton Island off the west coast of Hudson Bay, the sixth child of Qayarjuak and Tagalik. She was one of twenty children born to Qayarjuak and his two wives. In the same year, far to the south, in Napanee, Ontario, I was born, an only child. Emiline and I met and became friends in 1968 in Churchill, Manitoba. Twenty-seven years later we are still good friends, both now living in Rankin Inlet, now Nunavut, married with children! This is also the story of my daughter, Tagalik, the *abbaq* (namesake) of Emiline's mother. She is nineteen years old.

Emiline spent the first three years of her life living in a traditional hunting camp where her father was the leader of a large family group. A skilled hunter, he was easily able to provide for his large family and was highly respected by all. Her early memories are of family, children and adults, living and working together in harmony. "I remember them, the men like royalty because they were the hunters and had to endure the hardships of the hunt, and the women just working happily, wherever I went ... they were busy and it was a comfortable feeling, like we belonged there and we had a home, we had a place. Whenever they were doing something, it didn't seem like they were grudging or hurrying but they were doing whatever they [could] at that right time."

Emiline moved to the small settlement of Coral Harbour at the southern end of Southampton Island when she was three or four. This move led to many changes — a separation of the households and the separation of her parents, for one. The influence of the priests was very strong in the settlements and so Qayarjuak had to choose to live with one of his wives. Tagalik, the older, set up her own household, not a widow, no longer a wife. This caused the young child Emiline much pain. "As I was growing up I remember so well my dad not being around anymore. As a child I think I made up my mind that if I ever had any children, I would make sure that they [had] a father, a dad, who would be there for them."

Moving from the land to the settlement opened the floodgates of change. There was no holding back the powerful influences of the Southern invasion. The Church and the School often replaced the authority of the elders. The priests jealously guarded their flocks from the encroachment of the "other church" and the virtue of the girls by dragging them to the altar to wed at fourteen or fifteen. "The priests used to control everybody ... Most of my sisters, I remember them getting married and they were crying, they were dragged to the altar and they were forced to say yes. One of my sisters never said yes, but she was married anyway. The priests and the parents made an agreement, and the young people didn't have any choice to say yes or no. The man I was supposed to marry in Rankin Inlet got involved with someone else, so I didn't marry him after all." But that was later, when Emiline was fourteen.

Her childhood years were not unhappy ones. In between the chores of fetching water for the households and washing clothes, seeking a place in the family by serving and helping wherever she could, there were the games of childhood: Amarujak, played on the crisp winter snows under the cold light of the Arctic moon, the thrill of catching birds in fall or the little ugly fish in summer. Then there was the fun of sneaking around the beach into the forbidden Anglican church out of sight of the binoculared eyes of Father Choque! School days passed in the "day school," which she cried to go to when only four and a half.

"I never did well in school ... I had some bad experiences that I haven't talked about ... that really ruled my life, I guess, for the rest of my life. Bad experiences at Coral [Harbour] ... when I was too young. I remember the men ... whenever you start to get to a certain point in your age they started being interested around you. And I remember men going around chasing women, and the women were literally scared but nobody really helped them. If they raped somebody, it wasn't considered rape. It was the men's right. Maybe it was different for others, but it was hard for me. My mother was grieving for the loss of her husband and she was also out for a long time with TB."

When Emiline was in Grade Eight she moved to Baker Lake with the Area Administrator and his family. It was while in Baker Lake that she was ordered by the priest to go to Rankin to marry. But that was not to be. While in Rankin "I met a nurse who really helped me. She trained me in being punctual and [taught me] other work habits and I worked with her as an interpreter in the Nursing Station. She encouraged me not to get married because I was too young."

Emiline went on to work at the hospital in Fort Churchill, and then went down to Ottawa for upgrading and business college. After working in several southern cities, she returned to the North in 1969 and married Kowmuk. "It was sort of arranged; the generation that I grew up in had a strong influence on me, even though I went down South to school and worked there for some time ... it was still in me ... when I got back. They hinted here and there that I should get married. It felt like home, I wanted my dad so badly and Kowmuk attracted me. He did a lot of things like my dad and he was a hunter. It felt good to be home." Emiline married Kowmuk in 1969. No one had to drag her crying to the altar!

She has fulfilled her desire to grow up to be a good wife, and to have children. Emiline and Kowmuk have five adopted children, and Emiline, like many women in Canada in the 1990s, struggles to balance her duties as wife and mother with a full-time job outside the home. She works for CBC North as a radio reporter.

My journey began in southern Ontario. Seeking adventure and a place to belong, I moved North in 1968. Moving North for me, first Churchill and then Arviat, was about wanting to change. From my first meeting with my Inuit students at the Churchill Vocational Centre, I admired their quiet, respectful demeanour and the way they loved and supported each other. Attracted to a culture where the good of the community took precedence over individual needs, I sought a job as a social worker in Arviat. In this small isolated community, I found that people were not valued for their possessions or level of education or class. Nor were people judged for their misdemeanours. Elders taught me to look to the inner person and to have patience with people — to understand that people are always growing and changing as their *ihuma* develops. And I learned from Emiline to trust and believe in God, the Creator of all, and in Jesus His Son.

In 1970, I also had hopes that the new territorial government would be different from the rest of Canada; that it would be based on a more equal sharing of power. Unfortunately, that was not the case. The patterns of colonialism were too entrenched and there was little or no respect paid to Inuit culture and laws.

Far removed from my roots, I forgot about politics in the struggle to become the best "Inuk" wife that I could be. With four children and a series of on-again, off-again jobs, there was little time for anything but surviving and building a strong family unit.

Tagalik Kathleen Pemik, my oldest daughter, was born in 1975. Although the daughter of a "mixed marriage," she says she never felt different from other Inuit children. Fully fluent in Inuktitut, of all my children she is the one who seems to have the heart and soul of her Inuit ancestors. When I look at her I wonder sometimes how did I mother this Inuk child, where am I in her?

Like many young women in the Arctic, she dreams of a healthy, loving relationship with a "special" man. Having gone through two abusive relationships already, she has learned that women have to speak out and stand up for themselves. In her own words, "Women have more power in the family, now ... I wouldn't want to be a woman before. Now, they're not scared to say what they think, most of the time. My dreams for my children ... do what you want to do without worrying about other people, be the best you can be, and for my daughters ... never let any man walk all over you."

In several generations and even in our lifetime, Emiline's and mine, the lives of Inuit have gone through tremendous changes and upheaval, changes which have rocked the very structures that gave families strength and kept their society healthy. In the past, the roles of men and women and children were very clear. Each had an important part to play in life, and relationships were based on mutual respect. The survival of all depended on it. That heritage is now blurred by a history of colonization and social turmoil. But there is great hope. With the settlement of the Inuit Land Claim comes the promise of the federal government to create a new territory in Canada in 1999 — *Nunavut*, "our land." One of the changes in government being considered by the Nunavut Implementation Committee is the proposal for gender equality in the New Legislative Assembly. Each riding would have two elected representatives, one man and one woman, recognizing that the population is 50 percent women and 50 percent men and that the leadership of Nunavut should reflect that. John Amagaolik, chair of the NIC says, "It is now necessary to make sure that both sexes play a role in the leadership of society. If we are brave enough to accept gender equality in our legislature, Nunavut will be the envy of other jurisdictions in and outside of Canada."[39]

And I would add, Emiline Kowmuk's memories and the dreams of these three women of Nunavut will come together in a society where men and women work together in harmony.

FREEDOM TO SPEAK
MY MIND

Keith Louise Fulton

-<o>-

I HAVE SPENT MUCH of my life dodging words that pin me down: girl, wife, mother. And now, no more. I claim these words — and lesbian, too — as possibilities in the independent lives of women. In this account, lesbianism must be the aspect that makes these stories important to include because it would be on that basis that they would be excluded. That is lesbian invisibility: stories that are awkward to tell, that are heard differently, that are eliminated in accounts of generation.

So I am writing not about three generations, but about three people in a family: myself, my partner and friend Sally, and my daughter Emily. I would have loved to include my mother, but she is dead now. In some ways her death gives me permission to speak, for there is nothing left that I can do to help her and every reason to work for the changes in the world that could have made her life better. When I feel discouraged by the slowness of changes for women and men, I remember that the women's movement has made a difference to me: it has changed my life.

My mother was educated at university, but worked inside the home. I was a tomboy, and the expectations that I must grow up to be ladylike were increasingly humiliating to me. I loved the desert-like plains of Montana and the mountains to the west, but I began planning early how I would leave to find some space. My role model was my mother, her life and her dreams. Like her, however, I went to university and then put aside my own plans as I adapted to life as a married woman.

I am forty-nine, of Scottish/English descent. I have two grown sons and a seventeen-year-old daughter. I married when I was twenty-two. I wanted to be rid of "girl," and maybe even "woman"; I didn't want to take on "wife," but it happened anyway. When I became pregnant, I was no longer considered a serious graduate student; it took me ten years to figure out how to respond to that lesson. Since leaving the marriage twelve years ago, I have raised my children and become a professor of English and Women's Studies at the University of Winnipeg. From 1987 to 1992, I was the first to hold the Manitoba Margaret Laurence Chair in Women's Studies.

Sally lives with us, though she has her own house down the street. Reflecting on our shared lives, Sally says, "I have known dignity in this relationship for the first time in my life; I have known respect, support, and have learned to get those things back. I had to get to be the age I am to get to know that." Now she is able "to recognize the anger and abusiveness with which I was raised and to do something about it." She has also created a home: "I bought this house and have done an enormous amount of work here. When I look at it, I think I'd like to have a house like that! And I do! I do non-traditional things."

Sally's mum did non-traditional things, too, for her brief life, but the contexts for her marriage and death on Vancouver Island are depressingly familiar: she married when she was eighteen and pregnant, and died when she was twenty-nine, hemorrhaging from a self-abortion. In between, she had four children and did the hard labour of a small farm: "My dad was a logger, so my mom did all the chores. She was very athletic and strong, both fun and funny, an intimidating person. She dressed in Dad's work shirts and pants and old hats and swung around that farm like she had everything in control. She chopped wood and dug ditches. She scythed the fields with a hand scythe. She could build just about everything with a hammer and a saw. She could do plumbing, electrical work and the mechanics on the car. She could run. She could do a handstand from a standing position with her hands on the edge of the table, and she would do headstands on chairs and really neat hand flips. And she could shoot a gun." If safe abortion, or even contraception, had been available, Sally says, "I might still have a mother." She was nine when she lost her.

Sally lived with family members, in foster homes, in a Catholic orphanage, and, after her father died, with her grandmother. "She always called me a whore and a trollop and said I would end up in jail one day and why did I bother going to school. I was quite determined that I wasn't going to be any of these things ... so eventually I left."

She was sixteen and had already begun to recognize her attraction to other girls: "I did know that whatever this was called, it was bad ... I certainly knew that I couldn't ask about it." But when Sally at age nineteen went to the University of British Columbia through the help of foster parents, she learned the name — homosexuality. "I found out that I wasn't the only one who was like that. Thank god. It was like coming home." There were no models, however, for how to be a lesbian, nothing in movies or in books. But Sally had made a triumphant discovery: "I didn't have to be with a man." She could have a same-sex relationship, though it took years to find out how to have that relationship: "Now I understand that the two people in a relationship must retain their autonomy. Nobody owns anybody."

It also took years for Sally to understand another experience that started long before her mother died and ended only when Sally was twelve: "I was sexually abused by a man in the neighbourhood. I didn't tell." When her father gently asked his small daughter about it, she denied everything. "I was terrified if my mom knew this, that she would go — and I [had] heard her say this — and 'shoot the son of a bitch.' And I knew my mother could shoot. She shot her way all over that farm and I knew that. And I was afraid that that's what my mother would do, and she would go to jail."

Today Sally works as a counsellor in the battered women's movement and has worked for twenty years as a counsellor in the Manitoba Youth Centre.

Sally has helped break the silences about abuse and about lesbians, but she is still surprised at the change: "Damn, this is going to be neat, I hope. When I think of [Keith's] daughter now who has grown up most of her life with lesbians, she knows she has a choice. That whatever she chooses to do she will be loved and supported. What a difference! In the universities now, there are women who stand up as lesbian, so girls sitting there in class, terrified of their feelings, they have the knowledge that — holy shit — this is okay. I can be this."

So, the most important social changes for Sally? "The women's movement, the civil rights movement and the lesbian movement." Politics are everyday realities in our home.

Emily grew up in this home with two older brothers. She was four when the marriage ended and we moved to Winnipeg. What she likes about her family "are people trusting my judgement for things in my life." The most "amazing" change for her happened last summer, "when I realized that I could do things for myself and stand up for myself. And I really decided not to live my life by anybody else's standards." That year our apple tree, which we had named Emily when we planted it six years before, bloomed for the first time! Her role models have been her brothers and her mother: "My brothers are important for what it's like to be a kid growing up. They show [me] not only what good things I should do, but also things that now I think I won't do. My mum shows me what it's like being female. I've got a good relationship with my mum. She's a strong person. I don't always agree with her, but it's okay to not agree with her."

Having a mother who is a lesbian "really pushed politics into my face. You couldn't get away from it. Life politics. It's always there. And I think it gave me maybe an analysis of life that other people around my age didn't have. In that sense, I'm glad she's a lesbian. It's also given me opportunities to think in ways other people haven't had. It means, I think, my eyes are more open to the world. But that's also because we have been very open to talking about things. It's also been hard sometimes. I'm put into positions of defending my family and I know it separates me quite a bit from people my own age." Now, however, "a lot of my friends at school have quite different views on homosexuality. I helped normalize it for them ... my mum's like a lot of other people's mums in that she works and makes me lunches on occasion and all that stuff."

Emily sees society changing in her own school: "I see people my age following fewer roles — actually very few people date. The prime requirement for going out with someone is being a really good friend." She sees the society becoming more open: "It's no longer acceptable to be racist with the people I know, but I go to a school where there are something like forty different languages spoken by the students and lots of different races, classes and cultures. Only a handful of non-Aboriginal people are more than first generation Canadians." Nevertheless, "there are more subtle race issues that most certainly still exist." The political issues are also personal: "It is becoming less acceptable to be sexist, although that's still a struggle ... so right now women have the responsibility to stand up for ourselves and change some things." But there Emily and a few others often find themselves working alone: "It's not easy for anybody to stand up for themselves. And it would be nice to have some help sometimes. And I talk to people afterwards and they say, 'Ya, I really agree.' So I say, 'If you'd said that about ten minutes ago in front of everybody else, it would mean a lot more.' Like it's one thing to hold a belief, it's another actually to put yourself on the line and speak it."

Asked about her spiritual beliefs, Emily turns to physics: "There is something really cool about our entire universe ... I can't help but think that people do have souls, and not just people, but places and animals have souls, too." She talks about "some resilience of spirit to make people keep on living okay lives after bad things happen." Discussions of spiritual matters take us back to gender: "Every now and then I sort of wonder about the fact that the cycles of women's lives just in menstruating coincide with the cycles of the moon. I think that ties us to our planet a little bit more, if we let it. But I think everybody has a role to play, men and women alike, to look after our planet and each other. You can't just put that on one sex."

Emily reflects on the changes she sees between her life and my mother's: "I think I've both given myself more freedom and been given more freedom to speak my mind. In a sense, she always played deaf as well as being deaf. She didn't hear things because she couldn't do anything about it anyway." For me, I am struck by my daughter's description of herself. My mother had encouraged me by saying, "Keithie, you can be anything." I had no idea how that could be true. Now, Emily says to me: "I can make my own decisions and be who I want to be. My life has changed, but yours has, too, a lot, I mean if you think about where you grew up to where you are now."

And I do think about where I grew up — the fields of crested wheat, yucca and sagebrush and the rim rocks where I learned to climb. Where I am now, however, is a different kind of space made by knowing how profoundly I am a woman and how fine it is to love women. That joy and acceptance changes everything. What I had wanted to be was myself.

Notes

1. Deborah Romeyn, "My Mother's Eyes," on *Distance in Her Eyes: A Gift from the Prairies*, Winnipeg: Bo Jess Records Compact Disk, 1997.

2. See Maureen Fitzgerald, Connie Guberman, and Margie Wolfe, eds., *Still Ain't Satisfied! Canadian Feminism Today* (Toronto: The Women's Press, 1982); Angela Miles and Geraldine Finn, eds., *Feminism: From Pressure to Politics*, 1st and 2nd eds. (Montreal: Black Rose Books, 1983, 1989); Nancy Adamson, Linda Briskin, and Margaret McPhail, *Feminist Organizing for Change: The Contemporary Women's Movement in Canada* (Toronto: Oxford University Press, 1988); Sandra Burt, Lorraine Code, and Lindsay Dorney, eds., *Changing Patterns: Women in Canada*, 1st and 2nd eds. (Toronto: McClelland and Stewart, 1988, 1993); Joan Turner, ed., *Living the Changes* (Winnipeg: University of Manitoba Press, 1990).

3. Adrienne Rich, "Transcendental Etude," *The Dream of a Common Language: Poems 1974–1977* (New York: W. W. Norton and Company, 1978), 72–77.

4. Margaret Laurence, *The Diviners* (New York: Bantam, 1975), 247.

5. Margaret Laurence, *Margaret Laurence: Dance on the Earth. A Memoir* (Toronto: McClelland and Stewart, 1989), 19.

6. See Audre Lorde, "Poetry Is Not a Luxury," in *Sister Outsider: Essays and Speeches by Audre Lorde* (Trumansburg, NY: The Crossing Press, 1984), 36–39.

7. The "Persons Case" is a fascinating story. See Alison Prentice, Paula Bourne, Gail Cuthbert Brandt, Beth Light, Wendy Mitchinson, and Naomi Black, *Canadian Women: A History* (Toronto: Harcourt Brace Jovanovich, 1988), 281-282.

8. Miriam Toews, *Summer of My Amazing Luck* (Winnipeg: Turnstone Press, 1996) and *A Boy of Good Breeding* (Toronto: Stoddart Publishing Co., 1998).

9. Canada, *Women in Canada: A Statistical Report*, 3rd ed. (Ottawa: Statistics Canada, 1995), 133.

10. Both *Canadian Women's Studies* and *Atlantis* have issues in 2000 that focus on immigrant women.

11. See Samuel W. Corrigan and Robert C. Annis, "Aboriginal Settlement in Manitoba," in John Welsted, John Everitt, and Christoph Stadel, eds., *The Geography of Manitoba: Its Land and Its People* (Winnipeg: University of Manitoba Press, 1996), 18 n, 132.

12. John Welsted, John Everitt, and Christoph Stadel, "Manitoba: Geographical Identity of a Prairie Province," in Welsted, Everitt and Stadel, eds., *The Geography of Manitoba*, 3.

13. Canada, *Women in Canada*, 148–149.

14. Keith Wilson, *Manitoba: Profile of a Province* (Winnipeg: Peguis Publishers Limited, 1975), 18.

15. Ibid.

16. Corrigan and Annis, "Aboriginal Settlement in Manitoba," 127.

17. Ed Whitcomb, *A Short History of Manitoba* (Stittsville, ON: Canada's Wings, 1982), 14–15.

18. See Susan Jackel, "First Days, Fighting Days: Prairie Presswomen and Suffrage Activism, 1906–16," in Mary Kinnear, ed., *First Days, Fighting Days: Women in Manitoba History* (Regina: Canadian Plains Research Centre, University of Regina, 1987), 53–75.

19. In 1984, the Charter of Rights Coalition (CORC) was formed in Manitoba to educate about the effects of the Charter guarantees and to implement women's equality. While it no longer exists, the Canadian group Legal Education and Action Fund (LEAF) does. It was formed in 1985 "to advance the equality of women in Canada through litigation, law reform and public education using the Canadian Charter of Rights and Freedoms." See Berenice B. Sisler, A Partnership of Equals: *The Struggle for the Reform of Family Law in Manitoba* (Winnipeg: Watson and Dwyer Publishing, 1995), 217–223.

20. See Linda Kealey and Joan Sangster, eds., *Beyond the Vote: Canadian Women and Politics* (Toronto: University of Toronto Press, 1989).

21. Francis Marion Beynon, *Aleta Dey* (1919; reprint, London: Virago Modern Classics, 1987).

22. See Emma LaRocque, "Native Writers Resisting Colonizing Practices in Canadian Historiography and Literature" (PhD dissertation, University of Manitoba, 1999).

23. John C. Lehr, "Settlement: The Making of a Landscape," in Welsted, Everitt, and Stadel, eds., *The Geography of Manitoba*, 92–95. See this essay for further discussion of immigration policies and groups and individuals who responded.

24. Katherine Martens, "Introduction," in Katherine Martens and Heidi Harms, eds., *In Her Own Voice: Childbirth Stories from Mennonite Women* (Winnipeg: University of Manitoba Press, 1997), xix-xx.

25. Ibid., xxi.

26. Though education is clearly a factor in women's financial well-being, Statistics Canada indicates that "women with university degrees earned on average $41,228 and females with a grade eight or less education had a yearly salary of approximately $20,580" (Canada, *Women in Canada: A Statistical Profile* [Ottawa: Status of Women Canada, 1994], 10).

27. Doug Nairne, "Manitoba Labelled Child Poverty Capital," *Winnipeg Free Press*, 3 December 1998, A6

28. John Lyons, "Manitoba's Native Kids Stalked By Death: Report," *Winnipeg Free Press*, 7 January 1999, A7.

29. Canada, *Women in Canada*, 10.

30. Ibid., 70.

31. Manitoba Women's Advisory Council, *Facts on N.W.T. Women*, June 27, 1995.

32. Paula Bourne, "Women, Law and the Justice System," in Ruth Roach Pierson, Marjorie Griffin Cohen, Paula Bourne, and Philinda Masters, *Canadian Women's Issues*, Volume I: *Strong Voices* (Toronto: James Lorimer and Company, Publishers, 1993), 339.

33. Mona Brown, "Introduction," in Sisler, *A Partnership of Equals*, 10.

34. Sisler, *A Partnership of Equals*, 223.

35. This was in 1990. Margaret Laurence had done her Bachelor of Arts at the University of Winnipeg.

36. June Menzies then persuaded the Manitoba government to contribute $250,000 over a period of five years. Her analyses and lobbying skills were also critical to women's efforts to reform family law, as Berenice Sisler documents. Indeed, feminists working in multiple locations have been both typical of and powerful in the women's movement in Manitoba.

37. Dan Lett, "Turning A New Page in Our History," *Winnipeg Free Press*, 1 April 1999, B2.

38. See the opening dedication, "A Living Commitment," in Joan Turner and Carol Rose, eds., *Spider Women: A Tapestry of Creativity and Healing* (Toronto: J. Gordon Shillingford, 1999), 318-321.

39. Linda Pemik noted in 1999 that while it is encouraging to know that there are leaders in Nunavut who are looking for ways to change the status quo, the voters soundly rejected the idea of gender parity; the one and only female minister played a very voluble and visible role in opposing the idea.

Study Questions

1. What language did you learn as a child? Is this the language of your ancestors? What social conditions have affected your language use?

2. Many of these stories refer to families that were blended or chosen or that combined different ethnic heritages or classes. Is there any story here that is similar to a family that you know? Choose that story and compare it to the family you know.

3. Consider Yvette's mother's story of coming to Winnipeg. What social and cultural conditions contributed to her move here?

4. Are there any similarities that you can find between different stories in this chapter?

5. How is theatre used to create discussion about events and ideas? Do some research on how women used theatre to win the vote. Compare that drama to a play you know.

ONTARIO

Nottingham Island, •
Northwest Territories

St. Albert, Alberta •

The Pas, Manitoba •

Winnipeg, Manitoba •

• Shawville, Québec

Brockville
Ottawa
Sherwood Springs
Toronto
Oakville
Burlington
London
Windsor

ONTARIO WOMEN

Greta Hofmann Nemiroff

-◄◦►-

WHEN PEOPLE MENTION "CENTRAL CANADA," they are usually referring to Ontario, if not to Ontario and Québec combined. However, because of Québec's distinct cultural character, it is usually Ontario which is intended. Covering about 916,733 square kilometres[1] between the 40th and 50th parallels, Ontario touches each of the Great Lakes in the south — Lakes Superior, Michigan, Huron, Erie and Ontario — and spreads north to the Hudson Bay. It is bounded on the west by Manitoba and on the east by Québec. Parts of southern Ontario share a border with the American states of Minnesota, Wisconsin, Michigan and New York.

The varying landscapes of Ontario were first the home to Aboriginal peoples — the Cree, Aniishinabek, Mohawk and Algonquin tribes lived well from its copious lakes, rivers and forests. But from the mid-eighteenth century, Ontario has been "settled" and "resettled" by a wide variety of immigrants.

While both Aboriginal and European women had deep responses to the landscape around them, their attitudes differed radically. For Aboriginal women, the land has a spiritual meaning related to their sustenance:

> Within the oral traditions of the various and distinct peoples called Aboriginal, the understanding of nationhood is rooted in a spiritual world view that recognizes a unique bond between the land as the source of sustenance and the people whose responsibility it is to take care of the land.[2]

Pauline Johnson (1861–1913), an Aboriginal poet, celebrated the beauty of the landscape:

A thin wet sky, that yellows at the rim,
And meets with sun-lost lip the marsh's brim.
The pools low lying, dank with moss and mould,
Glint through their mildews like large cups of gold.[3]

European immigrants from more moderate climates seemed to regard nature in fundamentally pragmatic terms, as was recorded by Catharine Parr Traill in letters home to England written in 1832 to 1835:

The sensation of cold early in the morning was very painful, producing an involuntary shuddering, and an almost convulsive feeling in the chest. Our breaths were congealed in hoar-frost on the sheets and blankets. Every thing we touched of metal seems to freeze our fingers.[4]

On the other hand, many immigrants eventually learned to appreciate the landscape even in hardship, as described in 1852 by Traill's sister, Susanna Moodie:

Every object had become so dear to me during my long exile from civilized life. I loved the lonely lake, with its magnificent belt of dark pines, sighing in the breeze; the cedar swamp ... my own dear little garden, with its rugged snake-fence which I had helped Jenny to place with my own hands, and which I had assisted the faithful women in cultivating for the last three years, where I had so often braved the tormenting mosquitoes, black flies, and intense heat, to provide vegetables for the use of the family.[5]

The "dark pines" of the landscape inspired the more contemporary poet Gwendolyn MacEwen (1941–1995) to transform nature into a metaphor for human emotions:

But the dark pines of your mind dip deeper
And you are sinking, sinking, sleeper
In an elementary world;
There is something down there and you want it told.[6]

From the Aboriginal point of view, European immigrants invaded Aboriginal land, formed colonial governments in which the Aboriginal peoples were not represented and imposed land treaties that "limited

Aboriginal land use" and cleared the way for further immigrant settlement.[7] Much of the recorded history of Aboriginal life in Ontario focuses on men; however, the role of Aboriginal women in maintaining the culture and healing the deep wounds of colonialization in their communities is becoming increasingly visible to the world.[8] Sylvia Maracle knows she must return to her roots in order to move forward:

> The fact that I am a Mohawk woman means to me that I have a license to make changes in the world. I have my instructions from the beginning of time to look at the world we live in, to challenge and encourage people to return to our roots. Some of my great aunties, who are still alive, don't bat an eye in telling someone they know, or someone they don't know: "This is what has to be done."[9]

This spirit has moved Ontario Aboriginal women to form very active advocacy groups such as the Ontario Native Women's Association, which has chapters throughout the province. The ONWA, founded in the 1970s, addresses legal, social and political issues affecting Aboriginal women as well as organizing social services for Aboriginal women and their families within the community. As well, since 1958, Aboriginal women have played an important role in Native Friendship Centres throughout Ontario.

The European settlement of Ontario began in the seventeenth century. The first wave of European settlers were the French men involved in the fur trade. After the British conquest of 1759, the immigration of English-speaking people increased dramatically. With settlement came the creation of English-speaking communities and institutions. United Empire Loyalists left the United States during the revolution of 1776 and settled in southern Ontario. During the mid-nineteenth century, one of the Underground Railways brought African-Americans escaping the slavery of the American South to Chatham and St. Catharines on the Niagara Peninsula. By 1850, Francophones had settled in the areas of eastern Ontario, moving into northern Ontario from the late nineteenth century up until the Depression of the 1930s.[10] Subsequent groups of European immigrants came directly from England, Scotland and Ireland; others immigrated from Scandinavia, Holland, Germany and later from Italy and Portugal. Jews escaping persecution in Eastern Europe began to settle in Ontario in the early 1900s. More recent immigrants have come from Caribbean countries, Central and South America, China, South Asia, India and Pakistan, the Middle East and Africa.

In 1995, the population of Ontario was 10,753,573 people, or 37.2 percent of the total population of Canada. Women make up 51 percent of that population. Sixty-two percent of Ontario's population claim ancestry from England, Scotland and Ireland; 12 percent claim French ancestry; 1.3 percent claim Aboriginal ancestry; and 15.6 percent are African, Caribbean, South Asian, Chinese, Filipino and West Asian. Of all the current newcomers to Canada, 55 percent settle in Ontario, making it a vibrant and multidimensional society.[11] While there is a diversity of population in most of the larger towns and cities of Ontario, the greatest concentration of racial and cultural minorities, excepting Aboriginal people, is to be found in the larger cities, especially in Toronto. In 1991, a majority of Ontarians indicated some connection to Christianity, although there is increasing diversity in religious belief in the province.[12]

Northern Ontario is sparsely populated, much of it inhabited by Aboriginal people in thinly spread out reserves, villages and towns. (There are also Aboriginal communities in southern Ontario.) This northern section has its own beauty, some rolling rocky country and small mountains filled with forests, rivers and lakes. It is rich in minerals, with many mining communities. Because of the long cold winters, northern Ontarians spend this part of the year in virtual isolation. Women are especially isolated — an issue that was addressed by the 1970s women's movement. To help combat isolation and speak to the needs of women in northern Ontario, numerous women's groups were established during this period. Some of these were the Sudbury Women's Liberation group; the Thunder Bay Women's Centre; the Thunder Bay Anishinabequek chapter of the Ontario Native Women's Association; and Franco-femmes at Hearst's Collège Universitaire. As well, *The Northern Woman Journal* was founded in Sudbury in 1973 as a forum for women to discuss social and political issues.[13]

The central and western sections of Ontario have fertile and productive farmland. Farm women's lives in these regions have changed radically since 1945, due to the increasing mechanization of farms, better roads and improved communication systems. Farm women have always participated in farm production while providing reproductive

and personal services in the home. While many farms would have col-
lapsed without their labour, women's contributions to the management
of the farm and household have been rendered invisible. It wasn't until
the the 1970s and 1980s, when the farming communities experienced a
serious economic crisis and many families lost their farms, that Ontario
farm women's strength and perseverance became visible. They began to
organize to save their farms and to address the social and psychological
costs of the losses many were experiencing. New farm women's organizations were formed at the local, provincial and national levels, and
Women for the Survival of Agriculture was founded to meet such
needs. Concerned farm women in Bruce County set up a bankruptcy
counselling service and a hot line for suicide prevention.[14] As Ontario
farm women organized themselves and broke the silence of their isolation,
many of them began to take courses through their organizations and in
community colleges and universities where they demanded training in
farm management, agricultural production and other related subjects.
They also recognized the need for and began to organize women's shelters
in their communities.[15] By the end of the 1980s, there was an increase
in the number of women farmers, as divorced, single and widowed
women started taking on the primary responsibility of managing and
running farms. On the whole, they were better educated than their male
counterparts. But to keep their farms running, they had to supplement
their farm incomes with cash-paying jobs.[16] From the 1980s onward, a
majority of farm women have worked outside the farm to earn much
needed cash. In some cases both men and women have had to work at
two jobs, but it is the women who continued to hold down the third
job of household and family maintenance.[17]

Farmland gives way to a ribbon of heavy industry that crosses the
southern section of the province. Southern Ontario women make up a
large percentage of the labour force and have been central participants
in union organizing for many years. In 1972, for example, feminist groups
supported a strike against Dare cookies; 75 percent of Dare employees
were underpaid women. In 1978, a group of predominantly female
workers won a strike against the Puretex Knitting Company in
Toronto. In the late 1980s and the early 1990s, however, women workers
experienced a serious blow to their livelihoods when Canada became
party to the Free Trade Agreement (FTA) and the North American Free

Trade Agreement (NAFTA). These agreements made it more profitable for industrial companies to set themselves up in Mexico, the southern United States and developing countries where they could hire cheaper labour and maximize their profits rather than comply with minimum wage and workers' rights legislation in Canada. This trend in southern Ontario is part of the world-wide restructuring taking place under "globalization," and it has had tremendous effects on the women workers in the manufacturing sector as well as in other sectors such as banking and telecommunications. As early as 1985, Laurell Ritchie, a trade unionist, organized a meeting in Toronto to which she invited representatives from various groups most affected by these trade agreements. From this meeting emerged the Coalition Against Free Trade, which later evolved into the Pro-Canada Network. The National Action Committee on the Status of Women (NAC), an umbrella organization of women's groups throughout the country whose main office is in Toronto, joined the Pro-Canada Network and waged a strong campaign against these agreements. Along with NAC, other Ontario women's groups such as Nurses for Social Responsibility and the National Organization of Immigrant and Visible Minority Women of Canada voiced strong opposition to these measures. This was all to no avail — FTA was passed in 1989 and shortly after NAFTA came into effect. Ontarians, especially women, have suffered and continue to suffer the economic and social consequences.[18]

Because of Ontario's diversity of landscape and peoples, not all the issues facing women are the same. Many issues are informed or shaped by the physical, social and cultural locations of any one group of women. On the other hand, Ontario women face many issues in common, such as reproductive rights and health, violence against women, pay equity and equal participation in domestic and public decision-making. In the next section, we look how some of these issues affect women's work and women's lives.

WOMEN'S WORK / WOMEN'S LIVES

In the 1990s, Ontario women overall have experienced increased poverty because of the punitive policies of the provincial Conservative government. There have been cuts in social assistance programs and in other support services for women and children living in poverty. In addition, women earn lower incomes, which also have a disproportionate effect on children since 83.6 percent of all single-parent families are headed by women.[19] One of the first things to go under the Conservative government was the pay equity initiatives that if put into place would have helped to improve working women's wages.

Ontario's women live considerably longer than its men. In 1991, 63 percent of all people in Ontario over the age of seventy-five were women.[20] However, many older women have spent productive lifetimes of unpaid domestic work and have not accumulated pensions in the paid labour force and, as a result, are considerably poorer than their male counterparts.

In 1995, 60 percent of all women in Ontario above the age of fifteen participated in the paid labour force as opposed to 73 percent of men. The unemployment rate of women (9.6 percent) is marginally higher than that of men (8.7 percent), but only 49 percent of women who work have full-time employment and earn on average only $0.71 for every $1.00 earned by men working full-time. Women are overrepresented in part-time employment (51 percent of all working women as opposed to 39 percent of all working men) and on average earn only $0.71 for every $1.00 earned by men in this category. On the whole, the occupations of most women have not changed significantly since the 1960s when women began to re-enter the paid labour force in large numbers. Women workers are concentrated in sales and service, social service, education, health, and business and finance administration. In 1991, as a result of FTA and NAFTA, Canadian women lost 125,000 full-time jobs and 69,000 women took on part-time jobs, which had been newly created. Women, then, make up 71.1 percent of all part-time workers, with young women overrepresented in that category. Clearly this has a very negative effect on the lives of women in Ontario, the majority of whom want to work in the full-time labour force.[21]

In the 1990s in Canada, a larger percentage of women than men are completing high school and undergraduate degrees in university. Nonetheless, women are still concentrated in traditional fields such as education and nursing and are still only marginally present in engineering and architectural faculties. A larger percentage of post-graduate degrees was awarded to men than to women in Ontario in 1991, and male graduates from most university programs will continue to earn more than their female counterparts, although the gap is closing in some professions such as law, medicine and finance. This positive trend in women's education took place between 1951 and 1993 when women's level of schooling increased much more rapidly than men's. For example, the percentage of women who gained university degrees increased almost eight-fold in this period, while the percentage of men who gained university degrees increased about three-fold.

An incentive to improve the quality of education for women and girls came as a result of the report of the Royal Commission on the Status of Women (1967–70), which studied the underrepresentation of women in higher education. With the rise of second-wave feminism in the 1970s, much attention was paid to the effects of sex-role stereotyping in forming the low aspirations of girls in elementary and secondary schools. Feminist-inspired course outlines and materials relevant to girls have made considerable inroads at the elementary and high school levels in academic subjects as well as in sports and leadership training for girls.

The development of Women's Studies has more or less coincided with the second wave of the feminist movement. Through the development of Women's Studies programs in colleges and universities, and through the constantly increasing body of research in Women's Studies and other disciplines, women's experiences, concerns and ideas have been rendered visible, validated and theorized. From its very inception, Women's Studies has been concerned with maintaining a dialogue between academic women and women in the community beyond the academy. There are three reasons for this: Women's Studies arose from women's need to name, share and understand their own experiences; at the same time, women saw the need for change and organized themselves to that end; and the research and theoretical framework needed for feminist action often came from academic women who, through their own experience in universities, could identify with the marginalization most women in society experience. In the 1970s, some of the earliest women's groups originated in universities, such as at Carleton University in Ottawa (1969) and at Queen's University in Kingston (1972).

Since 1970, Women's Studies has grown to the graduate and doctoral level. The first doctoral program in Women's Studies was proposed in

1989 and opened at York University in Toronto in 1992. Several other Ontario universities offer master's degree programs in the field. In 1985 the Canadian government established five regional university Chairs in Women's Studies. The Ontario Chair was shared by the University of Ottawa and Carleton University. The mandate of these Chairs is to promote teaching and research in Women's Studies and to bridge academic, governmental and grassroots organizations.

The growth and development of Women's Studies curricula and degree-granting programs have stimulated Women's Studies publishing. Two of the major Women's Studies journals that exist today originated in Ontario: *Canadian Woman Studies/les cahiers de la femme* was founded in 1979 at York University, and *Resources for Feminist Research/ documentation sur la recherche féministe* in 1972 at the Ontario Institute for Studies in Education. These journals not only cover feminist scholarship but also address social and political issues of relevance to both the academic and activist and provide up-to-date coverage of the national and international women's movement. The 1970s also saw the founding of other education and activist-oriented publications that focus on women's knowledge and education: the Canadian Congress for Learning Opportunities for Women/Congrès canadien pour la promotion des études chez la femme (CCLOW/CCPEF) in Toronto, and the Canadian Research Institute for the Advancement of Women/Institut canadien de recherches sur les femmes (CRIAW/ICREF) as well as the Réseau national action éducation des femmes in Ottawa. These journals and organizations help to connect activist and academic women in the ongoing struggle to promote women's issues and improve women's lives.

Another aspect of women's lives that has been critiqued by second-wave feminism is religion. The Christian and Jewish religions have been critiqued as being partriarchal and often irredeemably sexist in nature. These critiques lead to the question of whether or not these religions can be reformed or if they should be altogether abandoned by women.[22] Within various religious denominations, women's groups have formed to press for change and have met with variable success. The United Church, for instance, ordained its first female minister in 1936; currently half the candidates for ministry are women. In some Anglican dioceses women are ordained. While some Catholic churches allow women to serve at the altar, this is not a general practice and the ordination of women to priesthood is a much debated and contested issue.

Many women have begun to search for spiritual expression outside the conventional religious institutions (churches, synagogues, temples). Some Aboriginal women have reclaimed their spiritual practices that had been lost through colonialization or marginalized within their own communities. Other women are focusing on forms of goddess worship, manifested by a "resurgence of interest in goddess symbols, usually a plurality of goddess symbols." Women who practice goddess worship claim that it can "be healing: a tool for ourselves, our internalized forms of oppression ... [it] can buttress our resolve and nourish our inner resources to deal with the oppressions that remain."[23] In addition, there has been a revival of the Wiccan tradition — the pre-Christian pagan worship of gods and goddesses.

Women's lives and women's work are deeply affected by their economic circumstances and their educational achievements. Women are affected by their individual circumstances, but it is through working collectively that women can bring about social, economic and political change that benefits women as a group.

WOMEN'S POLITICS / WOMEN'S MOVEMENTS

In the Canadian women's movements, there have been many meanings and nuances applied to the word "feminism," but most feminists would agree that at its most basic common denominator, feminism is concerned with the advocacy and protection of women's rights. Although there have been disagreements regarding fundamental characteristics of human rights and advocacy, it is clear that the exercise of political rights is an essential component of women's liberation. The first public feminist initiatives in Ontario took place in 1876, when Dr. Emily Howard Stowe of Toronto, influenced by such activity in the United States, founded the Toronto Women's Literary Club; its name revealed nothing of its intentions towards working for women's suffrage.

In 1882, the Club was successful in its efforts to win the right to vote in municipal elections for unmarried women with property qualifications. In 1883, under Dr. Stowe's leadership, the Literary Club changed its

name to the Toronto Women's Suffrage Association. The fight for
women's access to equal representation extended into the field of higher
education. In 1893, under the leadership of Dr. Ann Augusta Stowe-
Gullen, the daughter of Dr. Emily Stowe, the Ontario Medical College
for Women was opened, and in 1886 women were admitted to the
University of Toronto. Yet despite all the work of many Ontario
women from the 1860s onwards, it took decades for women to win the
vote at the provincial level on April 12, 1917. That, however, was a
Pyrrhic victory, because although women could vote, they did not have
the right to stand for political office. They won that right in April 1919
when the law granting women the right to stand for office in Ontario
was passed.[24] Agnes Macphail, who came from Ontario, was the first
woman to sit in the Ontario legislature, and in 1921 was the first
woman elected to the House of Commons. She has been followed in
the past many decades by other distinguished women parliamentarians
in both the provincial legislature and the federal Parliament.

Winning the vote did not ensure women's equality municipally,
provincially or federally. Over the next forty years — a time in which
Canada faced two World Wars, the Depression and various economic
booms and recessions — women began to realize that, although they
could vote, they were underrepresented in all seats of power, and fairly
powerless in their private spheres as well. Too many of them were poor;
all of them were relatively powerless in a society run by and for men.

By the 1960s, although women certainly wanted to attain equality
with men, they did not have access to analytical tools or a vocabulary
that would enable them to appropriate their own experience and express
it accurately. There were many factors that contributed to the rise of
second-wave feminism. Between 1951 and 1971 the proportion of
married women in the paid labour force doubled,[25] and attitudes towards
married women's labour force participation were changing. Not only
had there been serious changes in women's participation rate and attitudes
towards the workforce, but their expectations concerning their sexuality,
marriage and family life were also subject to changes brought on by the
development of the birth control pill in the early 1960s, the general
decrease in infant mortality since the Second World War and by a
greater social acceptance of divorce. The divorce rate in Canada had
risen from 88.9 per 1,000 in 1951 to 124.3 per 1,000 in 1968.[26]

Ironically, while science had developed methods of increasing women's control of their sexuality and fertility, most women in Canada could not legally have access to information on birth control, to actual birth control devices or to legal abortion until 1969. It is not surprising, then, that the criminalization of information and services, which women increasingly perceived as their "rights," played a large role in raising the political consciousness and organizing of Canadian women. The increased presence of women in universities (as discussed above) was an important factor in mobilizing women to action through the 1970s and 1980s.[27]

Throughout this period, women continued to have an active role in Canadian politics, although they did not uniformly define their participation as feminist in nature. Women had been active in maintaining the infrastructure of constituency associations in the Liberal Party even before they were granted the vote. In 1928, the National Federation of Liberal Women of Canada was founded and in 1973 the National Women's Liberal Commission, whose members included all women members of the Liberal Party, was established.[28] In 1947, the Progressive Conservative Party established the Women's Committee within the Progressive Conservative Association of Canada. This committee, like its Liberal counterpart, provided important services for the party.[29] The New Democratic Party (NDP) created the position of Director for Women's Activities in 1961, and by 1963 there were approximately 135 constituency-level women's committees. The Participation of Women Committee (POW) was created in 1969, and is still in existence.[30]

Another segment of political activity was the growing participation of women in the peace movement, which contributed to raising the consciousness of Canadian women to the role militarism and war played in controlling their lives. Although Canadian women participated in the founding of the Women's International League for Peace and Freedom in 1915,[31] it was in the early 1960s that women again perceived that they had a particular role and stake in preserving the world in the nuclear-bomb era. In 1960, a mass meeting of women for peace was called in Toronto; a year later the Voice of Women was founded (July 1961). The Voice of Women was to be a non-partisan organization with the objective of uniting "women in concern for the future of the world." Five thousand women joined up in its first few months of existence. In

1962, Voice of Women organized a "peace train" to Ottawa led by its second president, Thérèse Casgrain, who transformed it into a bilingual organization.[32] The organization would develop its interests in many areas throughout the 1960s to the present day with chapters in several provinces, some of which eventually presented briefs to the Royal Commission in 1968.

In the mid to late 1960s, the American Civil Rights Movement brought the issue of race discrimination to the forefront of American and Canadian society. The media exposed most Canadians to the turmoil in American cities and campuses where struggles for civil rights were being fought for African-Americans. The Civil Rights Movement had a strong influence on both American and Canadian women in their search for gender equality. Here in Canada, women began to press actively for rights for women and other oppressed groups. "The ideology of equal opportunity and elimination of institutionalized discrimination based on group membership, affected Canadian perceptions of social reality."[33]

A key player in the effort to ensure gender equality through legislative means was the late Honourable Judy LaMarsh, a member of Lester Pearson's Cabinet representing an Ontario constituency in the 1960s. She describes her effort to influence Prime Minister Pearson to set up a royal commission to study the status of women in Canada:

> Nothing was so hard to accomplish during all the time I was in Cabinet as the appointment of a Royal Commission to inquire into the Status of Women. Not long after I took office, I broached the matter with the Prime Minister, pointing out to him that President Kennedy had recognized the signs of unrest among women of his own country and had set up just such a commission ... In early 1965, Pearson seemed at last to be prepared to accept my advice and to set up such a commission ... When I mentioned a Royal Commission to a national women's meeting, there was an immediate and scathing reaction from some of the responsible press of the country. Pearson backed off as if stung with a nettle ... I have no doubt in my own mind that I would have been unable to convince the Government to set up the commission without the remarkable organization of Mrs. Laura Sabia.[34]

In 1964 Laura Sabia, a broadcaster, school board member and alderman from St. Catharines, Ontario, was elected national president of the Canadian Federation of University Women. In 1966, she

> invited the national presidents of some thirty-five national women's organizations to a meeting in Toronto to discuss strategies for change and for achieving equality ... We took a momentous decision. We decided to fight together for a Royal Commission on the Status of Women. We established the Committee on the Equality of Women. I was appointed Chairman. Women in Canada were on their way! We asked Thérèse Casgrain, with her newly formed Fédération des Femmes du Québec, to join us. Her reply was a resolute *Oui* ... In November, 1966, seventy-six of us, representatives from thirty-five women's organizations set off for Ottawa to meet the Prime Minister and the Cabinet.[35]

In January 1967, there were rumours that the Prime Minister and Cabinet had turned down the request for a royal commission. A reporter for *The Globe and Mail* telephoned Laura Sabia to inquire about future strategies for her committee. Although she had neither strategies nor a mandate to respond to such questions, she gamely countered that he should not "underestimate women, there were many things we could do." When asked what they were, she responded that she could "march two million women to Ottawa."[36]

Sabia was quoted in an article in *The Globe and Mail* of January 5, 1967. The article claimed that she had "given an ultimatum to the Government: establish a royal commission or face the consequences." Sabia certainly attributes the establishment of the Royal Commission to that "off-the-cuff" comment: "The power of two million women was beginning to be awesome. The fear of two million women marching on Parliament Hill sent the politicians scurrying back to their drawing boards. The Prime Minister reopened the file and appointed the Royal Commission on the Status of Women."[37]

The process and interplay of pressures that brought the Royal Commission on the Status of Women into being foreshadowed strategies that the Canadian women's movement was often to use in its dealings with the state during the next three decades. Successful lobbying has usually been the result of the combination of three elements: media visibility ("The whole world is watching!"), vast numbers of women with at least one visible and media-worthy leader, and internal pressure from women within the state apparatus.

One important result of the Royal Commission was the creation of women's groups throughout the country. In the five years immediately following the Royal Commission, numerous feminist groups formed themselves. Some of these groups were reformist, some were radical and some were front-line service groups. As well, most of the already established groups, which had contributed to the struggle for the Royal Commission and had submitted briefs, continued their activities and evolved into other organizations. For example, Laura Sabia's Committee on Equality for Women evolved into the National Ad Hoc Committee on the Status of Women in Canada in 1971, which then evolved into the National Action Committee on the Status of Women in 1972. That spring, NAC held its first conference, Strategy for Change, and over 500 women attended.[38] That same year Women for Political Action formed in Toronto with the aim of getting more women into public office. In 1973, the first Conference of the National Congress of Black Women of Canada was convened in Toronto by the Canadian Negro Women's Association. The Congress has met since then at regular intervals in various cities throughout Canada.[39] Between 1971 and 1974, many other feminist groups were founded: the Canadian Advisory Council on the Status of Women (1973–1993); the Ontario Committee on the Status of Women (1971–1996), which later became the Ontario Advisory Council on Women's Issues; the Canadian Association for the Repeal of the Abortion Laws (which became the Canadian Abortion Rights Action League after 1980); the Native Women's Association of Canada; the Association of Indian and Inuit Nurses of Canada (originally called the Registered Nurses of Indian Ancestry, this was the first Native professional organization in Canada); and the National Association of Women and the Law. In 1975, women celebrated the UN-declared International Women's Year and the beginning of the United Nations Decade on Women. While Canada did send a delegation to the UN conference in Copenhagen, many women's groups took this occasion to publicize how little the federal government had actually done to implement the recommendations of the Royal Commission and to effect the significant changes demanded by the women's movement.

The struggle leading to the creation of the Royal Commission on the Status of Women and the feminist discourse that developed between the 1960s and 1980s primarily represented the standpoint of the white, middle-class, heterosexual, somewhat educated women in Québec and Canada who had (albeit limited) access to the state and media apparatus by virtue of their race and class connections. While it is true that in both the years preceding and following the Royal Commission's *Report*, numerous non-white, non-heterosexual, non–middle-class women's groups were founded, the "public image" of the late-twentieth-century women's movement supported by the state and represented through the media was of a white, middle-class, heterosexual group of women.

This insistence on "a shared female experience of oppression" perilously neutralized crucial differences between degrees and kinds of oppression. Many early writers of feminist works in the 1960s and 1970s in Canada were "women cushioned by high education, material privilege and the benefits of white domination. However disadvantaged ... [they] may have felt] ... as women, ... [they] experience[d] great privilege in terms of race and class."[40] In the 1970s, the analysis that took place within women's groups, publishing collectives and the academic milieu was often informed by the resultant spirit of "naive" feminism in which an area of "women's experience" common to *all* women was posited and from which large scale pronouncements could be made on women's conditions and needs. The majority of women in Canada whose ruminations on this subject were first heard were white, European, heterosexual, educated, able and middle class.

It was in the 1980s that the strong, united voices were heard challenging the white middle-class feminist hegemony in Canada. While many white feminists described their sense of "invisibility" in white patriarchal institutions, it emerged that there was a large and diverse population of feminists who felt "invisible" in what they identified as a "white women's movement." The 1980s marked a period that saw the formation of numerous feminist groups representing the differentiated and sometimes overlapping needs of women of colour, immigrant women, lesbians and disabled women. Caucuses representing various groups of women sharing a specific identity would form at national meetings, and a politics of difference was articulated which was resistant to sentimental and homogenizing notions of "sisterhood." As Marlene Nourbese Philip writes in retrospect, "The challenges posed by Women of Colour show that women's experience is mediated by multiple and overlapping determinations."[41]

When feminists of colour, Aboriginal women, immigrant and working-class women began to critique the "privileges" of white mainstream feminists in Canada, it was often difficult for white women to accept or even understand their views. Most of the white, middle-class women who worked to achieve the Royal Commission and to form women's organizations in its aftermath, sincerely saw themselves as a part of a vast group of women who had always been treated as second-class citizens. They analyzed gender differences in access to education, jobs, wealth and power and saw *all* women as disadvantaged. Since they focused on gender oppression, it was difficult for them to accept that although all feminists are aware of gender oppression, there are other factors that determine how women experience oppression. Jaya Chauhan, writing in 1993, points to the interlocking systems of gender, race and class that the women's movement was forced to see: "My awareness of gender oppression is inextricably tied into my experience of oppression as a non-white woman. The link between violence and sexuality is something you live rather than something you theorize about because both are triggered by gender and racial fascism."[42]

The naive feminism of the 1960s and 1970s defined itself as "transcending" differences between women. Gender alone was sufficient to link all women in one common battle. The desire to "transcend" differences was well grounded in the western liberal and even socialist ideologies where much of early feminist political thought in Canada was rooted. Over time, the critiques of the "white women's movement" brought forward by women who regarded themselves as excluded, forced many primarily white, middle-class feminists to understand that "rejecting a traditional model does not eliminate basic organizational and political questions. Leadership, decision-making, recruitment, the composition of the membership are key considerations for any organization, regardless of political orientation or vision."[43]

In the 1980s and 1990s, numerous women from other classes, races and ethnicities articulated their distance from the "mainstream" women's movement. Aboriginal women pointed out that they could not feel "sisterhood" with women who continue to benefit from the ill-gotten gains of the male-dominated colonial powers that stole North America from its Indigenous peoples. Activist Donna Kahenrakwas Goodleaf writes:

> What is the position of the white feminist movement on the liberation struggle of Indigenous peoples? As an Indigenous woman, I have studied the deep contradictions, elitism and white supremacy in the mainstream primarily middle-class feminist movement. Feminist theory and practice that focus only on male supremacy, without analyzing the impact of colonialism, race and class, reveal the narrow-minded thinking of white, middle-class women who make sexual politics the top priority. This creates a "politics" that is Euro-supremacist and exclusionary ... feminists appear to share a presumption in common with the patriarchs they oppose, that they have some sort of inalienable right to simply go on occupying our land and exploiting our resources for as long as they like.[44]

There has been a clear call on the part of many feminists to understand the relationship between the "racism, heterosexism, ableism and classism of the mainstream women's movement" and those "institutions, economic practices and cultural expressions that structure the dominance in society at large of white, heterosexuals, the able-bodied, and the middle to upper classes."[45]

Indeed, an argument has been put forward by feminists of colour that if white women are serious about wanting equity for all women in Canada, they must in fact melt into the background and give up their places to women from various designated groups. Twenty years after its creation, NAC built diversity into its mandate and committed itself to a politics of inclusion. Sunera Thobani, elected NAC president in June 1993, put out the invitation to all women to work towards a more inclusive vision of Canadian society:

> Today, feminism stands at a crucial juncture. Either the women's movement will forge ahead under the leadership of the women most marginalized in society, and make its commitment to the politics of inclusion and diversity real ... Or it will be contained within the status quo, as the women who have benefited from the struggles of the past help shut the doors on the majority of women who still continue to be excluded and silenced.[46]

The insights of women of colour, Aboriginal women, women with disabilities, lesbians and bisexuals, and working-class women are essential requirements for contemporary feminists in Canada. A politics of inclusion/difference means including and recognizing the many different interpretations and realities of women's lives and values so we can scrape away the detritus of patriarchal, racist, classist, ethnocentric and heterosexual definitions.

Over the past 140 years, many women and women's groups in Ontario have struggled to achieve equality and equity for women. In the struggles, women have been forced to recognize what unites them but also what separates them. There are numerous local and national feminist groups to be found in Ontario, whose staff and members work hard to realize the aspirations of their members and of all girls and women. Sometimes groups must work alone; other times very successful alliances have been struck. Ontario has all the human and natural resources needed to become a society where all people are equal at every level of their being. Whether or not women and the women's movement succeed in realizing this end is dependent on their capacity to think clearly, develop workable strategies and form the alliances necessary to bring about much needed change in the twenty-first century.

PREFACE TO THE WOMEN'S STORIES

Although various means were used to involve students in this project, the women in this group were ultimately brought together by the fact that all but one had been students of Greta Hofmann Nemiroff at Carleton University or at the Unversity of Ottawa during her tenure as Joint Chair of Women's Studies from 1991 to 1996. Extensive effort was made to find participants who were widely representative of the vast diversity of population in Ontario, but in the end we are the women who volunteered and who followed through to the completion of this project. While some of us had never met before the group formed, by the end of this process we were to know one another quite well. At the beginning there were six of us plus Greta at the meetings, but only four of us completed the work. Some evenings we met in the seminar room of the Women's Studies house at the University of Ottawa. The meetings were potlucks, with everyone bringing some food to share. Our meals were deliciously unbalanced, leaning heavily towards elaborate calorific desserts, and we all muddled through our work sustained by infusions of sugar and some protein along the way.

There were many moments of intensity and we shared frustrations, surprises and sadnesses with one another. We were able to critique only some of the texts, giving feedback and advice to one another. The group came apart before the task was completed since some of us had to return to homes far away for jobs and family. It was heartening to hear how pleased and honoured families were to be included in this snapshot of twelve Ontario women taken in 1995. It will mean a lot for the writers to see themselves published. This chapter, then, is the result of some soul-searching, discussion, conviviality, mutual support and plain hard work.

WINGS OF FREEDOM

Jennifer Anne Larkin

宗教
housewife.

—◦—

A bird should not be caged I say — The wings it has should set it free.
Soaring freely, gliding upwards,
Boundless possibility.

Once a cage is placed around it, door shut tight, the wings grow stiff.
Hopes and dreams slowly snuffed out,
Stifled in captivity.

Then one day the latch is broken, fearfully the bird takes flight.
No question now it will be mighty,
Graced with opportunity.

A LONE CRY WAS HEARD in the night air, Adrienne Lacroix (Larkin), my father's mother, just moments old, was greeted by her mother, Ida Pelletier (Lacroix) and the midwife responsible for her delivery, Lea Laderoute (Pelletier), Ida's mother. Three generations of women were in the same room to document the occasion: a mother and her child, the child in turn giving birth to a child ... such was the way of life here in the 1920s. "I was born in Ottawa on October 30, 1921, at home," Adrienne recalls. "My grandmother brought all our family into the world ... she was a midwife." The birthing ritual was a common occurrence in the Lacroix residence. "Well, it's a good thing [my mother] stopped at eleven," reflects Adrienne, "because she had ten miscarriages and twenty-one pregnancies. It's no wonder she died very young at fifty-five years of age. She was married at eighteen and was just a housewife. Ahh, those days women were treated like workhorses ... they stayed in the home and had babies. Mother was very talented. No one ever really knew it, though."

Being the youngest girl, raised in a staunch Catholic family with many siblings, was difficult for Adrienne. She could not recall ever being told of her mother's hopes for her, "She had a lot of children, I don't think she had the time. When I was young, god, I don't think I ever got hugged by my mother. I don't show affection like some people; I just keep it inside. That's from being a child who was hurt ... I felt I was always left behind in my family." Adrienne never really had "a special girlfriend" and dealt with many things in isolation. Gifted musically, Adrienne resorted to expressing herself through other means: "I'd come from school and I'd get on the piano ... and just let it all out. Never took any lessons but I loved it. I was kind of like a loner ... an independent. I hurt sometimes [but would] ... keep it all in and say to hell with them all. When [my sisters would] go out [without me] I'd say, 'Well go ahead and look for boyfriends. Whenever I find one I'll have him. I won't need to look for him, he can find me.'"And find her he did. Adrienne dated Joseph Larkin for five years, and as soon as they could afford it, they were married: "I couldn't go to university. I wish I had. [Being a woman had] ... nothing to do with that choice, it was money. The women today ... have the opportunity to be more educated. The more educated a woman is, the more likely it is that her children will be educated."

With a strong independent nature as her driving force, Adrienne tunnelled much of her energy into working in the paid labour force. "Oh, dear God in heaven, I worked at everything I could get my hands on!! In 1939 the war came, so I went to work at a manufacturing company making tents [for the army]. Then I went to the government in 1944. In 1947, Joe, my husband, was able to keep me at home to have my four children. So, after all that, I went back to work in 1960 when my children were more or less raised pretty much. [At that time my youngest child was three years old.] I was young and I knew I couldn't spend the rest of my life as only a homemaker. I wanted to see what was going on in the world. A lot of other women looked down on me, though. At first I used to think ... I should be home, but then I started thinking, 'Do you have to have the children hanging on your tails all the time? I am not just a scrub woman!!' ... I felt I was wasting any talents I had, so I went out and I proved myself."

As far as balancing work and managing a household, "Joe and I both worked together ... that's the best way to be. I don't think one person should have to do it all. Joe figured if he was sitting in the living room reading the paper, it was time lost ... time we could spend together. Joe never sat with the children to teach them, though; after he'd done his day's work he was tired, he'd had enough. So I figured that was my time. I used to love it, just to sit with them and teach them the best that I could."

One of the most important things to Adrienne is to "be your own person and be independent. I wouldn't want my daughter and grand-daughters taking orders from a man, 'cause I never have. They're not superior. Women have the brains to do anything." As far as feminism is concerned, "I have never been into the women's thing. I always thought of being with my husband, but I think it is good if women are fighting for something they want. I found that some of the feminist girls bring the men with them, too. A man could fight beside his woman if he believes in it."

- At age seventy-three, Adrienne feels, "I have achieved all I am ever going to achieve in my life, I'm too old." She struggles with arthritic knees, doesn't invest much time in her talents for music, knitting or sewing any more, but her relationship with Joe has remained strong. "[We've been together] for forty-eight years, coming up fifty. That'll be nice, I hope I make it." A message Adrienne has about relationships is, "I think having a sexual life ... is fine, but finding love and compatibility in a person is everything, like what Grandpa and I have. I'd be a lot worse without Joe, I'll tell you that much. I'm telling you, if Grandpa ever dies, watch out. Just put me in a home and tie me up. I'd be lost without Joe, I really would be."

Ida Pelletier, wings clipped, died with only her offspring to show for her life's work. Adrienne had a "mere" four children and chose to "break free," soaring away from a life as a housewife. She gave the world the man who would become my father. Her influence lives in him still, so indeed the story continues through the children. Women wearing their bodies down past all repair from perpetual pregnancy did not end in Adrienne's era though; nor did the trend of women choosing to stay home with their children.

Frances Ethel O'Connor (Martin), a vibrant woman, artist and singer, became a mother at age twenty-one when she bore her first child, Donna Mary Martin (Larkin), my mother, into the world on May 27, 1946. Frances continued to conceive for fourteen years straight, leaving five girls and seven boys in the world to carry on her heritage. At age fifty-eight she passed on, her body ravaged by cancer, after a life caring for a family of fourteen. This bird's voice may have been prematurely silenced but her spirit lives on in those she left behind. She will not be forgotten.

I grew up in "a male-dominated home [where] ... the girls did the bulk of the chores," recalls Donna. "I had an authoritarian father who is ... very self-centred and is also an alcoholic, which ... crippled the family. His behaviour was never challenged." Eldest of twelve, denied a childhood and burdened with responsibility, "I was numb to my reality, but ... vowed at a very young age that no man would ever dominate me.

"University was not an option for economic reasons and the stress factor within my family [was too much anyway]. It was always something I dreamed of, but it didn't happen." At age twenty-two, Donna married William Joseph Larkin, Adrienne's son. She worked as a secretary for years and reveals, "we were expected to make coffee and bring it in on trays. I was never sexually harassed but would not have tolerated it. In the '60s a woman's job was not considered a career, though." As Bill advanced in "his career," transferring from city to city, Donna followed without question; they settled for twelve years in St. Albert, Alberta, and raised their family of four. "Creating an equality situation within the home was important to me ... my spouse is very supportive ... but I often tried to ... control everything in the home to my standards, in an attempt to create ... a perfect existence unlike ... the chaos of my family of origin. In doing this, however, ... I began living as though my needs were not important ... and ... started to break down. I tried to be like my mother but felt I failed continually. I couldn't confide in my mother my deep depression or discontent with my own life; she saw me as having everything ... you would ever want, but I had a hole in my soul that I couldn't express to her."

As a homemaker, Donna did much volunteer work but mainly devoted her time to her family. "Being there, ... sharing with my children ... and seeing them embarking on their own journeys in life has been very gratifying. The pay is 'the shits,' though! Much of what I do within the home is taken for granted ... is not valued as work. I get frustrated ... that there are not enough hours in the day to accomplish all that I want to do for me. More importantly, however, what you teach your children goes out the door with them into the community ... it affects our future generations. There has to be more recognition given to those who stay at home and mould these young lives. I have fought for years with the question, 'What am I worth?' Being unpaid in this profession demeans the task of teaching, [but also] ... contributes to the shredding of women's self-esteem."

In between two sets of children, "I ran my husband's office doing secretarial work for about a year and a half. I found it difficult to maintain the home the way I had it without going to work." Because of this experience, Donna feels that, "the quality of life deteriorates ... in some facets when both parents work. I personally don't think you can effectively balance the two without a great deal of sacrifice."

Donna places great value in the empowering relationships in her life. She feels blessed with a "rock solid relationship" with her husband, but also feels that "the affirmations women give one another can't come from men. There's not the same depth." Donna's search for deep emotional support has been satisfied by several femal mentors. "[They] were all very catalytic in bringing me to where I am today, in affirming me. Not getting the affirmation I looked for in my husband was hard until I realized ... my husband's inability to affirm my talents was his fear that every time he saw me forging ahead, he thought he was losing part of me ... it's a threat to their male security ... that things will start to change." Donna's introspective nature has enriched her life considerably; she is always looking to improve herself. She takes personal exploration classes, reads a great deal and does daily meditation in an effort to attain balance and serenity. "The biggest part of who I am is my spirituality. Because of female suppression [and] ... the dogma that was shoved down my throat growing up in the Catholic Church, I have lost faith in organized religion, but my core beliefs in a higher power have only become stronger. My need for control is gone and I am far more accepting. I hopefully act as a beacon to other people as they see me becoming ... more peaceful." Another influential aspect of Donna's life has been her involvement in active recovery programs to heal the pain caused by the alcoholism that has consumed her life since childhood.

Donna hopes her daughters will "reach their potential with serenity, rise above all that stands in their way, celebrate themselves and remain connected to people who support them. I've always said, 'Never give yourself away cheaply, every time you give a piece of yourself to someone ... [it's] gone forever.'" In relationships, Donna hopes her daughters "have mutual respect ... communication at a deep level, and the ability to ... celebrate one another as individuals and not do as I did and unknowingly live my life through others and become a shadow of a man over the years!

"I now feel I am capable of doing anything I set my mind to. Fear used to hold me back, fear of moving out of the shadows of my mother and my executive husband climbing the ladder." With wings outstretched Donna is now exploring her many talents, works with a special-needs child and gardens daily. "I have been a teacher a long time. I would for once like to be a student." Happily, she reveals, "I am soon beginning university and am fulfilling a dream at the age of forty-nine!" It's never too late for a bird to take flight.

I, Jennifer Anne Larkin, was born October 7, 1972, in Ottawa. I am Donna's first-born daughter. At age five I was afflicted with the whooping cough. I needed to become very self-sufficient to survive the ordeal, which further intensified my already independent character. My childhood was wonderful. My mother gave me the freedom to explore my imagination, celebrate my uniqueness and discover my talents. She never thwarted my free spirit from soaring. The gifts she has given me are many.

At age nine, my place in the family dramatically changed. My mother had two more children and I began taking on responsibilities similar to those my mother had taken on in her youth. I was often in the kitchen with my mother, developed a passion for cooking and helped out often with minding the "little ones." I feel fortunate to have had this experience.

There were differences, which perhaps were unintentional, in the way males and females were treated in the family. My parents always seemed more overprotective and questioning with me than with my older brother. Expectations concerning household responsibilities seemed to be placed more heavily on me as well. I often was at home baby-sitting while my brother was out socializing, and I frequently cleaned up after dinner while the boys watched sports.

Feeling overshadowed by the presence of two new babies in the home, I often felt I shouldn't bother anyone in the family with my problems, so I shared very little. In school, I always felt very different from everyone. I was also mature beyond my years, separating me further from my peer group. I spent my entire adolescence rebelling against the world, experimenting with everything and searching for answers.

I used my creativity as an outlet for all the bottled emotions in my life. The theatre became my second home and a place for self-expression. Becoming a performer was monumental in shaping the person that I am today. I know now that I need to express myself through creative means in order to feel totally fulfilled.

I am often seen by others as a very confident person. Because of this, I felt I couldn't express what was troubling me or show people my weaknesses for fear of disappointing them. Unfortunately, I spent so much time protecting myself, I shut out many potential relationships, denying myself the level of human connection we all crave in the process. I now realize the importance of empowering relationships and have happily discovered it is possible to reap the benefits without losing who you are as an individual.

My strong need to be an individual is very significant, however. Seeing girls unquestioningly lose their identity for the sake of "popularity" made me cringe growing up. Stereotypes of women were reinforced as they acted dumber than, weaker than or less than who they were. I made the choice early to be true to my convictions and conform to no one. I have not escaped unscathed in the process, however, and have been most severely affected by body image in my lifetime. Much of my youth was spent concerned that I was not thin enough, pretty enough, hairless enough or good enough, and no attempt to be a strong liberated woman altered that fact. I continue to try and break free of the insecurities imbedded in me, but society just perpetuates the problem, especially for women. We must have faith that with persistence we can change anything. Women's equality is something humanity as a group can work on together. Women do not need to do it alone!

Education plays a key role in attaining equality and freedom. It opens up the world and reveals all the possibilities, empowers you to be strong and never allows you to limit your vision for the future. Although I am still searching for a career direction, my insatiable desire to learn drives me forward. I also nourish myself by keeping physically active, writing and exploring my spirituality (outside the confines of structured religion).

My job (supervisor of security at a civic center in Ottawa) is challenging. As a female in an authority position, I often feel like I need to prove myself and am ever leery of possible sexism. Much goes on that wouldn't if I were male. I was also sexually assaulted by two "friends" at age fourteen, and have fallen victim to various forms of physical and verbal abuse. Being a fighter, my need to challenge others to work for change has never been stronger.

I don't know what is down the road for me as far as marriage and children are concerned, but I know in my heart that I will not be satisfied with my life if I don't give back to the world what my mother gave me — life to continue the everlasting chain.

So, as far as I am concerned, my wings are outstretched. I continue to soar, searching for my path in life. I have been snared by the occasional chain, but I believe my will can break through anything that holds me back. I will do my best to ensure that my wings, and the wings that follow me, are never clipped. The story continues.

leery

MAKING IT AS A WOMAN IN A MAN'S WORLD

Jane Zigman p ass

-◄o►-

GENERATION 1: DOROTHY
(JANE'S MOTHER)

BORN OCTOBER 7, 1917, on a farm in Sherwood Springs near
Brockville, Ontario, Dorothy was the sixth child of three boys and five
girls raised by Georgina May Widdows. A petite woman who "came to
Canada from England when she was twenty-five," May ruled her brood
with an iron fist and, occasionally, the switch. In Dorothy's opinion,
however, they "were one big happy family and always had lots to eat.
My role model was mostly my father. He sort of ruled the roost, most
men those days did. Mother was pretty hardheaded betimes, and pretty
pushy too, but she went along with my dad mostly. My mother worked
in the house, she baked, cooked, milked cows and helped my father in
the fields on the farm. She never worked [outside the home] until my
dad was older, after we lost the farm. My father was not a good man-
ager, [but] he wouldn't allow her to look after things. A man was the
boss, he was the king of his little domain."

According to Dorothy, "My parents always knew I was a smart
kid." Hence, she aspired to create a better life for herself than the hard
life her mother had chosen. "I wanted to be a nurse all my life but we
didn't have the means. I didn't want to be like my mother. I wouldn't
choose the same role model now, because I think women are smarter
than men." Growing up in the Depression, she had to quit school with
only a Grade-Eleven education. "There was me and my brother and sister.

My mother couldn't afford to keep us going or buy clothes for us, so we had to quit. I was fourteen at the time and I went to work. There were no jobs then ... all you could get was housework. At age sixteen, I thought it was a great world to live in then. I don't think it is now. I was hoping that I could get a good job, better than housework. I would like to have finished my high-school education."

Dorothy married before the Second World War, and had four daughters with her first husband. "I did the domestic tasks, I looked after the house. The most gratifying element of family life was my kids, because I had them and I looked after them. The most frustrating element of family life was my husband running around after other women. When I was married, I worked for him, kept the books, washed wipers, and I got paid."

At the age of thirty-three, Dorothy moved in with her mother with her children. "I left my first husband because he was mentally and physically abusive and we were divorced. I married my second husband in 1968 and had a good relationship with him. [He died in 1978.] I paid the bills and I looked after things. In my first marriage, my husband was the boss but in my second marriage, I was the boss. Women are more into their own these days, they are not under a man's thumb as they used to be. When I was married to my first husband, I never thought I was worth a penny. It wasn't until I left him that I really found myself. It wasn't until I got into ... [factory work] that I found out I could do things, make money, save money. I never wanted to be a boss or anything like that. When I was working, we had a lot of fun, a lot of laughs.

"Now I am [retired and] independent, I do what I want. I have my pensions, I pay my bills and I feel good about myself. I live alone and I have no pets. Sometimes I get lonely but I don't mind it. I read books and I do crossword puzzles. For my daughters, I hope they get along in this world fine, make something of themselves. And my grandchildren, I hope they get good jobs.

"I don't have relationships outside my family, except bowling, lodge and cards. I don't think of myself as a caregiver, [although] I make cakes for my grandchildren. I am a Rebekah [Lodge member. It's a club for women that operates as an auxiliary to the Independent Order of Odd Fellows for men]. We believe in friendship, love and truth. We are all women in the lodge.

"I believe in Canada and the Canadian way of life. I have travelled to Australia, Tahiti, England, Florida, Texas, the Caribbean, the East Coast [of Canada] and Vancouver. I think this area is the best. I believe that women are smart, most women are morally superior to men. I think they should be put into Parliament. I think men are crooked and women should run everything. Yes, I do [agree that women contribute many hours of unpaid work to their families]. I think women should have a fifty-fifty share of pensions.

"[The most important personal change in my life was] my divorce from [my first] husband. [The most significant social change which affected my life was] women in the work force. My daughters' [lives are very different since they] have [had] more opportunity and education."

GENERATION 2: JANE
(DOROTHY'S DAUGHTER)

After my parents' separation when I was two, I grew up in a female environment with my mother and sisters, two older and one younger. We were all equal except for size and age, my older sisters being a little more equal. We did have male contact since my father visited daily when business permitted. I modelled myself after my parents, trying to emulate the best qualities from both my self-educated, businesslike father and my independent, self-sufficient mother. My evaluations of them have not changed; thus I would still choose the same.

At sixteen, I was a rather conventional teen looking for a boyfriend and concerned about my appearance with little idea of my goals in life. Growing up in a small community during the age of rock and roll, hippies, free sex, drugs and the women's movement, I missed it all except the rock and roll. I had little involvement in the '70s counterculture, since I was marginalized from groups who might influence my choices. I do not doubt that these factors affected my outlook and actions. Since I was assumed to be smart by my parents, it was simply taken for granted that I would go to university to acquire a profession. Rebellious and unsure of my abilities, I opted for what appeared to be an easier route.

After one year of teacher's college, I was hired to teach elementary school but began taking university courses immediately in order to advance in pay and qualifications.

With little faith in marriage or interest in raising children, I married despite an already dysfunctional relationship. I soon realized that "happily-ever-afters" are figments of collective imaginations but seldom realized in real life. Thus, after nine years of incompatibility, I became a single parent of three children with limited resources to support them. Since jobs were impossible to obtain, I started my own graphic and sign business, rented rooms and operated a mini-golf park, which supported us for almost ten years.

While all of the relationships in my life were important, the one that had the greatest impact was my disastrous marriage, which confirmed my former low opinion of the institution of marriage. Attempting to correct the problems of my parents' relationship, I managed to re-enact the whole scenario, only to discover that there was no solution. After navigating a series of disastrous relationships, I am now involved in a friendship that includes trust, acceptance and, especially, humour. Having demonstrated the pitfalls to my children, I hope that they will finally see that good relationships are possible. Like my mother, I expect and hope that my daughters will make better choices in careers and relationships to create more interesting and satisfying lives. As a good listener, I seldom interfere in the affairs of other women. With my children, however, I try to steer a safe course, offering advice in certain situations and biting my tongue in others.

By taking the harder route and overcoming obstacles along the way, I have gained confidence in the belief that I can accomplish any task worth pursuing with hard work and ingenuity. I suspect that because few options were available to me, in fact, my choices have been different. I am currently finishing my honours degree in psychology with a concentration in Women's Studies and plan to continue with graduate work, to what end I do not know at this time. I trust that it will become clear as I progress.

Coming from a small-minded community like Brockville, it is refreshing to live in a city like Ottawa where people accept you for the person you wish to be. My favourite form of recreation is spending quality time with good friends and family, reading an interesting book or engaging in simple pleasures like walking or dancing.

Raising my children alone after my divorce forced me to re-evaluate my priorities and to structure my life to suit my interests and abilities. The advent of birth control would qualify as the most important social change in my lifetime. I am sure that my mother and grandmothers would have welcomed the option to control the number and spacing of their children. Fortunately, my daughters have a greater degree of choice in relationships and lifestyles since feminism has reduced the pressures that compelled women to fulfill prescribed roles in society.

GENERATION 3: RACHELLE (JANE'S DAUGHTER)

The oldest of three children, Rachelle claims her role model was her mother. "She was a working mom and she had her own business. Now, I don't really think much about role models. I don't know, I'm pretty much my own person, I try not to model myself [after anyone]."

Being the oldest daughter, however, has it's drawbacks, since "everyone has some things to do but I feel that I have the largest share. [I] make supper, do the dishes, pretty much everything … [the] things that everyone else doesn't do." As a student in university with a part-time job, her most important relationships may be only beginning to develop. "I guess," she says, that "these include my family and some of my friends, not my old friends, but new friends in Ottawa, at work. I don't want marriage or children, but I would like to have a relationship, someone to talk to or do things with." Despite being raised by a single mother she feels that, "I [can] take anything I [want] at university. I [have] to do the housework but I don't feel the need to be a wife or a mother or a teacher.

"At sixteen, I was working and going to school. I was more crazy than I am now, [I] did more crazy things then. I used to talk to a lot of people on the phone. I'm more tame now, just work and go to school and go out once a week. I think my mother just wants me to be successful and rich, not be married and not have kids, and to be rich.

"The era I grew up in probably masculinized me more. What era is this, Generation X? I don't think I was a 'groupie' to follow what other people were doing. People expected me to be responsible and I am. They expected me to be thoughtful and nice and I am, [as well as] polite and giving and [hard working]."

Her own attitudes regarding her personal abilities have undergone some transformation. According to Rachelle, "some things have gone up and some things have gone down. In school, I don't think that I'm that great but in other things I've done better than I thought I could. Especially the physical side, I feel a lot stronger, more capable and more confident. [I am very exercise conscious.] I probably would still have taken psychology. I want to help people, but I don't want a PhD."

As for religious orientation, "I pretty much listen to most spiritual religions but not too many really appeal to me. The only one that sort of appeals to me is Wiccan. I like Wiccan because it's pretty much non-structured, and I like astrology.

"I don't think women have to be better than anyone or anything, they don't have to be morally superior to anyone just because they've been socialized to be more sensitive. It doesn't mean that they have to be, men should be able to do that, too.

"My race is white. British is more what I identify with, I'm also half French but I don't really identify with it. I'm partially Russian and Irish, which is all right on St. Patrick's Day. My religion is non-denominational; social class is middle class. Sexual orientation … not really sexual. I am completely able. [These factors have had] absolutely no impact on my life. I used to think religion was more important, but now I don't.

"My home is where my hat is. It's only important because there are people here [in Ottawa] that I like. If I could bring the people [that] I like to BC then I would like it there, too. I guess [living in] Brockville has affected my life. My parents' divorce has also affected my life.

"I have not been active in volunteer, women's or political organizations. Feminism means being for women, that's it. Media attention makes women look bad, but [it has] not [affected my life] too much. My personal relationship course [at university] has effected the greatest change [in my personal life]. [My life is different from that of my grandmothers and my mother since] I'm not married, I don't have any kids, [and] I haven't been beaten. [What do I think of this interview?] Too much!"

LOOKING THROUGH DIFFERENT EYES INTO A COMMON FUTURE

Karen Campbell

◄◦►

I'VE HAD A VERY DIFFICULT TIME trying to tell the lives of my foremothers. Even though they've given me their own words, I find that I seem to lose them through the telling. They don't fit into sentences or parcel themselves into issues; you can't hear their smooth voices on the page, or see the light or the anger in their eyes.

Margaret Campbell, my grandmother, is of French and British descent and was born in Winnipeg, Manitoba. Her family moved to London, Ontario, when she was in her teens. She became a teacher by profession and continued to take university and other courses throughout a good deal of her adult life. She married a minister of the United Church and raised three children. They've been together for over fifty-two years. The Campbells lived in many different communities in Manitoba and finally settled in Burlington, Ontario.

Susan Anderson (Nakalook), my mother, is Inuit and was born on Nottingham Island in the Northwest Territories. When Susie was a little girl, she fell into a bonfire and received third degree burns to over 50 percent of her body. Three men, working at a weather station on the Island, saved her life. They cared for her by communicating with doctors through a radio handset, until the weather allowed flying her to the closest hospital in The Pas, Manitoba. While Susie was being nursed back to health, the people living in her community were "relocated" to another island by the federal government. Susie was unable to find out where they had been moved to, and never saw her birth mother again. Since she was too ill to go home, Susie stayed in The Pas with the young minister and his wife (the Campbells), who took care of her when she wasn't in the hospital. Unfortunately, at that point in history, it was deemed inappropriate for a white couple to adopt an Inuit child, so Susie was sent off to a residential school. For more than a century, hundreds of Aboriginal children were forcibly taken from their families and sent to schools run by religious orders, who taught them how to assimilate into Euro-Canadian society. For some children this was an opportunity to learn, but for most the experience produced intense psychological scars, since they were dislocated from their families, were prevented from speaking their languages and were often subject to various forms of abuse. Luckily for Susie, she couldn't stay in the school for long, since her growing body required constant skin grafts and lengthy stays in the hospital. When Susie was eighteen and no longer legally defined as a ward of the Crown, she was adopted by the Campbells. Even though her formal education as a child was quite sporadic, she went through college and became a nurse. After more than thirty years of turbulent relationships, she married a lovely, kind Ojibway man, and settled on his home reserve in southern Ontario.

I am my mother's only child, and I am adopted as well. I grew up all around southern Ontario, but stayed the longest in Mnjikaning (Rama) First Nation, which is where I call home and where my parents still live. I am soon beginning graduate studies in social work in Winnipeg. I am the keeper of my mother's story — I have lived with and told her history since I was a child. I am now fortunate enough to begin to have the stories of my grandmother to keep and tell as well. At many times in my life I have felt overwhelmed by my mother's past — it is impossible for me to have an identity separate from what has happened to my mother, since I have been affected by her life as much as she has. Fortunately for us, she had the influence and care of some very good people along the way, like my grandmother.

The elder women in my family are both exceptional; my mother for her strength and sheer will to survive, and my grandmother for her wealth of kindness and love. It was these strengths that brought them into each others lives, and into mine. In some ways it feels as though the women in our family did not come together by chance, that there was some sort of fate engineering our choices. Although we are three very different women, we draw our strengths from similar places, and we have our eyes set ahead on a common future.

One aspect of our lives that we all agree is essential to our very being is a profound sense of spirituality. My grandmother has always been actively involved in the church, the Anglican Church when she was growing up and the United Church after her marriage. "I don't know what I would do without the faith that it has given me," she explains, "the beliefs, the confidence in something better in this world. It's been one of the biggest influences in my life ... [and] it has deepened over the years to the point that I couldn't be without it. I need that communion with other people and that feeling that a supreme being is there and that I can call on that when I need it. I've needed it many times in my life and found that it [has] never failed me."

My mother's experience with religion has been much less homogenous. She now follows the traditional path of the Ojibway, which she is learning from various elders, especially her husband. "As I was growing up, I was forced to believe in different religions, but now I feel at peace living within Aboriginal spirituality. Most of us involved in the residential schools have turned against or away from the churches and turned to Native spirituality because it is all-encompassing. There are no strict rules and regulations and it's not something that can be forced on anyone. It's a person's choice."

I've been lucky to grow up with diverse spiritual influences. I've been able to take what speaks to me, and leave what I felt was harmful. A belief we all share is that women are central and integral to spiritual life, they are the leaders, the caregivers and the strength of the community. I have a less formal experience of religion than my foremothers and feel a more general and basic spiritual connection with the earth and other peoples.

My grandmother and my mother are both very artistic, and find a grounding for their self-confidence within their recreation. My mother sews and spends a great deal of her time, both dreaming and awake, creating ideas in fabric. My grandmother finds expression and confidence through the theatre. "I was never a person who had much confidence in myself," she says, "but over the years, I found that I'm much more capable than I ever thought I was, and I think that's come out through encouragement from other people ... particularly in the way of theatre. Taking courses at university and being on stage helped me a lot. Then I ... tried to direct shows and I found I was very capable and it literally changed my opinion of myself." She spent over twenty years devoting her time to helping in the production of musicals, particularly with the Burlington Light Opera Society. This has given her a sense of connection with the wider arts community. "I identify with women who are working to do something for their community; women who are educators, caregivers, who are working for the culture, the beauty of our country, not only in theatre but in art and music; [women] who are doing those kinds of things to make our society a better place for everybody to be in."

Although my grandmother found confidence and community through her recreation, my mother needed to look some place else. There was a constant void in her life left by her early loss of her biological family, some of whom she was able to trace. "When I found my family after searching for forty-two years, it made me realize I had to come to terms with who I really am and to take pride in my own heritage. It changed the direction of my life ... and helped me to come out of myself, to be honest and stand and say this is who I am, this is where I was born, this is what I can take pride in." Once she found what she was searching for, my mother became much more vocal about the rights of Aboriginal peoples, particularly women. "I am part of a movement to make change so that our children and future generations never go through the residential school system. I am a survivor ... a survivor of Canadian history."

My mother began organizing with other women, and for a few years had a very active role with the Ontario Native Women's Association. However, she feels alienated by the women's movement and by feminism. "I don't like the word used at all. I think it means a real radical type female. In one sense I would say I'm a feminist but not the radical type that throws their bras around and that type of thing. I believe in women's rights, women's issues and women's voices, but in a soft gentle way."

My grandmother echoes these ideas: "In many ways [feminism] has become a dirty word. I think that the feminist movement has had some very poor leadership [by some] very angry people that have led it way down the garden path and have made people feel they don't want anything to do with it. I think it's a shame because there's a place for it. I'm a feminist up to a point, where I feel women should have an equal chance and opportunities with men ... but when women try to push men aside I can't go with it."

Unlike the other women in my family, I feel very comfortable identifying with the term "feminist." In fact, I feel I've gained a lot of my sense of self through my personal activism, largely within the women's movement. Although my mother and grandmother do not consider themselves feminists, they embody and believe in feminist ideas and have personally worked to change the lives of women, and I am sure we all agree that all our lives are very different than the women's who have come before us, greatly due to the women's movement.

My grandmother feels that changes in women's lives are "multitudinous," and that women now have much greater "freedom to be and freedom of communication." Although she had plentiful opportunities in her youth, as a woman she was still limited in her choice of career. If she had had the opportunity to change some of her decisions, she would have loved to work in theatre or television, something she did not have a chance to explore until later in her life. When my grandmother envisions my life and those of my daughters, she "hope[s] that they will find their place in the world today and that they contribute ... I want to see women contribute more than they ever have because I think they have an important role to play in our future." It is only because of the greater freedom and opportunities available to women now that they can contribute in this manner. It is because of these same gains that I can actively call myself a feminist, where I feel that my mother and grandmother cannot.

The biggest change in my mother's life did not relate to improvements for women, but rather to changes in the lives of Aboriginal peoples. "I am not living my own cultural life like my grandmother and my mother. I've been forced into another life which was not mine." My mother's greatest wish is to learn more about her culture and to re-learn the language that was taken from her as a child. As part of her healing, she shares her story with others to give them hope or simply to help them understand the harm of cultural ignorance and interference. She and her husband volunteer almost full-time, teaching people about their traditions and about their lives.

Even though the lives of my foremothers have been very different, they both describe their personal growth in the same terms, as finding tolerance and acceptance of others and themselves. Although they started at different places, and have taken very different journeys, they are now at a point where their ideas converge and they can go into the future along the same path. My grandmother realizes that over the years she has "become much more tolerant of things and people. I am more tolerant of ethnic groups that I felt at one time were invading the country and I didn't want them here. Now I've met so many that I've grown to know and to love that I feel a profound respect for people who maybe hadn't had the opportunities until they came to Canada. I've also become more tolerant of people who have had more opportunities than I had. At one time I think I experienced a lot of jealous feelings about people who could go to university and could do things until I realized that I had opportunities, too, and I made the most out of them." My mother has also become much more accepting of who she is: "I've had a lot of growth. I still have a lot of healing to do but I am more accepting of my own and other people's faults ... more patient and understanding where before I wouldn't tolerate or accept differences. I am more at peace with myself and with other people, and happy with my home life."

Like my foremothers I need to learn from the kind and gentle teachings of elder women, to learn tolerance, love and self-acceptance. In the Ojibway tradition, the seventh generation is the one to set all nations on the path to healing and acceptance — to reconcile our differences. In our family, three generations of very different women have all managed to begin the journey on this path to reconciliation together. However, as one of the seventh generation, I hope I can learn from the stories of my grandmother and my mother and reach the same peace within myself.

WOMEN'S VIEWS
OVER THREE GENERATIONS

Susan Castle

◄○►

THE THREE GENERATIONS OF WOMEN I discuss here are my grandmother, Pat Brown, my mother, Carroll Castle, and me, Susan Castle.
Some areas of our lives appear similar, as do the feminine views and
emotions we share, but in other areas the opportunities and lifestyles
we have known are so different that the fifty-nine years separating us
seems like different lifetimes rather than different generations. One thing
common among all of us is that we are women and we face many similar
challenges. There are three important and constant themes throughout
the lives of my grandmother, my mother and myself that I focus on:
our early family lives, educational opportunities and spirituality. I focus
on these since they appeared and reappeared throughout my research.

Each of us grew up in different situations with varying degrees of
typically feminine domestic duties. My grandmother grew up during the
Depression on a rural farm near Shawville, Québec, where she had a lot
of work to do at home. She participated in the domestic responsibilities
of cooking, cleaning, washing and so on, and the boys helped their father
do the outside chores with the crops and animals. There were no other
families nearby who could help out, so the responsibilities were left up
to them, because it was next to impossible to hire someone during such
difficult economic circumstances. When asked how she felt about the
daily responsibilities laid upon her, her mother and her sister, my
grandmother simply stated that "on a farm everyone had to help out,
and that was the way it was." When asked how these responsibilities affected her way of thinking, she said that "a woman's place should always

· 198 ·

be at home with her family, if she chooses to have one. Women are moral beings and are the nurturers when it comes to the family. However, should a woman choose not to have a family she should do her best to excel in whatever path she chooses." Throughout her life, my grandmother has been a homemaker and has worked hard at her job; my grandfather was the sole breadwinner working in their family-owned garage. I know she has greatly supported everything her daughters and granddaughters have chosen to do in their lives. I know she is very proud of the fact that I am a university graduate.

Growing up, my grandmother loved baseball. In fact, she was even better at the game than most boys. In our interview she told me that if women in her day had had the opportunity to play professional baseball or if she had been a man, she would have tried to play in the major leagues. Today, she is still a huge Toronto Blue Jays fan and watches almost every game on television while wearing her cap.

My mother, Carroll Castle, grew up in Oakville, Ontario, where we still live today. Shortly after my grandparents were married, they moved to central Ontario and had five children, the first of which was my mother. At that time Oakville's population barely exceeded thirty thousand. As one of two daughters, my mother helped out around the house assisting my grandmother with domestic responsibilities. Her three brothers had paper routes and helped their father in the family-owned garage. The home responsibilities that my mother's generation took part in were similar to those of my grandmother's. There was no immediate family close by; However, another family who lived upstairs in their home became their "extended" family. (My mother could not pronounce Mrs. Sommerhill's name, the woman who lived upstairs, as a child, so she spent the rest of her life calling her "Fumfum" and her husband "Green Fumfum.") My mother attended school nearby and had a lot of friends both at school and within the church. My mother has always been fond of her family and, most importantly, of her own mother. They are very close and live only blocks away from each other. My mother admires my grandmother for all that she has done with her life. [Recently,] my grandmother was given an award by the Oakville Rotary Club for her participation in the community. This was the first time this award had ever been given to a non-Rotarian. I also have spent my entire life in Oakville. Today the population has risen to one hundred thousand. As a child I had to clean my room and put my clothes in the laundry. However, aside from that I had no real home duties.

In my family home, the responsibilities between my parents were fairly equal. My father did the grocery shopping, baking and vacuuming, and my mother did a lot of the cooking, cleaning and laundering. When either one of them needed support, the other was always willing to help out. This could be a result of the ever-changing world and the realities of both of them working. My mother worked part-time as a nurse at the Oakville hospital until she became full-time. When my younger sister, brother and myself were growing up, we always had a parent around. My parents seemed to plan their time wisely; my father would work all day and then my mother would work the four p.m. to midnight shift while my dad was at home with us. When we started school, both my parents took on more responsibilities in the community, which I believe encouraged us to participate both in social and extracurricular activities.

It appears that throughout the three generations, our lives have kept pace with the new opportunities for women who could enter the workforce and become educated, as society slowly accepted women as independent people. Times have changed since the Depression and the Second World War, when women worked in factories to support Canadian forces overseas. Today, women fight for equal rights in the workforce and the community. These social changes have helped women progress to where we are today. In addition, new laws protect us and as a group we strive for educational and economic independence.

During the Depression there were very few educational opportunities for young women in rural Québec, especially for poor families. My grandmother's family suffered many economic tribulations when her father was accidentally shot in the leg by a child who was shooting at targets on a tree. Consequently, his leg was amputated, and he was in a Ottawa hospital for six months after almost losing his life in the incident. This left my grandmother's family with less help on the farm and with greater economic hardship since her father could not earn extra wages working for neighbouring farmers. As a result, they became very poor. There was no extra money after his accident for my grandmother or her siblings to obtain any formal post-secondary education. My grandmother wanted to become a nurse. In fact, when I asked her what job or career she would choose if she could have any one she wanted, she replied that she would still like to be a nurse. However, she married and started a family and there was no time for her to get the education she wanted. Years later she was able to live out this dream through her daughters, who both became nurses.

While my mother was growing up, the educational opportunities for girls were mainly directed towards three different streams: teaching, nursing and administrative work. Women chose which route they wanted to take in high school and took courses according to that choice. My mother attended the nursing school at the Salvation Army Grace Hospital in Windsor, Ontario. She chose this particular school because she wanted to make her mother happy, as it was important to her that she went to a Salvation Army nursing hospital. My mother feels that life was very traditional then, but given the opportunity to have any lifestyle, she would choose first to be independently wealthy so she could travel the world, and second, she would still choose to become a nurse.

In my educational career, I have had many opportunities to get whatever education I wanted. Today, it is not gender that stops students my age from getting a higher education; rather, it is the competition for spots within the universities. My parents and grandparents have been very supportive of me both financially and personally as a student, always encouraging me to study as much as I want and not to worry about any financial costs. This support is what all women deserve and need — it can give them the confidence to get what they want out of life.

As a sociology and Women's Studies student at the University of Ottawa, I have been faced with many gender challenges and issues that face women within the university hierarchy. Although I see how far women and education have come over the last several years, I do not believe that Canadians have reached the goal of equality. However, this study of three generations of women is an example of how women have advanced over the past fifty-nine years. It is also an example of women's strength and drive to grasp opportunities that come their way.

Religion and spirituality in various forms have been a part of all our lives as members of the Salvation Army Church. However, the views of religion have changed from my grandmother's generation to mine. It is not a matter of my mother and myself being less religious; rather, our thinking patterns have expanded on religious views.

Religion has been a very important part of my grandmother's life, starting at an early age. Her mother used to read Bible stories to her and her siblings on Sundays. She does admit that at the time she would much rather have scooted out the backdoor to go play baseball with her friends, but she believes that those stories created a base for her spirituality. Gran has been an active member of the Salvation Army Christian organization since 1955 and participates as a volunteer. She raised her children in this church, and some of them continue to attend. Her religion goes far beyond attending church; every decision that is made in her life involves the Lord and is carefully thought out. Her church and experiences as a young child have led to the volunteer work she does today. During the Depression after her father lost his leg, the children on the nearby farms used to call her a "poor kid," telling her that their parents had to give her family sugar or flour because they could not afford to buy their own. She explained that in those days you were not given money by neighbours; instead, they helped a family in need by giving food, quilts and other materials. The experience of hearing other children say these horrible things to her made her promise herself she would never let the same things happen to her children. This kind nature led her to helping the sick and needy through her volunteer work with the Salvation Army and in the local hospital.

My mother has grown up in the Salvation Army Church, and it is still a mainstay of her life. She actively participates in church groups and attends functions at our family's church in Toronto. She has developed many long-term relationships with people at the church and the Salvation Army nursing school she attended. Her view of the Salvation Army has changed over the years. For example, the Salvation Army is a strong advocate against drinking. However, my mother does not feel that drinking in moderation is wrong. It has been important to my mother that her children attend church on Sundays. She also had us attend youth group and sing in the children's choir. When I was older, I joined the adult choir and sang in it for five years.

Before I was born, my parents attended Yorkminster Citadel in Toronto, and they still attend that church. Since moving to a new city and starting university, I have found myself attending church less because I know very few people who attended the Salvation Army Church in Ottawa. This, however, is not the only reason I do not attend church often. I have found it difficult as a woman to agree with the religious teachings that support out-of-date views concerning women's place in society. I find that I am no longer drawn to one particular religion, but believe in several combinations of religions. In a sense I have developed my own personal spirituality with God that is not dictated but guided by spirituality and the understanding that women are more than what they appear to be.

Questions concerning women and Women's Studies demonstrate that we are becoming increasingly conscious of the advancement of women. For example, my grandmother believes that a woman's place is with her family. My mother in some ways is like her mother, but she strongly feels that women should do whatever they want as far as having children. She would advise her daughters to think twice before having children because the job prospects and standard of living in Canada are anticipated to decline.

Our three generations are vastly different in some areas. However, the challenges we face as women remain the same. Time has changed more traditional values and ideals over the past fifty-nine years, and it is our hope that the advancement of women will continue in the future.

Notes

1. Statistics Canada, "Profile of Census Divisions and Subdivisions in Ontario," *Profile of Census Divisions and Subdivisions* (Ottawa: Industry Canada, 1999. 1996 Census of Canada. Catalogue number 95-187-WPB), 22.

2. Madeleine Brant Castellano and Janice Hill, "First Nations Women: Reclaiming our Responsibilities," in Joy Parr, ed., *A Diversity of Women: Ontario 1945–1989* (Toronto: University of Toronto Press, 1995), 232.

3. Pauline Johnson, "Marshlands," *The New Oxford Book of Canadian Verse in English*, chosen by Margaret Atwood (Toronto: Oxford University Press, 1983), 60.

4. Catharine Parr Traill, *The Backwoods of Canada* (1836; reprint, Toronto: McLelland and Stewart Limited, 1966), 65.

5. Susanna Moodie, *Roughing It in the Bush* (1852; reprint, Toronto: McClelland and Stewart Limited, 1962), 231.

6. Gwendolyn MacEwen, "Dark Pines Under Water," *The New Oxford Book of Canadian Verse in English*, 389.

7. Castellano and Hill, "First Nations Women," 232.

8. Ibid., 233.

9. Sylvia Maracle quoted in Castellano and Hill, "First Nations Women," 246.

10. Linda Cardinal, "Making a Difference: The Theory and Practice of Francophone Women's Groups, 1969–1982," in Parr, ed., *A Diversity of Women*, 283.

11. "Profile of Census Divisions and Subdivisions in Ontario," 22–28.

12. Table 1, Profile of Census Divisions and Subdivisions in Ontario-Part A. 1991 Census (Ottawa: Statistics Canada, Ministry of Industry, Science and Technology, 1992), 26.

13. For a comprehensive overview of women's organizing in the North and selections from *The Northern Woman Journal* see Ruth Roach Pierson, Marjorie Griffin Cohen, Paula Bourne, and Philinda Masters, eds., *Canadian Women's Issues*, Volume I, *Strong Voices* (Toronto: James Lorimer and Company, 1993).

14. E. A. (Nora) Cebotarev, "From Domesticity to the Public Sphere: Farm Women, 1945-1986," in Parr, ed., *A Diversity of Women*, 212–215.

15. Ibid., 213.

16. Ibid., 218.

17. Ibid., 201.

18. Marjorie Griffin Cohen, "Feminism's Effect on Economic Policy," in Ruth Roach Pierson and Marjorie Griffin Cohen, eds., *Canadian Women's Issues*, Volume II, *Bold Visions* (Toronto: James Lorimer and Company, 1995), 282–336.

19. "Profile of Census Divisions and Subdivisions of Ontario," 30–32.

20. Ibid, 24.

21. Cohen, "Feminism's Effect on Economic Policy," 281.

22. Marymay Downing, "For Her or Against Her: The Power of Religious Metaphor,"

in Geraldine Finn, ed., *Limited Edition: Voice of Women, Voices of Feminism* (Halifax: Fernwood Publishing, 1993), 66–71.

23. Ibid., 77–78.

24. Catherine L. Cleverdon, *The Woman Suffrage Movement in Canada* (Toronto: University of Toronto Press, 1974), 19–45.

25. Alison Prentice, Paula Bourne, Gail Cuthbert Brandt, Beth Light, Wendy Mitchinson, and Naomi Black, *Canadian Women: A History* (Toronto: Harcourt Brace Jovanovich, 1988), 367.

26. Ibid., 322.

27. Ibid., 427–428.

28. Sylvia B. Bashevkin, *Toeing the Lines: Women and Party Politics in English Canada* (Toronto: University of Toronto Press, 1985), 114.

29. Ibid., 106–107.

30. Ibid., 110–111.

31. Dorothy Goldin Rosenberg, "Feminism and Peace," in Greta Hofmann Nemiroff, ed., *Women and Men: Interdisciplinary Readings on Gender* (Toronto: Fitzhenry and Whiteside, 1986), 523.

32. Kay Macpherson, "Persistent Voices: 25 Years with Voice of Women," *Atlantis* (Spring 1987), 60–72.

33. Cerise Morris, "Determination and Thoroughness: The Movement for a Royal Commission on the Status of Women in Canada," *Atlantis* (Spring 1980), 5.

34. Judy LaMarsh, *Memoirs of a Bird in a Gilded Cage* (Toronto: McClelland and Stewart Limited, 1969), 301–302.

35. Laura Sabia, "Fiercely Feminist," in Margaret Gillett and Kay Sibbald, eds., *A Fair Shake: Autobiographical Essays by McGill Women* (Montreal: Eden Press, 1984), 372.

36. Ibid., 373.

37. Ibid.

38. Prentice et al., *Canadian Women*, 349.

39. Esmeralda Thornhill, President of the Congress of Black Women of Canada, interview with author, Montréal, 19 February 1990.

40. Marlee Kline, "Women's Oppression and Racism: A Critique of the 'Feminist Standpoint,'" in Jesse Vorst et al., eds., *Race, Class, Gender: Bonds and Barriers* (Toronto: Between the Lines for the Society of Socialist Studies, 1990), 47.

41. Quoted in Carol Gabriel and Katherine Scott, "Women's Press at Twenty: The Politics of Feminist Publishing," in Linda E. Carty, ed., *And Still We Rise: Feminist Political Mobilizing in Contemporary Canada* (Toronto: Women's Press, 1993), 48.

42. Jaya Chauhan, "Involvement as Credential," in Arun Mukherjee, ed., *Sharing Our Experiences* (Ottawa: Canadian Advisory Council on the Status of Women, 1993), 176.

43. Gabriel and Scott, "Women's Press at Twenty," 39–40.

44. Donna Kahenrakwas Goodleaf, "Under Military Occupations: Indigenous Women, State Violence and Community Resistance," in Carty, ed., *And Still We Rise*, 240.

45. Ruth Roach Pierson, "The Mainstream Women's Movement and the Politics of Difference," in Pierson, Cohen, Bourne, and Masters, eds., *Canadian Women's Issues*, Volume I, *Strong Voices*, 190.

46. Sunera Thobani, "Making a Commitment to Inclusion," quoted in Pierson, "The Mainstream Women's Movement and the Politics of Difference," 210.

Study Questions

1. Spirituality and organized religion have played an important part in the lives of many of the women interviewed in this chapter. After rereading the parts related to religion, formulate an account of the roles (both positive and negative) that organized religion has played in the lives of these Ontario women and how they have addressed their spiritual needs. Do you perceive spiritual needs in your own life? If so, how do you address them? Back up your opinions with specific examples.

2. All of the Ontario women interviewed have worked hard in their lives. Do you think the work lives of the youngest generation of interviewees will be more satisfying than that of the other two generations interviewed? Do you think you will have a better work life than your mother and grandmother had? Back up your opinions with specific examples.

3. Ontario's population is a good example of the "Canadian Mosaic." Choose an ethnic group in Ontario and research its women and its organizations for meeting women's particular needs.

4. Aboriginal communities are spread throughout Ontario. Research their locations and draw a map of centres of Aboriginal people in Ontario. Research the issues which are particular to Aboriginal women and how they are organized to address these issues.

5. Jennifer Anne Larkin ends her piece, "Wings of Freedom," with the following remarks: "So far as I am concerned, my wings are outstretched. I continue to soar, searching for my path in life. I have been snared by the occasional chain, but I believe my will can break through anything that holds me back." Do you think this is a useful attitude for a young feminist to have? Can you apply it to your own situation?

QUÉBEC

Rivière-du-Loup
Québec City
Mont Laurier
Warwick
La Conception
Longueuil
Montréal

THREE GENERATIONS OF QUÉBEC WOMEN TELL THEIR STORIES

Huguette Dagenais

◆◆◆

IN GATHERING THE TWELVE LIFE STORIES that follow, our team wanted to emphasize the changes that women have experienced in Québec during the twentieth century. Convinced that it is within the heart of a single family that one can best observe the differences between generations, Chantal Doré, Nadine Jammal, Nadya Ladouceur and Sophie Pouliot interviewed their mothers and either their grandmothers or another member of that generation.

To fully appreciate these twelve life stories, one has to locate them within the Québec socio-historical context. Women's lives have changed a great deal during this century, so much so that it is impossible, in this short introduction, to comment even briefly on all the aspects of this rapid and profound, large and complex social transformation. Feminist historians, like the Collectif Clio in their *Histoire des femmes au Québec depuis quatre siècles*,[1] have superbly rendered past and contemporary women's history or *herstory*, as some prefer to say. In the following pages, I will essentially underline some of Québec's specificities pertaining to women's work and it's economic dimensions, family and the related questions of fertility and sexuality, and the role of the Roman Catholic Church as it influenced Québec women's lives over the previous generations. I conclude with feminist actions and the hope they inspire for the years to come, and then take a brief look at the methodology we used to gather these women's stories.

STORIES IN HERSTORY

The population of Québec, the largest of the ten Canadian provinces, is estimated at more than 7.4 million people, or one-quarter of the population of Canada. Most of the population (about 40 percent) live in the southern part of the province, particularly in the region of Montréal and in the St. Laurence River Valley, where the weather is more temperate than in the northern part of the province. About 700,000 people live in and around Québec City, the capital of the province, and close to 3.5 million live in the metropolitan region of Montréal. Immigrant groups are concentrated in the region of Montréal where they constitute about one-fifth of the population. The eleven Aboriginal nations, on the other hand, live mainly outside large urban centres, especially near the St.Laurence River and in the north of the province. The Mohawks, Montagnais and Cree make up 75 percent of the 66,000 Aboriginal people in Québec.

Québec is the only province in Canada where French is the official language and the language of the majority of the population. About 83 percent of Québec people identify their mother tongue as French; 9 percent identify their mother tongue as English; 0.4 percent have an Aboriginal language as their mother tongue; and 8 percent have another language (primarily Italian, Spanish, Arabic, Greek, Portuguese, Chinese or Creole). The English population, like the French population, has its own schools and universities and access to public services in its language. Immigrants who speak neither French nor English are referred to as "allophones." Most First Nations people speak English or French and many of them also speak their nation's native tongue. Like in the rest of Canada and the other industrialized countries, women form the majority (51 percent) of the population of Québec.[2]

Today, 60 percent of Québec people aged sixty-five or over are women; women's life expectancy at birth is about eighty-one years compared with seventy-four and a half years for men. However, older women are often in poor health. The gap between women's and men's life expectancy is much smaller when one takes into consideration the health condition of individuals who are sixty-five years old: between women and men who experience no loss in functional autonomy at sixty-five, the gap in life expectancy is 2.9 years only. In old age, women are also more often poorer than old men, especially women who did not participate at all in the paid labour force or who worked a much shorter period of time than the average male worker and therefore cannot benefit from private pension funds. This is currently the case for the majority of women over sixty years of age.

Nowadays young and middle-age women have more economic autonomy. In contrast to their mothers and grandmothers, over three-quarters of Québec women are now in the labour force when they are of a child-bearing age (between twenty-five and forty-four years of age). This means that living with a man or having young children is no longer considered sufficient reason for a woman to leave her job and the relative financial security that comes with it. From 1961 to 1991, the percentage of women with children under the age of three in the paid labour force increased from 28.5 percent to 62 percent. On the other hand, this also means that, compared with the past, more women today face the difficult conciliation of work and family[3] on a day-to-day basis, since most Québec men still do not undertake their fair share of the domestic chores.

In the Québec labour market, female employment ghettos have not disappeared. In spite of girls' better grades and a lesser drop-out rate in high school on the average, women are still largely concentrated (over 40 percent of them) in office work, sales, food services, nursing, and pre-school and elementary education — occupations which are not among the best paid in the country. The fact that women now form the majority of university students should not make us forget that university educated women constitute only a small minority of the Québec female population and that they are still highly concentrated in nursing, the humanities and social sciences.

Also, women in the labour force are more than twice as likely as men (27 percent compared with 11 percent) to be part-time workers which, of course, means that they earn less pay. Even among full-time employees, the average income of men is still 1.33 times that of women. If this inequality is due in part to blatant sexism in the sexual division of labour (salaries paid to women in the "feminine" occupations being generally lower that those paid in "masculine" ones), it is also related to the unequal division of parental and domestic labour in the home. Thus many women employed full-time work less hours per week than men because they want to have more time to fulfill their domestic responsibilities.

Also, among the forty-five to sixty-four age group in particular, women who have come back into the labour market after years of taking care of their marriage and children have less seniority and receive lower salaries than their male colleagues. As we can see, in the (not-so-distant) past, the family really did determine the destinies of many Québec women.[4]

The older women who tell their stories in this chapter testify to the primacy of family in their lives. They also speak to the authority men hold over them — their fathers, grandfathers and husbands — in a time when divorce was impossible for Catholics, which all of them were. No wonder radical feminists of the 1960s and 1970s have been so opposed to the family! However, as anthropologist Renée Dandurand reminds us,[5] what second-wave feminist theoreticians radically denounced is the oppressive character of non-egalitarian family as being the main institution of patriarchy. Feminists, like most women in Québec, Canada and elsewhere in the world, have never renounced family relationships and the experience of motherhood, but at a price. Two of the women in the stories stress the difference between their own relationships with their partners and those of their parents and grandparents; a third woman ended a relationship because of the authoritarian attitude of the man.

Marriage nevertheless is losing some of its popularity, especially among young people: more than 60 percent of Québec women between twenty and twenty-four years of age who live in a couple-relationship are not married and many will continue living with the same partner without marrying him. As a consequence, more than half of the children born in Québec today have non-married parents. In addition, divorced women and widows remarry less, and less rapidly, than men in the same situation. One family in seven is headed by a single parent and, in 80 percent of the cases, those families are headed by women.

Children remain important in women's lives; about three-quarters of women in Québec are mothers. However, to the great indignation of certain demographers, beginning with the cohort of women born in 1943, women now give birth to fewer children than are necessary to replace the previous generation (2.1 children per woman). The number seems to have stabilized at 1.6 children per woman. It is not the lowest in Canada nor among western nations but it is certainly interesting to observe it in Québec. On the one hand, any decrease in the Québec population reduces its proportion among the Canadian one, with obvious political consequences in terms of the recognition of Québec as a distinct society. On the other hand, the popular image of our female ancestors is that of mothers of very large families. At the beginning of the eighteenth century, women had effectively an average of 8.4 living children. Nevertheless, as historian Marie Lavigne reminds us, the decrease in the number of births is not a recent phenomenon in Québec; it began in the middle of the nineteenth century. Looking only at averages does not give a socially accurate picture of the demographic situation. For example, while 6 percent of the women born in 1913 had more than ten children, 20 percent had only one or two and 23 percent had none. The decrease in the birth rate in Québec is due mainly to the quasi disappearance of the phenomenon of women having more than six children.[6] Nonetheless, rates and numbers can be useful social indicators. Thus, the fact that women born in 1920–21 had an average of 3.59 children[7] while their granddaughters born in the 1960s had 1.6, signals changes in the society as a whole (urbanization, progress in schooling, economic crisis, wartime needs for female labour power) as well as in the way women and families consider children's and women's roles in society.

Whatever women's personal reasons for having fewer children (poverty, health, desire to give each child better care and education, professional aspirations for themselves), one cannot help but be impressed by their determination to control their fertility. If the grandmothers in these stories came from large families or they themselves had numerous children by the standards of today, their daughters on the whole had fewer children. Above all, they didn't want to have as many children as their mothers! And the granddaughters, who are in the midst of graduate studies, count on having only one or two children. But in the past things were not that simple. The Catholic Church, in particular, with its emphasis on virginity — for women especially — before marriage and its prohibition of modern contraception and abortion has used the considerable authority of its clergy to promote large families. Even the mothers who were in the prime of their lives in the 1950s experienced pressure from priests on the subject of family size: *empêcher la famille*, to use birth control, was a mortal sin that a woman had to confess to a priest in order to be absolved. To be sure, women, who not only had to bring children into the world but also to feed and educate them, did not submit entirely to these precepts, but the pressures were no less painful for them. Due to the lack of understanding of certain priests, some women distanced themselves from or virtually cut off their contacts with the Church.

Since the Quiet Revolution of the 1960s and the condemnation of "the pill" by Pope Paul VI in his 1968 *Humanae Vitae* encyclical letter, the Catholic Church has lost almost all influence on a couple's sexual behaviour. As Nadya Ladouceur shows in her own story, the Church's current influence on Québec society comes from its social actions and positions (for the poor, the unemployed) and from its most radical and marginalized (by the Church's hierarchy itself) sections, such as those who practice liberation theology.

If the negative influence of the Church is well known, one tends to forget that other factors have been as important in denying women control over their fertility. Information, for one: before 1920 women did not know how their menstrual cycle functioned. Of course doctors could have informed and helped women but, as we can see through Margot's story in Chantal Doré's narration, many of them were not willing to do so. Even after more information on reproduction became largely available, at least to the more educated classes, the Canadian Criminal Code continued to prohibit publicity and sale of contraceptives as well as information on contraception until 1969. The Parti Québécois, which was elected for the first time in 1976 and whose membership included many militant feminists, put in place family planning clinics that also provided abortion services. However, this did not change the Criminal Code. Abortion remained a crime in Canada untill 1988, despite the fact that tens of thousands of abortions were performed every year in Québec alone.

In these conditions, it is no suprise that *la grande opération*, as people of past generations referred to hysterectomy, was considered by some Québec mothers of large families (as well as by some doctors) as the most effective way to avoid pregnancy (which it is, of course), especially for women approaching menopause. Even today, while access to contraception is no more an issue, many women thirty-five years and older choose sterilization under the safer and milder form of tubal litigation (and more and more men undergo vasectomy) once they have completed their families. Oral contraceptives remain popular among young women eighteen to twenty-four years of age, but the possibility of severe side effects and health hazards (cancer, in particular) associated with the use of the pill over a long period of time are now common knowledge and make this method much less attractive for middle-aged women than it was two decades ago. Moreover, a large number of abortions are still performed in Québec every year (about three abortions for every ten births), especially on women of roughly the same age (fifteen to twenty-four).

Many hypotheses come to mind. Here are a few, expressed under the form of questions worth reflection. Are Québec women using sterilization and abortion because they do not trust their partners and thus have the assurance to be in full control of contraception? Would there be as many sterilizations if more research had been done and more male contraceptives were available? This question cannot really be answered except by the formulation of other hypotheses, but the following questions deserve additional empirical research. Would more women have one or two more children if men really did their share of domestic and parental duties? And what about men who do not want children? Doesn't that too play a role in women's decision to avoid or terminate a pregnancy?

Talking about birth control is also implicitly talking about sexuality and *la libération des corps*, the liberation of bodies, an expression used by the Collectif Clio when looking back at the 1970s in Québec. Sexuality is no longer a taboo in the province. Many parents are more at ease discussing sexuality with their children. There is more sexual freedom for women; they can express their sexuality more openly and can more easily express their desires and feelings to their partners and initiate sexual relationships. Young women in Québec today enjoy a sexual freedom never heard of before. As well, lesbians can live more openly, even though they still experience discrimination because of their sexual preference and lifestyle.[8] In fact, sexual freedom and access to contraception seem taken for granted by younger generations, judging by my own undergraduate students' reactions when I raise the subject during my course on feminist approaches in anthropology. Many young people apparently have problems believing that sexuality and control over one's fertility could have been the object of such repression in the history of their own country and their own families!

However, greater sexual freedom is not revolution. Indeed, gender relations have changed considerably but not entirely, not radically. There remains inequality in relationships between men and women when it comes to sexuality, and to work, and income as we have seen. For example, "negotiating" the use of a condom with their sexual partners is still a challenge for many single women, especially those in a new relationship. To avoid loneliness, a woman will not always push a man to use a condom and can therefore put herself at risk of becoming infected by HIV and of developing AIDS (not to mention getting pregnant and being infected by STD).[9] Also, which young woman today has never experienced the double standard of morality that still applies to sexual behaviour?

Violence against women remains a major social problem. Not all acts of violence, of course, take the form of the massacre at the École Polytechnique in Montréal on December 6, 1989, when a young man killed fourteen young women before killing himself. Marc Lépine shouted his hatred to the students he killed by saying: "You're all a bunch of feminists."[10] But murders of women by their partners has become an ordinary *fait divers* in Canadian newspapers, now that the media are more sensitized to the seriousness of the problem. The Collectif masculin contre le sexisme has counted 518 such murders between December 6, 1989, and November 17, 1998, in Québec alone.[11] And yesterday, on June 11, 1999, in Saint-Jean-sur-Richelieu, a man shot and killed his wife at the refuge for women victims of domestic violence where she was living. She had left him a month ago because of his psychological violence against her. In a case like this, psychological violence usually means that the woman has received threats from her partner and is afraid for her life. In its report, the press also published a reference from Statistics Canada to remind people that in 1997, according to police reports, 31 percent of women victims of violent criminal acts had been attacked by a spouse, compared with 4 percent of men.[12]

Information and education are essential ways to raise consciousness on such social problems and to keep memories of past miseries alive, so that change can occur. It is reassuring to see that education remains an issue for women in Québec and that women continue to attach much importance to girls' education. Many mothers see education as the way for their daughters to ensure their own autonomy. The four narrators in this chapter provide examples of families that value education. The attention presently given (and rightly so) by the government and the media to adolescent boys' high drop-out rate from high school should not reduce the attention given to girls' education and their professional orientation towards non-traditional sectors.

Another theme commonly found in these stories is that of women taking care of family members. The health and well-being of a mother, a brother, a father-in-law or another family member appear to have been the responsibility of the women who are grandmothers today. It was the same for many women of the following generation and, taking into account the lengthening life span and current Québec policies of homecare for the aged, the young women who are the daughters today can anticipate that their family responsibilities will increase equally in the future. In fact, this is very much an issue in Québec right now. With the actual restructuring of Québec's health and social services and the shift to ambulatory care, many of these changes are being effected without adequate public or private homecare services. This concern is the focus of feminist researchers and of the Québec women's movement. Women have reasons to worry: Who will take care of all the convalescent and the elderly whose care requires time and emotional investment? Is there not an implicit assumption that women will be the ones doing it? After all, women have done this very efficiently in the past and, to a large extent, today they still are more reliable caregivers for sick and older parents than men. But what if love is not sufficient?[13]

NO TIME TO REST!
FEMINIST WORK IS NOT DONE YET!

Obviously feminist work is not done yet and the struggle for equality and justice for women is far from over. However, I would like to end this brief introduction on a more hopeful note. Sophie Pouliot regrets that her generation, "which is harvesting what feminists have sowed," is also a generation "which too easily forgets that women's lives have not always been so easy" and many women of her generation often think likewise. But there are young women who do remember. In 1994 a scientific survey conducted for the Québec Conseil du statut de la femme showed that 51 percent of Québec women considered themselves feminists. Even more interesting is that 61 percent of female students considered themselves feminists,[14] which is equal to the percentage (60 percent) of women 55 to 64 years old who have experienced first hand the profound social changes discussed above. Compared to the dynamism of Québec feminism and feminist research,[15] this percentage may appear quite low (the glass is almost half empty). However, in light of Québec women's lives in the not-so-distant past, and considering the still marginal situation of women's/feminist studies in the education system and the sexism that still prevails in contemporary society (thanks in large part to the media's representations of feminism and feminists),[16] this result brings some hope that the glass is more than half full.

Hope is also what inspires the mobilization of a large number of women around social issues, as was the case during the 1995 Women's March Against Poverty, organized by the Fédération des femmes du Québec, the largest organization of women and feminists in Québec. While some people were proclaiming the end of feminism and the arrival of "post-feminism," about 20,000 women participated in the Women's March Against Poverty, which ended with a huge demonstration in front of the National Assembly in Québec City on June 4, 1995. During the ten days preceding this event, hundreds of Québec women marched to the capital from Rivière-du-Loup, Longueuil or Montréal, singing as they went the theme song "Bread and Roses to Change Things." All of Québec resonated with their song; even the media followed the marchers from town to town. The women went to receive responses to their demands from the premier and other ministers, of whom three were women who are known to be feminists. Their demands related particularly to the increase of minimum wage, pay equity, public housing and the recognition of women's social and economic work. The demonstrators did not receive all that they demanded but, as was emphasized the following days in the daily papers *Le Soleil* and *Le Devoir*,[17] the marchers were not sent away empty handed. They had made only some modest gains, but they had established a movement committed to these objectives. So much so that in 1996 a similar march mobilized women all over Canada and culminated in a demonstration in Ottawa.

So many women in the streets for a demonstration of such scope for women's solidarity! We had not seen that in Québec for some time! Expressed openly and proudly by so many women, feminism was in the forefront of the media and the centre of public attention for several weeks. The Fédération des femmes du Québec is presently organizing an even bigger event, the Marche mondiale des femmes en l'an 2000 contre la pauvreté et la violence envers les femmes. At the time of writing this introduction (June 1999), close to 1,950 different groups from 135 countries have registered as participants. Between March 8, 2000, the day of the launching, and October 17, 2000, they will be organizing actions around their respective national priorities pertaining to poverty and violence. The march will culminate on October 17, when women from all over the world gather at the United Nations in New York City. This creative initiative will renew energy, solidarity and hope for the worldwide continuation of women's struggle begun by previous generations, as described in the life stories of the women who participated in this project.

THE WAY WE WORKED

The generations of women who were interviewed for these stories are, in three of the families, Québec women with Francophone roots and, in one of the families, women immigrants from Egypt. Only in one of these families are the three generations of women specifically from Montréal. Although one can observe through these twelve narrations the growing social mobility and urbanization in Québec from one generation to the next, these stories cannot represent the cultural, linguistic and geographic diversity within Quebec. For example, no First Nations narrative is included here; although some First Nations students showed interest in the project, they did not follow up. As for the disciplines of the team members, two of us are are from anthropology, two from sociology and one from communications; three participants were at the time students at Laval University and one at the Université du Québec à Montréal (UQAM).

The stories which follow offer a synthesis of twelve lives, gathered through interviews based on a set of broad questions or *guide d'entrevue* prepared by myself and Sophie Pouliot following a discussion with the whole team. The guide comprised two large sections. In the first section, pertaining to personal life, the questions guided each woman through the following themes: her family of birth, socialization and education, the family formed by the woman herself (visits, marriage, maternity), domestic work, reconciliation of paid work with family and household obligations, social networks and community involvement. The second section evoked these women's perceptions of changes since their childhood in their own lives and in the situation of women in Québec in general. The interviewers also had access to the English questionnaires used by the other groups in this project across Canada, and some drew a few questions from them.

In my twenty-three years as a university professor, I have rarely encountered as much enthusiasm on the part of students for a project, especially for a demanding project that had neither credit nor financial remuneration attached to it. Since all the students had wanted for a long time to better understand the experiences of their mothers, grandmothers and of women in the preceding generations, they told me that the project gave them the occasion to do this, and I can witness that they took on this opportunity with pleasure.

The women who were interviewed, on the other hand, were sometimes astonished that their lives could interest our team to the point of being included in a book. "My life isn't interesting, it's just an ordinary life," said one of them, who added with humour that "if there was not enough useful material in this interview, one could just perhaps add it on at the end."

The enthusiasm for the project did not always prevent problems from arising. It did not take long to realize that it is not as easy as one thinks to interview people from one's own family. Some subjects (contraception, sexuality, money) have been taboo for a long time in the relations between parents and children in Québec, and it is often much easier to speak freely about them with strangers than with family members. As well, in all families, there are painful events on which people do not wish to dwell, and this had to be respected.

Neither is the interview a simple technique. It takes good preparation and time to collect a life story, and it requires a great capacity for listening and a great respect for the individual rhythm of the subject. With older women, who tire quickly, it often took more than one interview. As for self-interrogation, making a narrative of one's own life, as did the four investigators, it is not something one is accustomed to doing, especially if one is an anthropologist or a sociologist.

Memory rarely follows chronological order; it returns gradually and in snatches, one thought inspiring another, and so on. Memory is selective: souvenirs are constructed and reconstructed in terms of a person's current perceptions, which may explain why the women interviewed had a tendency to present the good rather than the bad sides of their lives; at least that is the interpretation made by the interviewers. This interpretation may also be very different from that of the people who are interviewed. "I thought I knew all the history of my mother ... In fact I didn't know all that much," said Nadine Jammal. The three other students had more or less the same experience with one or the other of the two women they interviewed.

Moreover, there were ethical considerations: How can one respect the anonymity of people and the confidentiality of their information when the project is about one's own family? There is no easy answer to this question and it concerned us from the beginning. All the women interviewed agreed that their life's stories could be published, but we decided to use only their first names. The students referred to them, of course, naturally and not without a certain pride, through their family relationships as "my mother," "my great-aunt," "my grandmother." Therefore it was not rare that an interviewer, becoming a narrator, had to make choices regarding the information to be divulged, and also how to do this so that the text would not embarrass the women she had interviewed. The interests of the women who told their stories had priority over the book.

IRÈNE, MARGOT AND CHANTAL:

A CHRONICLE OF THREE GENERATIONS

Chantal Doré

-◄O►-

> Women's History — a reality where women do not always leave a mark, which must make us remember that they, on the contrary, leave important traces related to the daily, to the repetitive, to the maintenance of life, to that which is perishable but nonetheless indispensable, to that which "makes sense" instead of that which "marks an epoch."
>
> — Micheline Dumont and Nadia Fahmy-Eid, "Temps et mémoire," *Recherches féministes* 6 (1993), 1–12.

BRIEFLY, HERE IS THE STORY of three Québec women, my great-aunt Irène, my mother Margot and myself. Our three women's destinies cover the twentieth century and bear witness to the transformation of values and social roles of women in Québec. I will focus especially on our respective childhoods, our experiences of motherhood and our family lives.

Irène was born in 1913 in Mont-Laurier, a small town northwest of Montréal. At the age of twenty, she married and went to live with her husband on a farm. After his death in 1966, she came back to Mont-Laurier where she lives to this day. In 1972, she remarried and lived, as she says, "a second life" with Arthur until his death in 1994.

Margot was born in 1925 on a farm in Mont-Laurier. After the death of her mother, she and her young brother were taken care of by her paternal grandparents with whom she lived until her marriage at the age of twenty. She left Mont-Laurier to live in La Conception, a village about 150 kilometres north of Montréal.

As for me, I was born in 1960 in the same village. I left the family home when I was seventeen to continue my studies in Montréal and then in Québec City, where I now live.

VERY DIFFERENT CHILDHOODS

Irène is the second of a family of twelve children, comprising six boys and six girls. Her father was a farmer and daily labourer and her mother worked in the household and on the farm. As for Margot, she was the second in a family of three children; she has two brothers. Her father was a farmer and lumberjack and her mother was a housewife. At the age of five years, she lost her mother who was about thirty years old at the time, and she was taken in by her paternal grandparents who brought her up with her younger brother; her older brother lived with their father. The "adoption" of orphans by relatives was a common practice of the time, even if the people who adopted the children had already raised numerous children. In this way, Margot and her brother joined two cousins who had also lost their mother. Despite their grandmother's handicap of having had a leg amputated several years before, the grandparents willingly took in these newcomers. Margot describes the role played by her grandparents very well: "Grandfather had a large farm for that time: twenty, twenty-five or thirty cows. It was virtually the refuge of all the orphans, and of nephews who had lost their mothers or, when they were out of work, they went to work for my grandfather."

While Irène and Margot passed their childhoods and the first years of their marriage in a milieu of poverty, this was not the case with me. I am the youngest in a family of five children: three boys and two girls. My childhood coincided with the prosperity which characterized Québec in the 1960s and 1970s. In addition I was fortunate that my father had a prosperous business with an uncle. My mother, Margot, did all the work associated with the home. Unlike my great-aunt and my mother, who had an average education for their time, I was able to benefit from the access to higher education accorded to girls as well as boys, although there is still strong sex segregation in the disciplines.

GENERATIONS FOLLOW BUT DO NOT RESEMBLE ONE ANOTHER

The largest contrast between these three generations certainly is to be found in the size of families. Irène had nine children, Margot had five, and I have one child. The conditions in which we experienced pregnancy, parturition and motherhood in general are also very different.

My great-aunt and my mother gave birth to their first children at home in the presence of a doctor and a midwife. Their other births took place in hospitals with the help of a doctor and nurses. Irène had her last two children in a hospital, "because it was more modern, and also I had children who could look after the household at that time." After their virtual disappearance during the middle of the twentieth century, midwives were to return in a clandestine manner during the 1980s. That is how I myself gave birth, like Irène and Margot, in a hospital with a midwife and a doctor in attendance.

The father's role at the time of the birth seems to depend to a large extent on where the birth takes place. In the past, because births took place at home, the father was often present and helped the doctor and the midwife by supporting his partner. As soon as births began to take place in hospitals, the husband was somewhat eclipsed in a situation in which he no longer had a role to play. "Parturition" was the business of the hospital personnel. Things were different for me. My husband could participate in our daughter's birth due to the struggles of women over the last two decades to achieve a much better if still insufficient recognition of the role of the father at the birth. When Irène and Margot gave birth, nursing babies was not "in style"; mothers gave their children cows' milk. I, however, nursed my daughter for several months.

Have the conditions of maternity improved over time? Today, the improvement of economic conditions and the reduction of family size allows mothers to give more time to their newborn children. Nonetheless, even if women have succeeded in having their right to paid work

recognized, it is still difficult for them to reconcile work and family responsibilities. On the other hand, although many working women have
access to paid maternity leave, there is no such support for students
such as myself!

There has been progress in the techniques of birth control, a concern
of all of us, which we each resolved with different effectiveness in different
contexts. For my mother and my great-aunt, the rules of the Catholic
Church were clear and without appeal: one must never practise birth
control. Women nonetheless used their good sense to put brakes on the
authority of the Church. For Irène, the margin of movement was very
small but she tried to exercise a certain control over pregnancy by assid-
uously practising her faith. She explains:

> – Oh yes! You had to have children. Oh yes! Because he [the priest]
> refused us confession if we used methods of birth control.
> – And did you use them?
> – Well, we counted the days a bit, ... but it was not really exact.
> – But you wanted to limit it a bit?
> – Of course, because ... look at my sister Régina who had seventeen.

In Margot's generation, women had more control over their fertility.
Many were willing to defy the authority of the Church on this issue.
Margot certainly was one of those:

> If you went to confession and told the priest that you had used
> birth control ... he made you promise not to do it again. But that
> meant nothing to me. I promised him, and I took care anyway. I
> didn't want them! There was no question of having as many as my
> aunt Irène who had a large family herself ... I wanted to have some,
> but not that many.

If the desire was there and the information was more or less accessible,
the taboo that existed around contraception made asking for complete
information on the subject a matter of shame. Besides, wrong information could cause results that were the opposite of what one wanted.
This is what happened to Margot, who had her first child after ten
months of marriage:

> I wanted to wait two years after my marriage before having chil-
> dren. But doctors weren't very forthright at that time and I was too

embarrassed to ask how to follow the Ogino method; at the time it was the Ogino method which was in style. And also, I didn't understand everything at all. And being too embarrassed to have it explained to me again ... I was discouraged by the first, but you know ... But the second, I was really disappointed: fourteen months later.

On the subject of reproduction, we should note that in Québec the high rate of hysterectomies is a concern. My great-aunt, like so many women of her generation, had a hysterectomy at the age of forty-two and my mother had one at sixty.

As for sexuality, at the time of Irène and of Margot, it was considered, at least by the still very influential Church, as being contrary to the principles of the Catholic religion. According to Irène, any clothing could be considered to be too revealing of the body and could attract public disapproval for the woman who wore it: "It was very severe, you know. I saw them refusing communion to women because they were considered too *décolletées*. Nowadays they go up and out (laughter). At that time there was no question of it."

The negation of sexuality imposed by the Church led to a particularly severe surveillance of dates between young men and young women. For Irène and Margot, all dates were closely supervised by their fathers. Irène's father would say: "Going around town amounts to running from man to man." In Margot's case, the two families knew one another very well and Eudore's family had a good reputation: "They were one neighbour away from us." As for me, I went out with the man who was going to be my husband for some time before I introduced him to my parents.

While my great-aunt and my mother left their homes to marry at the age of twenty, I left home to study, and it was only at the end of my twenties that I met my husband. In addition, even though the family is still important for me, my social environment is wider and more varied than those of Irène and Margot. The greater mobility of young people today increases the possibilities of meeting, of belonging to groups, and as in my case, of becoming part of networks of students and professionals.

For the two generations of women who preceded me, work took place in the domestic setting. While Irène made all of her children's clothes without exception, Margot bought clothes, especially after her first two children. As for me, who knows nothing more than sewing on buttons and repairing a seam that has become undone, I buy all the clothes that we need.

The role of care-giving was also important throughout my mother's and great-aunt's lives. As well as taking care of her nine children, Irène had two husbands whose state of health required care; the first one was sick for eight years and was confined to the house for the last three years of his life. Irène's care and psychological support of him were given at the expense of her own health. The last months of her second husband's life also put her emotions and physical strength to a test. As well as having five children, and after having taken care of her grand-parents in her youth, Margot at different times looked after her father, her father-in-law, her close relatives and finally her husband. I myself have taken care of my child with the help of my husband. Since women in Québec can expect a life span eight years longer than men's, I too in my turn will probably take care of those close to me.

The relationships between men and women have also changed a great deal. Women now have much more autonomy in terms of their husbands. What Irène said about elections makes one laugh nowadays:

- Did you always vote like your husbands?
- Oh, yes! At the time, oh, yes! Not in my second marriage, but in my first. That cancelled out the vote (laughs).

MANY CHANGES, BUT INCLINATIONS REMAIN

Throughout the life stories of Irène, Margot and myself, one can see the changes which took place in Québec in the twentieth century, and especially during the "Quiet Revolution" of the 1960s. Women have experienced changes in education and contraception, seen a more discreet presence of the Church and received support from the state for paid work whether or not they were mothers. Rigid traditional roles have given way to a certain pluralism of models and a wider range of professional and social choices for women. As well, the movement from a low to a middle socio-economic status for Irène, from a low to a high economic status for Margot and from a high to a low economic status for me, reflects very well the economic evolution of Québec. The economic restructuring of the 1990s has tended to increase unemployment, especially among young people and women, and, since the 1980s, the difference between the rich and the poor has been increasing.

These questions bring us back to the statements of Dumont and Fahmy-Eid quoted at the beginning of this work: that is to say that women's history always concerns that which "makes sense" instead of that which "marks an epoch."

From Egypt to Québec:
JEANNETTE, MIMI AND NADINE

Nadine Jammal

◄○►

JEANNETTE

MY GRANDMOTHER IS DEAD. In order to attempt to understand her life, I interviewed Jeannette, a woman of her generation who is about eighty years old. Jeannette was born in Haifa, Palestine. She had two sisters and two brothers. As a boarder with the Sisters of Nazareth, Jeannette says she had a "very disciplined education: with them one knew which was the right road." Her family left for Port Said, Egypt, after she had finished her studies, when she was about eighteen years old. The family was not limited to the father, mother, brothers and sisters; there were also aunts and cousins who took part in all the important decisions.

Jeannette married "before the age of twenty," she said laughing, but with a certain pride. "That was not late." At that time, in the Middle East, what was important for a girl who wanted to marry was to have received a "good education" and to be an "honest woman." For a boy, what was important was to have "a good situation in life." To the great displeasure of her parents and all the cousins, aunts and uncles, Jeannette broke her engagement fifteen days before the wedding date because her fiancé made the mistake of casting doubts on her morality.

> He was a wonderful man but jealous. He insisted on telling me that I had done some things which I had not done. Nevertheless, we had not met by accident; it wasn't as if we were making a love match. No, our two families knew one another; he knew that I came from a good family and I knew what was right!

It certainly must have taken much courage to make this break since she knew that this would cause gossip. "The whole world was talking about how Jeannette had left Emile and how Emile had left Jeannette a few days before the wedding." She renewed the relationship with her fiancé nine months later. After having told me this, she explained that "life in a couple demands compromises if one wants it to last."

Immediately after her marriage, Jeannette quit her job as a teacher. She had two girls and one boy. At that time, there was no question of a woman working outside the home; she had to stay at home to look after the children. Even today, Jeannette considers it "normal" that the man works outside the home and the woman looks after the children: no one else can have the feelings that a mother has for her children. For a mother, having someone else look after her children, even her husband, is "wearing on the nerves." According to Jeanette, women's work outside the home has caused the breakup of the family.

Like my grandmother, Jeannette did not emigrate of her own voli- tion. She followed her daughters when they migrated to Montréal after the nationalization of the Suez Canal (1959) because she wanted to be near them to make sure they were in good health. In those days, in the milieu where Jeannette grew up, a European milieu where children studied in French schools, they were convinced that they no longer had a future in Egypt.

When her husband would show a desire to leave, she would answer: "Good, you will leave alone!" A few days after one such exchange, he died of a heart attack. "He left for good," she said. Even though her marriage had been "arranged," Jeannette seems to have loved her hus- band a great deal: she burst into sobs when talking about his death.

According to her, women were happier in Egypt than in Canada: "We had our problems, our preoccupations, but we didn't have the oppor- tunity to make mistakes; you had to conform to certain principles. In addition, today's mothers do too many things at once." Jeannette's daughters have divorced and she has never accustomed herself to this situation. She is convinced that it is western culture that is responsible for that. "At home, divorce did not exist. Our religion did not permit it."

Today, what counts the most for her are her children. The most important event in her life was her husband's death: "He gave me the blow of leaving after twenty-three years of marriage. I found that very hard. Luckily, I had my mother and my whole family to console me!"

MIMI

My mother, Mimi, was born in Port Said, a town on the Mediterranean coast in the north of Egypt. She was the second in a family of five children. She has many bad memories of her childhood. Her father had already been married twice before marrying her mother, and he had enough children not to want anymore. When her mother communicated for the first time that she would like to have a child, he accepted this against his will, saying that he would agree if the first child were a boy. Mimi explains:

> The first child arrived; it was, as it was supposed to be, a boy. But afterwards my mother wanted another son so that the older one would have a playmate, and it is I who arrived. I think that I didn't at all fulfill my father's wishes, neither did I fulfill the criteria of the time for beauty. I was small, dark, quite thin, and very quickly I had the insolence to talk back to my parents.

Since she was the eldest daughter, Mimi was responsible for her brother and sisters: "My eldest brother, because he was a boy, could go wherever he wished, but I, every time I wanted to go somewhere, I had to take along my two sisters and my younger brother. Wherever I went, I had to take them." Mimi was fourteen years old when her father suddenly died. All at once she found herself at the head of this little family: "I have never understood why I gave myself this responsibility at the age of fourteen. Probably because I sensed that my mother was very vulnerable from the moment my father died. I remember that we were all afraid of losing her."

Because she herself had to leave school to look after her youngest sister and her father, my grandmother insisted that her daughters finished their *baccalauréate* at all costs. Since my grandfather was the director of a school, he of course expected the children to have good marks. However, he didn't pay much attention to problems they could have in school and never congratulated them on their good results.

Religion had a very important place in Mimi's family life, not only because she went to a school run by nuns, the Convent of Bon Pasteur, but also because her father was very religious:

> We always had a priest for dinner on Sundays, even if sometimes it was an absolute scoundrel who was currying favour with my mother. But him, he saw nothing. He went to mass every Sunday and took communion regularly. He also was charitable: he donated money to an orphanage near us, very discreetly but generously.

scoundre l

It was in church that Mimi met my father. She had vowed to go to church every day if she were hired by the Suez Canal Company. My father at one time wanted to become a priest, but he was very moved by this pious young girl who went to mass every morning! They went out together for a long time — eight years before getting married. My father vacillated between the priesthood and marriage. Mimi was very popular because she was considered a "good" young girl, that is to say, well brought up, responsible and ethical. Given my father's reserve, my mother was far from believing in the beginning that he was interested in her.

My mother married at the age of twenty-six. She had three daughters. If the birth of the first two were planned, that of the third was not. Contraception was forbidden by the Catholic religion, so she and my father used the "rhythm method," which this time did not work. "The birth of the third daughter took us off course a bit because it happened at the time when we were to emigrate and we knew absolutely nothing about the future."

Mimi left her job as a secretary and started it again after her arrival in Québec in 1962; her eldest daughter was four years old at the time. She found it difficult to reconcile work and family responsibilities, and she returned home to look after her children for about four years before continuing her studies in translation. Far from opposing her return to the labour force, my father encouraged her to do so.

Immediately after immigrating, my father worked relentlessly to support his family. Because he had returned to his studies at that time, he often had to bring his work home. My grandmother, who lived with us, did much of the domestic work. When Mimi got home in the evening, she did the work that her mother had not been able to do during the day:

At the beginning I found that very difficult ... I took you to the daycare, then I looked after your two sisters. I went to work in the afternoons so that I could look after you in the evenings. When you had all gone to bed after 11:00 p.m., I had to wash the diapers.

Mimi had left Egypt for religious reasons: "After the nationalization of the canal, the religious communities were invited to leave and we did not want you to go to government schools where you would learn the Muslim religion." Surprisingly, what struck Mimi the most on arriving in Québec was the difference in the relationship between men and women, which she found much more unequal here than in Egypt, at least in the milieu where she grew up, a Christian milieu which was urban and middle class. In Egypt, she says, "the woman had moral authority in the family. It was she who made all the important decisions. In comparison, when I arrived in Québec, the way in which men spoke to their wives shocked me. I found a terrible lack of respect there."

Certain conventions in the relationship between men and women also astonished Mimi and her sisters when they arrived in Québec: "the obligatory going out on Saturday nights, for example; anxious sitting by the phone because the chosen one might call that week. We didn't know those things in Egypt!" Eventually, in the 1960s and 1970s, marriage itself was questioned and many couples divorced. Mimi never accepted this practice: for her, a couple is made to last and a divorce is a catastrophe, above all when there are children. Because of that, she would have liked us to stay within the Egypto-Lebanese community in Québec and to marry Egyptians. "It seems to me that Middle Eastern parents inculcate in their children a sense of the perpetuity of marriage. In Egypt there was a feeling of security in marriage, which no longer exists here."

Nonetheless, despite her ideas about the family and divorce, Mimi was very sensitive to and concerned about the demands of the feminist movement in Québec:

> I think I was a feminist from the day when I started to think and that my feminism had been exacerbated by the difference between how I and my brother were treated within the family. Later on, when my daughters were born, I tried to inculcate them with the idea that girls can succeed just as well as boys in every domain.

NADINE

There have been many changes in the life of the women in my family since my grandmother's arrival in Québec. Religion is not as important for me as it had been for my mother and the women of her generation. I ceased to practise at the age of seventeen because I was disgusted by the positions of the Catholic Church regarding women. However, I retained a conviction, which my parents had given to me, that the essential message of Christianity is to concern oneself with others and to take action that there be more justice in the world.

The role of the father in the family and in the education of children has also changed a lot. While my father, perhaps despite himself, was forced by his times into the role of the *pater familias* who maintained law and order in the family, today my husband does not consider himself obliged to discipline our child. It is I who take this responsibility more often. Sometimes I find it a bit difficult, but basically I like it that my partner is an "accomplice" to his son; that relationship is precious.

Compared with women of my grandmother's generation, today's women have more breathing space. Perhaps it is true that our lives are more difficult nowadays because we have to make certain choices, but I prefer having the chance to make choices. Unlike Jeannette, I do not believe that it is preferable to stay out of contact with certain problems. I do not believe that there are things better kept hidden from children. When one adopts that attitude, it is really oneself whom one is trying to protect.

It was my mother's life that touched me the most during these interviews. I now understand why I always considered her to be a very militant and determined person. In fact, women of my mother's generation led many struggles, whose fruits we are now able to enjoy. If I am a feminist, it is certainly thanks to my mother. She always confirmed that women could excel in all fields and that no job should be refused to them because they are women. I do not understand, however, how she concludes that one of the important consequences of the feminist movement is the increased number of divorces, which still seems to be unacceptable to her.

Without doubt the adaptation to a new culture is a long and difficult process, especially for women of my grandmother's generation who did not emigrate of their own volition, but equally for women of my

pass
from
here
to
282

mother's generation. In effect, during the interview, in making reference to her original milieu, my mother said that, in her opinion, people are much happier in their family situations in Egypt than here. It is difficult for her to adapt to the idea that the couple is no longer eternal, and it must have been difficult for her to accept our ruptures, to support us in *rupture.* our heartaches, to understand when we said to her that "it's better this way." Nonetheless, I never felt that my mother disapproved of my choices. I always felt that no matter what decision I took, she would support me and offer her help.

Personally, I cannot imagine how I could be happy in the milieu which Jeannette and Mimi described to me, where the women had more obligations than rights. My mother confirmed that arranged marriages inhibit neither respect between mates nor do they inhibit the development of a kind of tender complicity. I do not understand how, in an arranged marriage, the partners could agree that the marriage must last despite misunderstandings and the lack of love. For myself, after seven years of living with my friend, and above all, after having had a child with him, I think that only the fact that I am deeply in love allows me to work through the problems and clashes of everyday life. I cannot keep from thinking that, during the interview, my mother somewhat idealized life in Egypt because it appears more acceptable to her than the idea in Québec that couples are not eternal.

Nevertheless, I do conserve certain values that were transmitted to me by my mother and grandmother; among others, family solidarity. In the spirit of my mother and Jeannette, family breakup is inconceivable. Personally, I can conceive of divorce; I understand that two people can no longer live together. That which I cannot accept is that one refuses to help oneself or to accept help from family members; I cannot conceive how one can definitively break relations with one's brother, sister or mother. Perhaps this is because my parents often repeated to me that love between members of the same family must be unconditional.

Education was also very important for the women in my family. Studying was not taken for granted for women in Egypt. My mother recalls that my grandmother fought hard for her daughters to continue their studies, especially since the family had become very poor after the death of my grandfather. Today, it is very important for me to complete my doctoral dissertation.

Another constant: mutual respect within the couple and the central role of women in the family. Jeannette broke her engagement fifteen days before the marriage because she thought that her fiancé did not have confidence in her. My mother always made the most of the important decisions in our family, and even today my father does nothing without consulting her. In my own relationship, despite occasional tugs of war, my partner and I have mutual respect and he never makes an important decision without consulting me.

How should I end? I have now fully become a Québécoise. In my values, in my ways of thinking, I identify myself with the people who live here; I participate in their struggles and in their projects. In the past I was often embarrassed during family reunions in restaurants to see thirty or forty people in our group. I thought that we took up too much space, that we spoke too loudly and that we were making too much noise. Now, however, when I hear Middle Eastern music, these are the happy memories which come back to me, the memories of a large family which was sometimes intrusive but which maintained solidarity despite disagreements and daily problems.

Between Women:
PAULINE, MONIQUE AND NADYA

Nadya Ladouceur

◄o►

May 14, 1995

Today is Mother's Day. I look at my mother and my grandmother sitting facing me, well dressed as usual, loving life. I find myself searching for the women hidden beneath their features. Do they have identities other than mother and grandmother? Who are they? Through this writing project, I will rediscover our lives as women; I will plunge myself fully into the search for my roots. I feel close to these women; we are all filled with dreams and ambitions; our lives are all touched by the same condition of being women. Having lived through different periods of time, but always in three working-class districts in Montréal, we three have experienced childhoods that were different but also similar.

Pauline, my father's mother, was born in December 1919. She says that she had a very short childhood. She, her father, her mother and her little brother were a happy family until she was twelve years old. The death of her father, in 1931, left all three of them in a situation of dire poverty. Taken out of school, she soon had to contribute to the family finances. At the age of thirteen, she worked throughout the whole week as a housekeeper and children's nanny for rich anglophone families in Notre-Dame-de-Grâce in Montréal. Badly treated and exploited by some families, she was too young to understand how to defend her rights. Afterwards, she worked for people who treated her well. Pauline spent weekends at home, where she took care of two young children and had to do the housework, sometimes with the help of a boarder. Her mother was excessively strict with her, and forbade her to go out in the evening and to entertain boys on their balcony. Pauline had only one desire: to work in order "to get out of this shack," which always sheltered six to eight people of whom she was put in charge. Pauline has sad memories of her youth.

As for Monique, she has very different memories of her childhood with her parents. Born in 1937, of a father who was a milkman and a mother who was a housewife, she is the fifth of six children. In order to help their relatives, her parents took in lodgers. Monique's mother looked after everything except washing the dishes and taking out the garbage, jobs given respectively to the girls and the boys. Happy in her family life, Monique was not as happy at school. Unlike Pauline, who had been withdrawn from school against her will in seventh grade, Monique quit school voluntarily after ninth grade. Every day she was ashamed of her clothes: her shoes were secondhand and her dress was cleaned only once a year. For Monique, who is very proud, this was an intolerable situation. She decided to enter the labour force and pay room and board to her parents.

I, who grew up alone with my parents, especially with my mother, knew a completely different reality filled with both sad and happy moments. Unlike Pauline and Monique, I did not grow up in a household full of activity; after my parents' divorce when I was ten years old, my childhood was marked by solitude. My world was composed of imaginary friends, dolls and the neighbours' cats, faithful companions. My mother did most of the housework and I received modest payment for the small daily tasks she assigned to me. First in the class, I didn't enjoy school so much as I knew that my academic success was of great importance to my mother. Luckily, I am of the generation of organized groups, and my childhood was filled with an uninterrupted series of groups. There were the Brownies (Jeannette's), the Girl Guides and the organization of family mass; I was part of a young people's group in the parish and I took part in a day camp in the district, and later in a youth centre, in addition to activities at school. My mother and my grandmother did not experience that kind of social life until much later in their lives when Pauline became a volunteer for her parish and Monique became involved in a vacation camp for low-income families.

The importance accorded to the extended family in the past seems to have been reduced from one generation to another. Pauline not only took care of her family, but also of retired people, neighbours and friends because they were having difficulties or they had no access to any form of social security. My mother looked after her own mother for many years. I, for my part, have not assumed such heavy family responsibilities, at least not yet.

MAY 15, 1995

I got a call from my associate, Mireille, with whom I have recently started a business. Contracts are starting to come in. At the age of twenty-five, I have just finished my *baccalauréate* in communications. I am making my entry into the labour force under very different conditions than those of my mother and grandmother.

From necessity, Pauline entered into the service of a well-to-do family when she was thirteen years old; she had to meet the needs of the family. She worked six days a week and gave her pay to her mother, who returned a very small allowance to her. On the other hand, Monique chose to enter the labour force at the age of fifteen; she wanted to earn money to support herself. She worked in different jobs in manufacturing, then in bars and night clubs, always looking for better pay. Since she lived with her parents, she paid them a small amount of money for room and board. For her, stable, full-time work was worth much more than staying in school. As for me, at the age of fifteen I started to work for my sister in a convenience store. I was not impelled there by necessity but by the desire to enter the adult world quickly and to have pocket money. I worked part-time, and my mother never asked for any money from me. When at the age of twenty I left home, work took on a new meaning because, henceforth, I would have to earn my own living. Since then, I have had various jobs in group facilitation, in management and in community organization. These days I am a professional who is starting a business.

MAY 16, 1995

My mother, my grandmother and I discuss the influence of husbands and families on women's work. I, who am not married, I alone make my own decisions, but things were very different for them.

After her marriage, Pauline stopped working in order to take care of the house and the children, like most of the women of her time. However, when her daughter finished her studies, Pauline found herself a full-time job as a cashier in a grocery store, because she wanted to give her daughter a beautiful graduation party. She worked at this job for twenty-two months until the day she got sick. Her husband, who did not like seeing her work outside the house, asked her to return to the home where, he said, she had enough work raising the children and doing housework.

Monique, who was an unmarried mother no longer living with her parents, quit her job as a waitress in a bar two weeks before her first child was born and quickly resumed working afterwards. Ten years later when she married, she left her job again to have a second child. Her husband, who preferred having her at home, strongly encouraged her to do so. However, his debts soon brought her back to the work force. Since then, she has never stopped working, sometimes at two jobs simultaneously, in order to pay all the bills and support the family.

MAY 17, 1995

Today my career possibilities do not seem to have anything in common with those of my mother and grandmother when they were my age. In Pauline's time, the Church was very influential and made women into "baby-making machines." For my mother, as for the majority of women of her time, the situation of the housewife was enviable if the child had been conceived in a marriage. Now, although there are still many social pressures, I have much more freedom and am less restricted by taboos. Perhaps because of the difficulties in her own life, my mother considers my studies and my career as important as family life.

MAY 18, 1995

Spring has returned, the quintessential season of lovers. I have the impression of coming out of a long sleep. Like Pauline and Monique, I experience the desire to be a woman in love before becoming a mother, but I think that our love lives rapidly turn into family lives.

One year after her marriage, Pauline had her first child; she had four children in five years. She looked after a large household with eleven people around the dinner table. She explains: "I was called upon to raise my brothers, my children, my neighbours, my cousins, but what can you do? You can't leave a dog outside ... much less people!"

Monique, a single mother at the time of her first child, had to confront the social norms of her time. She had to leave the family home because her father was very concerned about what people would say. After the birth of the child, she called herself "madame" so that her daughter would not be considered a bastard. Her entire life was devoted to fulfilling her child's needs.

As for myself, I had my first serious love affair with a man who had the custody of his two-year-old son. Very quickly the role of mother was forced on me. I discovered the reality of work and studies associated with daycare–supper–story–sleepy-time. Like Pauline and Monique, I was quickly separated from my freedom by this routine, which I could nonetheless avoid by returning to my own apartment. Apparently I led a double life, at that time. I now realize that even though I have more freedom, I look for the same kind of validation that my elders searched for, but the difference is that nowadays this implies not only family life but also professional life. Far from being able to replace one with the other, I must combine the two. As well, over our three generations, there is one constant in our condition as women: taking care of others.

MAY 19, 1995

But what exactly is life in a couple? When my grandmother was thirteen years old, a new boarder arrived at their house. He was a young neighbour of sixteen years whose sister already lived with the family. He became Pauline's ally in the face of her mother's strictness and, when she was sixteen, she was allowed to go out with him. When she was seventeen, they became engaged to be married the next year. She lived with him for forty-three years, until he died. When she talks about her life in a couple, she talks about a life *with* him, a life of sharing.

For my mother, on the other hand, relations with men were not absolutely reliable. Even on her wedding day, in the square in front of the church, an old suitor threatened to kill her. She went through numerous financial difficulties with her husband. After various misdemeanours on his part, she lost all hope of changing him, and so she left him, finding herself alone with a second daughter and the debts they had accumulated as a couple. Afterwards, she had some lovers, but her child was always an obstacle. Today, Monique's perspectives on life do not include men because "it's too complicated!"

Like my mother, I have always been attracted by older men. I had a relationship with a man who had a great influence on my life. Like many women, I left the relationship bruised and demolished by his dominating attitudes. Now I am suspicious; I am always afraid of making a bad choice.

MAY 20, 1995

My grandmother and I discussed solitude. For her, who has spent her life looking after a large family, her husband's death has created a huge void. It means that she is "all alone." Strangely, when I ask my mother what she considers the most difficult aspect of her life, she too answers that it is the lack of family life: no longer being able to have her children around, no longer looking after them, no longer being able to do as many things with them. Friends partially fill the void in painful moments.

MAY 21, 1995

I have just returned from a community meeting in my neighbourhood. We have been meeting for the last five years in order to share and reflect on today's society. I have developed a strong feeling of membership in my community, which represents a family to me, as do other social solidarity groups.

Monique also has good memories of difficult times in her life. There were three neighbours in the same situation and they organized themselves to survive and have a good time: "We were all in the same boat: without money and with young children." Often it was at Marie-Paule's vacation camp that they opened themselves up and spoke about their reality with other women, without hiding anything as they had in the past when you could only confide in close friends.

Friendship also played an important role in Pauline's life after she found herself single, following the death of her husband. It was her friends in the Golden Age Club, where she has been involved over the past fifteen years, who helped her survive this trial. Even now, she is a member of the board of the social club of the building where she lives with her best friend, who is like a sister to her.

MAY 22, 1995

I am absorbed by the desire to involve myself in the world, to participate in the transformation of society in order to make it more egalitarian. This desire was formed through international solidarity voyages that I have taken. When I discussed it with Pauline, we realized that we have the same ideals for change. She told me that, in her youth, there was a poll station in her house and that she would have very much liked to get into politics to change things, to "help poor people." My mother, without having wanted to get into politics, remembers great events which marked her, such as the election of 1976 when René Lévesque and the Parti Québécois took power. That event gave rise to her hopes of liberty and justice for the working class, of which she is a part.

MAY 23, 1995

As we tell our life stories, we realize, my mother, my grandmother and myself, how much we have been influenced by the institution of the Catholic Church. Pauline recalls one day, wanting to go to confession for Easter, but she did not know how to tell the priest that she had practised birth control by using a form of contraception. The first priest to whom she confessed refused to give her absolution. She went home in tears. Her husband, more liberated than she from religion, advised her to go and see another priest whom he himself knew well. That priest told her not to worry, that she had "done her part," and that now she had to raise her children. Pauline left the confessional reassured. Even now, she goes to church on Sundays and, if that is not possible, she watches mass on TV.

Monique as a young girl was totally devoted to the Blessed Virgin and even wanted to become a nun. However, when she became a single mother, she resisted the pressures of the Church. She remembers her last confession: the priest reproached her for living "in sin" with a man to whom she was not married. Thereafter she stopped attending church. She never went back except to accompany her children.

I grew up in the heart of a network that offered me an alternative Christianity as an extraordinary way of life. At a very young age, I participated in a family mass celebrated in the basement of the church — I also joined solidarity groups and have a community of friends who have helped me to realize my faith and to discover the liberation theology of South America. The Collectif L'Autre Parole has allowed me to link my faith with feminism. Strangely enough, even though I am profoundly Christian, I have always been on the margins of the Church, and have rebelled against even those margins. Here, then, are three generations, three influences and three realities!

MAY 26, 1995

Sitting in the living room, Pauline, Monique and I compare our different realities. We think that today's taboos are less important; women are more visible in society. But there is still much to do before women can thrive and take their complete place in all spheres of social, political, economic, cultural and religious life. Today, however, the march of 800 women against poverty is starting. They call for "Bread and Roses." They revive our hopes.

MARIE-BLANCHE, JUDITH AND SOPHIE:

A CENTURY OF LIFE IN QUÉBEC

Sophie Pouliot

◄◦►

THIS STORY TRACES THE HISTORY of three Québec women, my grandmother Marie-Blanche, my mother Judith, and myself, but on certain
themes this piece will cover four generations, thanks to the relationship
of my grandmother with her mother. Comparing our respective lives
allows us to follow the evolution of women's role in Québec society
over the twentieth century.

Marie-Blanche was born in Warwick in 1915; she was the eldest
daughter in a family of eleven children. She herself had thirteen children
of whom eleven survived. In her generation there was a large population
increase in Québec, but matters changed with the next generation. In
Marie-Blanche's time, the Catholic church proscribed birth control and
doctors did not sterilize women except in cases where pregnancy could
put their lives in danger. After having given birth to numerous children
at intervals of between one and one and a half years, Marie-Blanche
asked her doctor to help her prevent further pregnancies. He, however,
responded: "You are in good health, it can't be done," and he refused to
give her any means of contraception or even information on the subject.
It appears that the Church used disinformation as its primary way to
extol large families and force women to procreate in a society where the
majority of the population had little education, especially in rural areas,
and where isolation exacerbated the lack of information.

The conditions for giving birth didn't change much in the country
before the 1950s. For Marie-Blanche as for her mother before her,

when the time arrived for giving birth, a neighbour or a female member of the family came to the house to "attend" to her at the beginning of the contractions. When her labour was judged to be sufficiently advanced, they would call for the doctor who would arrive to "deliver" the child. When the doctor was late, the midwife took charge of the birth. My grandmother tells what happened with her second child:

> The woman came to attend to me, then we called the doctor, and he said: "When did labour begin?" I said: "Not long ago. I lay down at midnight and woke up at one, then I could see that I wasn't feeling well." He said: "Oh well, it has only been an hour, it will take some time longer. Call me back when the contractions have changed." When I called him back, my baby had already arrived. Madame Gauthier, the midwife, had delivered my baby.

It could also happen that there were complications at the moment of birth. In those cases, even the presence of a doctor wasn't always enough to save the baby. Marie-Blanche lost two babies at an early age; her mother also lost one.

Sisters-in-law or neighbours helped women to get back on their feet after childbirth. But for some of her children, Marie-Blanche also got help from a nurse, a service offered by her insurance company. In one case, her husband acted as nurse.

The scenario was very different with Judith. Born in 1948 at the height of the baby boom, she has had only two children. She had been married for three years before having her first child. During this period, she used contraceptives. Aside from the Ogino method, contraception was proscribed by the Church, but was accepted by the medical establishment. Judith's first child was planned as was the second child born five years later. Her family was limited to two children.

Contrary to what her mother and grandmother experienced after the first contractions, Judith was brought to the hospital where a medical team took care of her. She benefited from the modern technology of the time; to reduce her pain, the doctors gave her an epidural; they used chloroform for women in preceding generations. Her husband accompanied her to the hospital, but he was not present at the actual births.

For our three generations, and I include myself this time, the relationship between parents and children was characterized by a very close relationship with the mother, for girls especially. The image of the mother is very strong: she is at the same time a teacher, a psychologist, a professor and a nurse. The mother is characterized as being understanding, tolerant and open; one appreciates her methods of education and passes them on to one's own children. She is the true pillar of the family because she is strong and brings people together. Marie-Blanche describes her father as a loving man who played the role of family provider but who wasn't really involved in the education of the children, a task which was left to their mother. In the case of Judith, when he was present, her father had good rapport with his young children, but had difficulty in communicating with adolescents who then moved closer to their mother. As for me, I always had very good rapport with my parents, and both of them participated actively in my education. My baby sitter, with whom I spent a large part of my childhood, also played a large role in my development. During my adolescence, circumstances made me closer to my mother but now I am reaffirming my connection to my father. My parents knew how to complement one another, and to me they represent a model of stability.

In my family, children seem to have been treated more on the basis of their personalities than on the basis of sex, except in matters related to domestic work. At Marie-Blanche's house, in particular, as they grew up, the boys were asked more and more often to do women's and girls' work, housework. The numerous brothers and sisters formed a very united clan. I have only a younger brother and I have always kept up very strong ties with him. There are far-reaching connections within the family, which were previously maintained through helping one another and through frequent visits, most of which have slackened over time, notably because of the dispersion of family members for studies, work or marriage.

Expectations regarding education have grown in our family over three generations. For a long time people were happy to insist that their children knew how to read and write; this was considered sufficient to "make their way in life." Rural country schools in any case did not offer more than the seventh grade; if they did, only a minority of the youth could continue their studies. Marie-Blanche, like her mother before her, went only to the fifth grade. However, she and her husband considered it important that their children continue to much more advanced levels of education than they had. My grandfather wanted his children to have prestigious careers; like many others of the time, he would have liked to have a priest in the family. Marie-Blanche's concerns were much more practical: she wanted her daughters to study and have employment, which would allow them autonomy and choice. She feared that her daughters would become dependent on husbands whom they didn't love and would find themselves penniless if they didn't have a sufficient revenue to manage for themselves. Judith studied to become a teacher which, along with secretarial work and nursing, was one of the principal occupations of women at the time. My father finished his classical education and became a teacher, then a school director. I have completed the first part of my university education in anthropology and I intend to continue to a master's degree. My parents have always encouraged me to continue in higher education as they do my brother.

Marriage and the life of couples have evolved considerably over the three generations. Marie-Blanche married in 1942, during the the Second World War. She hardly knew her husband because they had only been going out for several months. She was twenty-five years old and he was twenty-eight. After their marriage, she left her work at a clothes factory to follow her husband to his place of birth. Because her husband's job kept him away for long periods of time, Marie-Blanche virtually raised her eleven children on her own. Judith met my father during her studies. They went out together for two years, during which time they got to know one another well. Their marriage has been maturely considered. Nonetheless, the two marriages happened in the same manner. Marie-Blanche and Judith both got married in the churches of their respective parishes in the presence of their parents and friends. The ceremony was followed by a banquet, which continued until late at night. I am not married; perhaps I will never be married because nowadays unmarried couples are accepted in our society.

As well, in our time, feminine and masculine roles are much less stereotyped than they were in the past; men take a greater part in the education of the children, and women contribute more often to the household revenue. As well, the couple's life is considered very important. Although Judith quit her job after her marriage to follow her husband, she knew that this situation was temporary. Marie-Blanche, on the other hand, could not return to work until her children grew up, and she had to take the necessary steps in secret. She only told her husband once she had a job, because she was afraid he would discourage her. His reaction had been very negative in the past. He said to her: "I always supported you and I can still support you. If you earn money, you keep it." That is what she did. She committed almost all her earnings to her children's education. He soon got used to the situation.

Judith never had to face that kind of attitude because her husband was very open to women's working. Moreover, she didn't like finding herself dependent on him after having had a certain autonomy. So very soon she started to be a supply teacher, and soon she was offered a full-time job at an elementary school. After each of her births, she had the right to a maternity leave, during which time she could rest and look after the baby. When she returned to work, she would have a baby sitter look after the child. Judith insisted on the importance of her work, which she considered essential for her own personal self-esteem. Her talents and aptitudes were recognized and valued at work. I myself am not yet in the labour market and my situation is perhaps somewhat different. There is little probability that I will benefit from the kind of job security that my mother experienced as a teacher; this simply will not exist any more or it will definitely be less. I probably will find myself in a very unstable job as a contract worker where, because of the competition, I will have to prove my competence every day. Nonetheless, I hope to work at something I like and that will allow me to travel.

Women in the labour force have very full timetables, which oblige them to be well organized, because the participation of men in housework is a relatively recent phenomenon. Marie-Blanche told me that when her husband was there, he would voluntarily take care of the youngest children, bathing them and changing their diapers, but she said that this was quite exceptional. He has always liked cooking and he made breakfast for the whole family. As well he would take the children to visit relatives in the country. But it was she who did all the rest: laundry, ironing, sewing and cooking were her daily tasks. The older girls helped with the dishes and housework, but the boys were not asked to do anything except work outside the house, sweeping up the yard or cutting the grass, and so on. Marie-Blanche also attended to the household accounts and managed the family economy. She described her workday in the period when she still had young children:

I got up in the morning, then when the children had left for school I would bathe the baby and give him his breakfast, I would give him his bottle, then I would peel the potatoes and prepare lunch; all the children came home for lunch ... After they had left again, I would put the baby to sleep and sometimes I would fall asleep with him. I would get up at three o'clock, finish washing the dishes and then I'd prepare supper.

And so on for about twenty years ...

Judith's daily life was different. Even though she admitted to having done the major part of the housework alone for a long time while my father worked on the outside of the house and did small repairs, she estimates that now tasks are more evenly divided between them. My father now does his part of the housework, such as laundry and dishes. In addition Judith is happy to be able to leave the household accounts, which she detests, to him. She thinks, however, that she didn't make her children participate sufficiently in the housework, but it is a bit late now because only my brother is at home. For the past five years, I myself have lived in an apartment, which I now share with two men. Even if the responsibilities are shared, I think that I am more likely to do the work than they who sometimes "forget" the tasks they were supposed to do. In addition, it is I who attend to the accounts for our shared expenses.

The very busy work days of Marie-Blanche didn't give her much time for social activities, especially when the children were still in the house. However, later on my grandparents joined a Golden Age Club, more for outdoor activities such as camping and touring in recreational vehicles: these are not your usual grandparents! Judith, on the other hand, chooses to take very little part in community organizations. However, she is part of a badminton league, which puts her in contact with women in the neighbourhood and she likes to work outdoors when her schedule permits this. She spends a lot of time with her family, "by choice, not by obligation." Although her best friends still are her sisters, she also has some other old friends on whom she can count. I myself have always liked participating in various projects and I consider myself to be very busy. I like organizing things and considering myself useful. While I like to be surrounded by people, I also appreciate solitude. My network of friends is mainly composed of students in anthropology, but

I have also kept some friends from high school who live near my parents and whom I visit when I am there.

When I asked Marie-Blanche what she considers to have been the greatest change in Québec society, she answered without hesitation that it is religion, the attitude of people to its precepts. Her own conscience is still disturbed, however, by the fact that so often people live together, have a sexual life and even children without marrying. Some of her children are in that situation and, even if she doesn't want to "judge" them, she finds it difficult to understand their reasoning. As a witness to the common-law arrangements of her children, she is astonished that after having made this choice, they decide nonetheless to have their children baptised and they take communion when they go to church.

For Judith, the most important change that she has witnessed is in the behaviour of men in Québec who, she says, having been hewers of wood, have now become "intellectuals." She is astonished to see them also "reinvent the world" and "discuss philosophy and politics" while, according to her, in the past "they were so proud of their physical strength." However, she finds that in Québec, people speak much more than they *do*; they accomplish fewer concrete things; they are also much less "manual" than before. The image she has is of men who have changed radically, "perhaps too much," in certain respects.

Otherwise, Judith considers that "men of Québec have come a long way" from the standpoint of sexuality; they are "less scrupulous" nowadays. She also notes changes in the Church's attitudes towards pregnant women, in the behaviour of men in relation to women at work as well as in the greater autonomy of women. She thinks there is a much greater openness to women in the labour market, and she rejoices that women can work in fields previously reserved for men. On the other hand, she does not approve of "radical feminism," which, according to her, puts "all men in the same basket" or which presents them as "our rivals." Judith does not consider herself a militant, but she affirms that "one must not let men create a place for us; if we want a place, we must take it ourselves." She says that she herself has never encountered those particular difficulties, but she thinks that "probably women have to be a bit more competent" to get managerial positions.

I, Sophie, am of the generation that is harvesting what the feminists sowed and that too easily forgets sometimes that women's lives have not always been so easy. I am from the generation where the women them-selves do not appear to see the use of feminism and even go as far as to rejoice that feminism is losing momentum. I am from the generation that thinks women have no more battles to fight, and that disappoints me. But it isn't all so dark: women have only begun to develop their great potential, more and more of them are attending universities and, bit by bit, they are entering fields previously reserved for men. The proportion of women in higher education is rising. The next steps will perhaps take place more discreetly, but in a useful manner: at least that is what I hope with all my heart.

Notes

The stories in this chapter were translated from the French by Greta Hofmann Nemiroff.

1. The Collectif Clio is formed by well-known and respected Québec feminist historians Micheline Dumont, Michèle Jean, Marie Lavigne and Jennifer Stoddard. The second edition of *Histoire des femmes au Québec depuis quatre siècles* (Montréal: Le Jour, 1992) is also available in English as Quebec Women: A History (Toronto: The Women's Press, 1986). Also see Marie Lavigne and Yolande Pinard, eds., *Travailleuses et féministes: les femmes dans la société québécoise* (Montréal: Boreal Express, 1983).

2. For demographic information on Québec, see Simon Langlois, "Tendances de la société québécoise," in Roch Côté, ed., *Québec 1998* (Montréal: Fides), 3–48; Suzanne Asselin, Hervé Gauthier et al., *Les hommes et les femmes: une comparaison de leurs conditions de vie* (Québec: Les Publications du Québec, 1994); *Femmes des années 1990. Portrait statistique* (Québec: Secrétariat à la condition féminine, Gouvernement du Québec, 1993); Louise Guyon et al., *Derrière les apparences. Santé et conditions de vie des femmes* (Québec: Ministère de la Santé et des Services sociaux, 1996); *Le Québec statistique. 60e édition* (Québec: Les Publications du Québec, 1995); *Statistiques sur le travail et la famille au Canada* (Ottawa: Conseil consultatif sur la situation de la femme, 1994).

3. For a historical overview of scientific research done in Québec on this topic and an extensive bibliography of more than 120 references, see Francine Descarries and Christine Corbeil, "La conciliation travail-famille," in Huguette Dagenais, ed., *Science, conscience et action* (Montréal: Remue-ménage, 1996), 51–71.

4. Which contradicts Sigmund Freud's now famous declaration that "biology determines women's destiny."

5. See Renée Dandurand, "Entre la quête de l'autonomie et le maintien des liens familiaux," in Dagenais, ed., *Science, conscience et action*, 31–50.

6. See Marie Lavigne, "Pour une approche féministe de la démographie," in Conseil du statut de la femme, *Femmes et questions démographiques. Un nouveau regard* (Québec: Les Publications du Québec, 1991), 205–213.

7. It is always strange to use fractions when talking about children, even though this is the way it is done in demographic averages and for the purpose of comparison. On the other hand, is it not time for scientists to study *men's* fertility rates?

8. On June 11, 1999, the Québec parliament adopted Law 32 on same-sex spouses abolishing any difference in the treatment of homosexual and heterosexual common-law spouses. See Irène Demzuk, ed., *Des droits à reconnaître. Les lesbiennes face à la discrimination* (Montréal: Remue-ménage, 1998).

9. See Nicole Dedobbeleer and Pauline Morissette, "Le sida et les femmes seules à la recherche d'un partenaire: un groupe à risque ignoré?" in Huguette Dagenais, ed., *Pluralité et convergences. La recherche féministe dans la francophonie* (Montréal: Remue-ménage, 1999), 217–242.

10. Every year on December 6, feminists and other women around the world remember this massacre through publications, memorial services, vigils, colloquiums, and so on. See Marie Chalout and Louise Malette, eds., *Montréal, 6 décembre 1989* (Montréal: Remue-ménage, 1990).

11. See Martin Dufresne, "Masculinisme et criminalité sexiste," *Recherches féministes* 11, no. 2 (1998), 125–137. This article provides examples of similar murders and references to several international Web site addresses of groups of fathers affirming their "rights" over their children.

12. See "Meurtre dans un refuge pour femmes violentée," *Le Soleil,* 11 June 1999, A1–A2, and "Le suspect sous examen. La violence familiale frappe surtout les femmes," 12 June 1999, A 21. On psychological violence, see Jocelyn Lindsay and Michèle Clément, "La violence psychologique: sa définition et sa représentation selon le sexe," *Recherches féministes* 11, no. 2 (1998), 139–160. For an overview of the research done on this topic in Québec over the last two decades, see Geneviève Martin, "La recherche sur la violence," in Dagenais, ed., *Science, conscience et action,* 121–148.

13. Nancy Guberman, Pierre Maheu, and Chantal Maillé, *Et si l'amour ne suffisait pas... Femmes, familles et adultes dépendants* (Montréal: Remue-ménage, 1991); Association féminine d'éducation et d'action sociale (AFÉAS), Denise Côté et. al., *Who Will Be Responsible for Providing Care? The Impact of the Shift to Ambulatory Care and Social Economy Policies on Quebec Women* (Ottawa: Status of Women Canada, 1998).

14. For the results of the whole survey, see *La Gazette des femmes,* March 1994.

15. See Dagenais, ed., *Science, conscience et action.*

16. For an example, see Micheline Dumont and Stéphanie Lanthier, "Pas d'histoire, les femmes! Le féminisme dans un magazine québécois à grand tirage: *L'actualité,* 1960–1996," *Recherches féministes* 11, no. 2 (1998), 101–124; see also Myriame El Yamani, *Médias et féminisme. Minoritaires sans parole* (Paris: L'Harmattan, 1998).

17. See Lise Lachance, "6,45$ l'heure, minimum," *Le Soleil,* 5 June 5, 1995, A1–A2; "Du pain et des roses. Début d'un nouveau partenariat," *Le Soleil,* 5 June 1995, A6; "'Au fond les filles, on a gagné beaucoup', Françoise David," *Le Soleil,* 5 June 1995, A6; and Lise Bisonnette, "Quelque pain et quelques roses," *Le Devoir,* 6 June 1995, A8.

Study Questions

1. In the introduction to this chapter, Huguette Dagenais formulates a few hypotheses under the form of questions. What other hypotheses could you make after reading the entire chapter?

2. What difference and what similiarities do you see in Nadine Jammal's family, an immigrant family to Québec, and the families of the three other Québec narrators?

3. How does social class articulate with gender in the lives of women from the four Québec families presented here?

NOVA SCOTIA

Cape Breton
Island

Glace Bay
North Sydney

New Glasgow
Pictou
Westville
Guysborough

Stellarton

Cape Chignecto
Truro
Preston

Dartmouth
Halifax

St. Margarets Bay
Chester Basin
Lunenburg
Bridgewater

LaHave
Digby
Shelburne
Yarmouth

Atlantic
Ocean

WOMEN'S CHANGING LIVES

by Linda Christiansen-Ruffman, Angela Dinaut, Colleen McMahon, Brenda Lee Regimbal, Paula Veinot

—◦—

THE GAELIC WORD FOR NEW SCOTLAND, Nova Scotia, may seem appropriate for this picturesque peninsula along Canada's Atlantic Coast. However, long before the Scots arrived, the Mi'kmaq, Nova Scotia's First Nations peoples, lived along the coast in winter and migrated inland along the river banks and lakes to fish in summer. They were first known by their colonizers as "Micmacs," but in recent years they have taken on their own tribal name, Mi'kmaq, and a renewed pride in their heritage.

The first Europeans, from France, settled along the Bay of Fundy from the early 1600s to 1750, although the Treaty of Utrecht in 1713 confirmed Nova Scotia as British. After years of promising neutrality, but refusing to take an unqualified oath of allegiance, some 6,000 of these French-speaking Acadian settlers were deported in 1755, an event commemorated in Longfellow's poem *Evangeline*. After the Seven Years' War, 2,000 Acadian families returned to Nova Scotia to find many of their former farms already occupied by the 8,000 New England Planters who had arrived from the United States between 1758 and 1768. The Acadians were re-settled in Cape Breton and from Yarmouth to Digby, along what is called "the French shore." Meanwhile, German families had settled along the South Shore of Nova Scotia, and their heritage is still evident in domestic architecture and food such as sauerkraut and sausages.

During the 1700s and 1800s, the British established their dominance in the province. Colonel Edward Cornwallis, who had been appointed governor of the colony, led settlers in the summer of 1749 to establish the provincial capital at the port which became Halifax. In the 1770s, settlers from Yorkshire, England, arrived in the Chignecto Bay area and Scots arrived in Pictou. The American Revolution brought a further 20,000 "Loyalists" to Nova Scotia of both British and African heritage. Around 55,000 British arrived in Nova Scotia between 1815 and 1851, and another wave of British immigration supported the expansion of the coal and steel industries of Cape Breton in the 1890s. The resulting English, Irish, Scots and Welsh traditions are evident today, particularly in the music, language and culture of the region.

Women and men of African heritage have lived in Nova Scotia since they came as slaves with a few early white settlers.[1] During the American Revolution an estimated 1,200 slaves came attached to white Loyalist households, but about three times that number came as Black Loyalists, having gained their freedom in exchange for their allegiance to Britain. They settled in and around the towns of Halifax, Preston, Shelburne, Birchtown, Annapolis, Guysborough and Digby. Some of these early Black Loyalists, disappointed by conditions in Nova Scotia, emigrated to Sierra Leone in 1791–92 as part of the "back to Africa" movement. In 1796 a group of Jamaican Maroons arrived to work on the Halifax Citadel; some of them were then sent to Sierra Leone in 1800. Another 2,000 Blacks arrived as refugees after the War of 1812.[2] These early Black settlers have made an important contribution to Nova Scotia's rich multicultural heritage. Over the years, many women from the Black communities have become well-known locally, nationally and internationally as artists, educators, civil rights activists and writers. Portia White taught in the small Black community of Africville on the Halifax peninsula before becoming internationally known as an opera singer. Carrie Best became a journalist and editor in the 1960s, before many women were recognized as professionals. Viola Desmond, an independent business women and civil rights activist in the 1940s and 1950s, became an important role model for many young Black Nova Scotians.[3]

Wars and economic hardships in Europe and promised prosperity in the new world led Italians, Scandinavians, Greeks and Eastern European immigrants to seek new lives in Canada. Until the advent of planes, most European immigrants to Canada came by boat and were "landed" in Halifax at Pier 21 after their voyage across the Atlantic. Some remained in Nova Scotia rather than moving west. In the 1960s changes to

Canada's *Immigration Act* removed some biases against racial minorities immigrating to Canada, but still required them to have superior job skills. Professionals arrived in Nova Scotia from the Caribbean, Africa and Asia along with "draft dodgers" from the United States. The Nova Scotian economy has not attracted large numbers of immigrants, however, and as Table 1 indicates, the majority of Nova Scotians in 1991 still have British heritage. In 1991 the 452,925 women in Nova Scotia constituted 50.8 percent of the provincial population.[4]

Table 1: *Population Estimates*

NOVA SCOTIAN HERITAGE, 1991
(Compiled from Statistics Canada, 1993)

BRITISH		FRENCH		OTHER EUROPEAN		BRITISH/FRENCH & CANADIAN	
English	256,265	French	11,845	West Eur.	34,395	British	1,890
Irish	35,850	Acadian	530	North Eur.	1,645	French	165
Scottish	17,665	Comb.	1,195	Scandinavian	1,525	Canadian	500
Welsh	1,000			East Eur	5,030		
Comb.	186,060			South Eur.	5,415		
Sub-Total	496,840						

English & French: 80,570   Total European: 641,545

ASIAN & AFRICAN		LATIN, CENTRAL & SOUTH AMERICAN	CARRIBEAN
South Asia	2,315	345	190
Africa	3,365		
East & SE Asia	3,330		

BLACK NS	ABORIGINAL	MULTIPLE
10,825	7,530	90,280

TOTAL NOVA SCOTIANS: 890,950

Socioeconomic Backgrounds of
Nova Scotian Women

Both Mi'kmaq and settler communities in Nova Scotia have relied upon the sustainable natural resources of fishing, farming and forestry[5] and on women's participation in this work. These sustainable resource industries provided livelihoods for early settlers and contributed raw materials of fish, kelp, maple syrup, fruits, vegetables and pulpwood to support small manufacturing plants. Along with the related tourist industry, they still contribute significantly to the provincial economy. Women's work in these sectors has been crucial although their work has frequently been invisible, unrecognized and unpaid, as has the importance of this sustainable resource sector in a world which has built an economic value system based on greed, exploitative growth and destructive technology.

Both the resource sector and women's economic roles have changed over the centuries. For example, in the fisheries, a cornerstone industry in the province, women have traditionally been responsible for salting and drying fish on flakes in the sun.[6] This dried salt cod, along with lumber, was a major trading export during the "golden age of wooden sailing ships" from the mid-eighteenth to nineteenth centuries. As processing technologies and the organization of work changed during the twentieth century, women worked for low pay in local fishplants that dotted the coast, processing the cod, haddock, halibut, herring, whale, lobster and scallops caught in Nova Scotian waters. In the last half of the twentieth century, the fishing industry's use of technology has led to environmental and sustainability problems. In the early 1990s, a moratorium was imposed on the cod fishery, which accelerated the closure of fish plants. Restructuring proposals undermined fishing communities and the employment gains women had been making in the industry, on boats as well as on shore, over the last twenty-five years. As the fisheries falter, women suffer loss, not only of their own economic and social positions, but those of their partners and their communities. As has happened in many resource industries over the years, the family enterprise was sustained by women's financial contributions from paid work in such jobs as domestics, clerks, fish plant workers, nurses and teachers.

While women's paid and unpaid roles in the processing sector and on boats have occasionally been acknowledged, women's role in the family business as "captain of the shore crew" has been virtually invisible. Women's indispensable work as business managers, bookkeepers, baiters, subsistence farmers, information consultants and repair supervisors has been critical for the viability of family enterprises. Yet, when the Canadian government compensated workers after closing down the cod fisheries, this women's work was not counted. Government policies, in fact, have favoured "professionalization," corporatization and commercialization of fisheries and have been designed to put family enterprises, often the most sustainable of fisheries operations, out of business.

Nova Scotian women, like women over the centuries in most of the world, have also been responsible for the ongoing unpaid domestic work of caring for families, raising children, doing "housework," and producing the next generation of workers. Through these unpaid and taken-for-granted jobs, women provide material support, spiritual guidance, emotional sustenance and managerial responsibilities for households and communities. In this work, women require knowledge of health, education, welfare, psychology, sociology, communication, economy and ethics, but women's skills, experience and knowledge in this work is unrecognized and unrewarded still today. So, too, is their multiple work burden.

Because of economic development policies that have imposed in-dustrial models on rural areas and marginalized Atlantic Canada, Nova Scotians have too often become economic refugees in their own country. During boom times in the rest of Canada, many Nova Scotians leave in hopes of providing more economic resources for their families. Thus Nova Scotia has experienced net out-migration in times of economic prosperity in Canada. During the last century, many young women left Nova Scotia to go "in service" as nannies for affluent Boston families.[7] When manufacturing in Ontario was booming, the majority of migrants headed there. During Alberta's economic boom, many Nova Scotians sought work in the oil industry.[8] When Nova Scotians "go down the road" for economic advancement, they often holiday or retire "back home." And they return home during economic down turns in the rest of Canada to find family support, content with the knowledge that they are not depriving their families economically during this period of living in Nova Scotia. We found that this migration pattern applied to two co-authors. One of us left Nova Scotia during the expanding mid-1960s to return fifteen years later; another of us left Nova Scotia during the Ontario "recovery" of the mid-1980s, to return in the early 1990s, during Canada's economic recession, and then to return again to Ontario once the economy there again grew strong.

Thus Nova Scotia — along with the other Atlantic provinces of New Brunswick, Prince Edward Island and Newfoundland/Labrador — is often referred to as a "have not province," because of high unemployment, frequent net out-migration and the lack of a large tax base. But ask Maritimers or Newfoundlanders about the place they call home and their response will often include a passionate knowledge and understanding of the land they love. Such passion is reflected in the province's rich art, music and poetry. It is also clear in the acute sense of place expressed by women who participated in our research. Almost all perceived themselves to be Maritimers first and Canadians second. Regardless of whether the women lived in rural or urban areas, or had left Nova Scotia and returned, they identified themselves as Nova Scotians and often recognized their strong ties to their region and local communities.

GEOGRAPHICAL BACKGROUNDS OF THE WOMEN

Most of the women who participated in this project reside in or around the port city of Halifax. This provincial capital and regional centre hosts a number of universities, which is where Women's Studies faculty developed the first joint graduate program at Mount Saint Vincent University, Dalhousie University and Saint Mary's University.[9] Halifax is the site of women's groups and services from the first and second waves of the women's movement and of the government-appointed Nova Scotia Advisory Committee on the Status of Women. As the largest city in Atlantic Canada, Halifax has attracted migrants in search of employment from more rural areas of Nova Scotia. The fact that the younger rather than the older generation of women is more likely to be born in and live in Halifax reflects this pattern.

Three women from the oldest generation live along the coast, south of Halifax. Lillian lives just outside of Halifax, in a small fishing community along St. Margaret's Bay. Sun Rose lives about a half hour drive from Lillian, on a Native Indian Reserve along a quiet dirt road that follows a winding river in Chester Basin. However, she does not own the land she lives on because it is part of federal reserve land that has been set aside for First Nations peoples. Margo lives less than an hour drive from Sun Rose along the Lahave River, just outside of the town of Lunenburg. Nearby in Bridgewater is the site of one of Nova Scotia's first women's centres.

Gertrude, another first-generation woman, now resides in Halifax, but she was born in Yarmouth County along the southern tip of Nova Scotia. From the town of Yarmouth, site of one of Nova Scotia's shelters for battered women, ferries cross the mouth of the Bay of Fundy to Maine. Around the western side of the peninsula, past the small French Acadian communities that line the shore, is Digby. Doreen, a second-generation participant, was born and raised in Digby County. Like many Nova Scotians from rural areas, Doreen moved to Halifax, became a nurse, married and settled in the city.

Two of the families interviewed are from the other end of Nova Scotia, to the northeast, on Cape Breton Island. The Cape Breton economy has been depressed since the 1930s.[10] Margaret, age seventy-three, lives in a senior citizens complex in Glace Bay, an industrial town. She was born in her house in the company coal town of Donkin (Dominion #6, fourth in line), where she lived with four sisters and two brothers. The people of Glace Bay migrated from the coal mines of Scotland to apply their skills in the coal mines of Cape Breton. Margaret's first paying job was in the "Sweet Sixteen Choir." She described how she "used to go around singing at the [community] halls ... We got paid twelve dollars for each show; that was big bucks then [during the Depression]." Throughout her life she also worked in a grocery store as a clerk and cashier, in a plant putting together radio parts, and cleaning homes. When Margaret married in 1943, she not only took her husband's name but also his Scottish ethnicity. Margaret's niece, Sandra, listed her ethnicity as Irish. Sandra was born in Glace Bay but has lived her married life in Halifax, working as a nurse, a supervisor nurse and a mother to two children. Sandra was raised Roman Catholic, but when she married, she switched to the United Church because she felt that "it was important to be the same religion as my husband." Although Jeanette, Sandra's daughter, was born in Halifax in 1972 to what she considers an upper-middle-class family, she describes her ethnicity as "Cape Bretoner," or "Caper."

The other Cape Breton family, also comprising strong, independent women, is from North Sydney, where the ferries connect Nova Scotia and Newfoundland. Mildred, the oldest, was a fisherman's wife, as was her mother before her. Mildred saw herself as the dominant parent and prided herself in the way she organized her home with little or no help from her husband. She remembers when the community provided her with a sense of support. "I was part of the great fishing industries in the world." Now that the fishing industry is no longer great and her husband has retired, Mildred feels a sense of loss; she appears to be grieving, as she says, "I still want to be the wife of a fisherman." Mildred's daughter, Karen, left Cape Breton for a career in the military, a career that brought her both personal and financial opportunities. She felt pride in her career and was thankful that the military had made her a more confident and capable woman. Like many Maritimers, Karen has now retired back to "dear Nova Scotia." In Cape Breton she has a sense of belonging to a community and her life is intertwined with those of her mother, her daughter (Tammy) and her young grandchildren. Tammy, a single parent, has also moved to her grandmother's town to raise her own family. She describes herself as a "converted Maritimer," who was "bred" to the Maritimes because of her parents' strong ties and love for the East Coast: "The Maritimes is a place that I have grown to love and admire, mostly because of the people and my family." Karen, Tammy's mother, believes that this sense of pride in being from Cape Breton is common amongst most Cape Bretoners. Mildred is clear that she is "a Cape Bretoner first and foremost."

GENERATIONAL BACKGROUNDS OF THE WOMEN

The three generations of women, born from 1910 to 1970, have been part of many technological, social and political changes, including changes in the strength and public profile of the women's movement. Our tentative generalizations in this section, where we locate lives of the three generations in the social context of the times, require additional research. In a further study, we might want to define generations more narrowly or by specific periods of history, so that we can better understand relationships between biography and history. We also might explore further our tentative finding that decisions made by women in one generation create a different climate and set of cultural expectations for subsequent generations. This pattern is consistent with the women's movement idea that the personal is political; women's daily decisions do have long-term consequences.

THE ELDER GENERATION

Women in the eldest generation were born between 1910 and 1929, during the latter part of what is sometimes called the first phase of the women's movement. Through the women's suffrage movement, Nova Scotian women won the right to vote in 1918, but before 1929 no Canadian woman had yet been recognized legally as a person.[11] This generation of women all grew up through the Depression years of the 1930s, and most of them were adults at the outbreak of the Second World War. We heard stories of gathering in the local hall to make up packages to send overseas in support of the war effort.

Socially, women in the elder generation were defined by their husband's economic status, and they defined themselves as fishermen's wives or minister's wives. This idea that women were wives and not members of the labour force was so prevalent that teachers, by law or convention, gave up their jobs once they married. Women's social identity was so subordinate that several women reported adopting religious and ethnic identities of their husbands to gain standing in their adopted communities. In the best of times, women took pride in seeing themselves within the community and family as caregivers and understood the important contributions they were making to lives around them. Yet many women also longed for their own social and personal space. One woman told how she found small community life to be oppressive, refused to become a fisherman's wife, left for the city and became a nurse.

Several of the women reported that they were raised in patriarchal homes, and later demonstrated an independence and pride in being able to run their own households without this domination. This suggests a conscious and concerted shift from patriarchal family patterns, which is consistent with pride in women's roles as nurturers, not just in their own families, but also within their local communities. This is also consistent with decisions made by this generation of women to reduce the size of their families.

All the women within the elder generation appeared to be independent and strong-willed. They had often faced adversity and created positive changes within their lives, such as abandoning destructive relationships. Defining feminism was difficult for many of the older women, and some thought that the (recent) women's movement had not affected their lives in any significant way. Margaret, a Cape Bretoner, was one woman from the older generation with a perceptive view of contemporary feminism. She defined it as "a woman using her own name, not her married one. She keeps her own identity." By this criteria, Margaret is not a feminist. She believes that a married woman should take her husband's name, like she has done in her life, as well as taking on her husband's Scottish ethnicity. On the other hand, Margaret would probably agree that she is a feminist by a definition developed during the suffrage movement, "a feminist is someone who refuses to be treated as a doormat."[12]

Only near the end of our analysis did we realize that this remark of Margaret pointed to generational ethnocentrism of our approach in identifying women by their first names. Several women in the first generation, but certainly not all of them, would have preferred a name like Mrs. John McDonald that reflected the way they lived their lives and derived their status as a wife in a community. Further research might explore the impact of the first phase of the women's movement on this generation of strong-willed and community-minded women, who had rejected some of the patriarchal family norms so dominant in their childhoods while accepting the family structure such as the role of wife.

THE MIDDLE GENERATION

The middle generation, born between 1937 and 1951, grew up in an ideological environment following the Second World War that attempted to remove women from the labour force by idealizing "the nuclear family." Technological advances had made work at home less demanding. Many of the second generation, born before the end of the

Second World War, were young adults prior to the feminist movement in the the 1960s. Others were young women during the emergence of this movement, which challenged female subordination. This group was most diverse.

Women of the second generation, like all generations, stressed the importance of family ties. In their first years of marriage, they reported having a well-defined sexual division of labour within the home. Almost all of them had lived traditional European lifestyles as part of a male-headed nuclear family. The most noticeable difference within this generation was that some of the women chose to develop alternative or different family lifestyles later in life. Some divorced or repudiated heterosexual marriage because it no longer satisfied their personal needs. Its idyllic image left unfulfilled dreams; its nuclear structure isolated women; and the activities in its sphere were considered worthless by an increasingly monied economy. Donna rejected European concepts of marriage for more traditional Native concepts and wished to raise her children independently. Jackie acted on her sexual preference and established a lesbian family with her female partner.

Unlike the previous generation, almost all middle-generation women stayed in the paid workforce after they married and had children. They cared greatly about their families, and several cared equally about their jobs. They, like their mothers, chose "pink-collar" jobs, including nursing and clerical positions. Two of the five women were underemployed; their education was well beyond what was needed to fulfill their work requirements.

All these second-generation women thought that there were more job and educational opportunities for women of the third generation as well as more personal freedoms and fewer social boundaries. This generation experienced tremendous social change and transition.

THE YOUNGER GENERATION

Many of the younger generation, born between 1959 and 1973, grew up along with the Women's Liberation Movement and the initiation and implementation of the Royal Commission of the Status of Women (1970). They saw that the struggles of their predecessors opened doors of opportunity in education and employment for women and that they are the beneficiaries of the women's movement. Support groups and programs are now in place for women in trouble, although funding is often precarious for these groups.

Young women recognize that social expectations of marriage and family have changed and that the family comes in various forms. They feel that they can live with a man or have children without being married, with little or no repercussions from society. Work within the family, both chores and child-rearing, is seen to be more equally shared with male partners, and many said that these changes have come about because of the struggles of the women before them.

Almost all thought that their mothers had played an important role in their development. They placed priority on independence and personal freedom and their own identity. Most of the women in this generation are in the midst of personal social changes; many had just finished university or were having their first child. Their personal lives were more in transition than older generations. However, they all appeared to be optimistic that their futures hold many opportunities.

In fact, almost every woman in all generations mentioned the now more abundant opportunities for women and fewer social and political constraints. In particular, women of the youngest generation believed that all doors are open for them. Many of the women (in fact, all of the youngest generation) said that the women's movement precipitated these increased opportunities.

WOMEN'S VOICES AND FEMINIST APPROACHES

These "findings" from three generations of women and the following women's stories are exploratory stages in developing a composite social portrait of the changing social landscapes in Nova Scotia during the twentieth century. Listening to voices of women allows us, *as individuals*, to empathize with women and to relate women's experiences to the context of our own lives. Listening to voices of women leads us, *as feminists*, both inside and outside the academy, to knowledge and understanding: we learn to appreciate multicentred women's lives and diverse realities, the sources of women's oppression, women's ways of creating change and women's movements. Women's voices challenge the persistent power of patriarchy and help us to change: to put an end to all forms of discrimination, to transform society and to revalue social relationships, and life itself.

Voices are always spoken, silenced and heard within social contexts. Feminist scholarship has grown from a discovery of the "malestream" or "patricentric knowledge" surrounding us — and enclosing us — in daily life, in economics, politics, bureaucracies, religions, universities and the media. Even in science and scholarship, which purports to be "objective" and unbiased, feminist scholars have found distortions that reflect the white, western, male, upper-class perspective of its theorists and researchers over the years.[13]

The voices of women, as well as women's realities and experiences, are sometimes suppressed and other times distorted by the gendered structure of knowledge that conceives of women as only functional to men. Patriarchy robs women of grounded autonomous voice and of human agency. Building a women's perspective on the world is difficult because names and words for many women's experiences do not exist, and when they do, they are not considered to be of value or significance. Grounded feminist research has developed in this context, with its focus on research by, for, about and (sometimes) with women.

Women's voices are a powerful resource for the creation of feminist knowledge and hence central to feminist methodology.[14] Women's voices, even though they are still inescapably filtered through patricentric language and concepts, guide us through to women's experiences. They are a starting point for a different comprehension of the world — one which values the unpaid work of women, for example, and refuses the pretences and indicators of existing antiwomen and exploitative systems of value and justice.

When we act as *feminist sociologists* and listen to voices of women, we interpret their stories within a disciplinary context. Unlike literature, for example, which encourages the development of individual voices and richer detail, a social science such as sociology urges us to discover similarities and differences and to make generalizations. As feminist sociologists, we seek to understand women's lives in specific temporal, geographic and relational contexts, within particular societies and cultures. In the process, women's experiences teach us about these contexts and lead us to theorize social patterns and structural interconnections. In this research on past and present experiences of three generations of women in Nova Scotia, we understand each woman's story in a number of ways: as an expression of a unique personal history; as part of a particular family history; as evocative of the social history of particular times in Nova Scotia; as suggestive of social patterns and structural interconnections, and as examples from which to discover patterns of change.

The Nova Scotian research was conducted as the major part of course requirements for a one-semester sociology course on feminist methodology at Saint Mary's University, taught by Linda Christiansen-Ruffman. The university context influenced our research, affecting its purpose, content and tone, and having methodological implications for every stage of the research process: design, sampling, data gathering, analysis and writing.

The course setting slightly altered the research design because students who had registered for the seminar were the pool of co-researchers and co-authors; Linda could not assume that these students would have access to two other generations of women in their own families because of deaths, refusals and distance.[15] Thus, the course required qualitative research from three generations, and most students chose to interview their partners' or friends' families rather than their own. In discussions of the emerging "sample," feminist students were particularly concerned to increase diversity; Colleen McMahon voluntarily interviewed an additional family.

Since only one student had experience as a researcher, we developed an in-depth interview instrument to guide interaction and information-gathering.[16] We "brain-stormed" questions and organized them around these topics: women's roles in family, society and the community; growth, dreams and learning; work at home and in the paid labour force; social location and community participation; effect of the women's movement; and other background or demographic "variables." Some students gathered almost all of their information through interviews and did not have the years of "participant observations" and reflections of those who focused on their own families. The lack or presence of the students' personal experiences with the interviewees, and the quality and depth of those experiences, affected analysis and writing, particularly the students' voices.

Both graduate and undergraduate student volunteers from the class worked beyond the end of term — editing their stories, analyzing

information from other classmates and co-writing sections of this introduction.[17] In analyzing and writing women's stories, the students sought
to find threads of similarity among the women in the three generations
of their families; they expressed their main themes of their stories in
their titles. They sought to find differences that could provide clues to the
structure and culture of generational variations among women over time.
This sociological approach led students beyond "their" specific women's
stories. Comparisons were made with others. In a typical sociological
fashion, one student analyzed all of the women's stories collected in the
seminar, using the lives of the people she interviewed as illustrations of
patterns she found. The class also reflected on patterns seen and insights learned. Unlike some sociology but like social history, our feminist
approach led us to see the participants' lives as part of social processes
in specific contexts. We analyzed the three generations of women "as
cohorts" in their historical context. If there had been more time, we
could have done more research in the archives and used previous research
to understand contexts more fully.[18]

CONCLUSION

We were surprised by the strength of women, especially in the first
generation. Our popular culture, based on assumptions of unilineal
progress, had created stereotypes that were shattered by these interviews.
We enjoyed hearing and sharing stories from all three generations.

We were also surprised by the optimism. We see persistent discrimination in all social institutions of society. In our eyes, the recession has
worsened the circumstances and opportunities for women. Restructuring
in Canada, like Structural Adjustment Programs in other countries, disad-
vantages women. Restructuring often means that new jobs are created for
men, women's jobs are structured out of existence, and women are
forced back into the home to do the caring work for which society no
longer pays.

Despite the optimistic outlook of many of our participants, we also
found that the unspoken stories hidden under the interviews reveal the
problems and pain that are also a part of life. Most of us, and particularly
women, have been conditioned to present the more positive aspects of

ourselves for public viewing. We also tend to protect ourselves and our families from the scrutiny of the public.

These tendencies prevent us from revealing our complete stories to others. Whatever their histories, however, the women interviewed emerged as strong and capable women who were able to confront adversity and create positive change within their social realm.

ESTABLISHING
INDEPENDENCE
A Struggle for Self-Determination

—◦—

The Elder: Sun Rose's Story

SUN ROSE, HER DAUGHTER AND GRANDDAUGHTER are all members of
First Nations peoples, the Mi'kmaq, and they are Status Indians within
guidelines of the *Canadian Indian Act*. Born in 1929 in Truro, Sun
Rose is widowed and lives with her son on Gold River Reserve. She is
the middle child in a family of five; she has one sister and three brothers,
who all still reside in Nova Scotia. Her mother and father, Teresa and
John Knockwood, provided for their family by creating Native crafts
such as baskets. Sun Rose has fulfilled many occupations with changes in
education throughout her lifetime. Before retiring, she was a community
drug and alcohol counsellor. She has six children, six grandchildren and
five great-grandchildren.

Sun Rose expressed how social and political mores have changed over
time since she was a girl: "When I was young I was protected, under
the care of Mum and Dad. As I got older, I left school after Grade Eight
to go out to work. During those times people looked for jobs without
qualifications. It was the same for the men, too." She worked in a factory.
Much later, Sun Rose returned to school twice, once in the 1970s to
complete a business college course and again in the late 1980s to complete
a degree in social work at Dalhousie University. She then became a
drug and alcohol counsellor.

When Sun Rose was living under the protection of her family, the
males and females in the family took on different domestic roles, and
the boys also had more privileges, such as going alone to the nearest
town. When her children were growing up, Sun Rose took on most of

the domestic chores. Now she shares her home with her youngest son, and the chores are divided equally.

Oral traditions, such as "story telling" and music, have always played a significant role in Sun Rose's life. She continues to love gathering together to socialize and to make music. Seven women within the Gold River Community are especially significant in her life, because of their social support and companionship.

Sun Rose's value system has changed over time. When she was young she thought it was important to marry. Now her ideals of marriage have changed: "Men and Women, 'marry and live happy ever after.' At the time I agreed, but today I do not agree; people do not need to live together forever. Today they do not 'live to death do you part,' and that is okay."

When Rose was young, she emulated "white fashions." Now she displays a pride in her Native culture. Rose has also rejected European religions and believes only in Native spirituality. She passionately stated: "I do not define myself with any religious denomination. Religious spirituality is fine as long as it is Native spirituality."

Sun Rose may have changed her ideas over time, but her perception of her physical self has not changed. She describes herself at sixteen as being pretty and dark; and at sixty-five she describes herself in the same way. The defining differences are not physical. Now she is an elder, a Mi'kmaq and content with her life. She stated that she feels "safe and enjoys being alone and independent." While she does not perceive herself as belonging to a community, she feels a part of the people who live near her.

The way Sun Rose defined "feminism" depicts her perception of women today: "I think at certain times a person has to do their duty, but it comes a time in life when she changes — changes the way she thinks, who she is. There is no weaker sex today. Women are no longer in the kitchen all day. They are in the workplace." Sun Rose closed the interview by saying that she thought the women's movement had helped to change her value system, particularly towards such beliefs as women not having to marry and making their own choices in society.

THE MIDDLE GENERATION: DONNA'S STORY

Donna is Sun Rose's daughter. She was born in Truro in 1951, and in 1995 she was attending Saint Mary's University in Halifax. Unlike her relatives, she was then divorced and living alone. Donna is the third oldest, with three sisters and two brothers who still reside in Nova Scotia. Her father's occupation, like her mother's, changed over time. When he was young, her father was a heavy machine operator. Later in life he became a drug and alcohol counsellor, as did his wife. Donna has four children and three grandchildren.

Donna's social values seem to be evolving much like those of her mother, Sun Rose. When Donna was younger, she felt that her destiny was to marry and have children. She remembers her mother's words: "She used to stress, 'marry a nice man and settle down.' I married, but didn't settle down, and didn't live happily ever after." Like her mother, Donna has changed her views and is now "dead against marriage." She does not believe that a person needs a piece of paper to develop a loving relationship.

Donna's ability to take on university and a single life did not happen over night. It has been a process of personal growth and a struggle to claim her identity as an independent Native woman. When she was younger, she accepted the negative stereotypes of Native people that are common among Euro-Canadians: "Mi'kmaqs, Aboriginals, Indians were considered drunks, quiet and [people who] did not try. In my mind I know that I am not that. I have worked hard to overcome such stereotypes. I make my kids aware that it is not true."

Donna fought drug and alcohol abuse, and it was not until four years ago, when she went to Red Bank, New Brunswick, to heal, that she was able to know sobriety. She feels that this was the most significant event that changed her life.

Donna hopes her children will develop into happy independent people like her role models: Auntie Mary, a strong independent woman who did what she always thought to be right, not necessarily what other people thought she would do; and Albert Lightning, a Cree elder, who taught her to be proud of her heritage. She feels that her daughters have more freedom than she did, partly because she promoted their independence.

Donna has a strong concept of who she is as a person, but does not consider herself as belonging to any country or community. One reason for this may be that she is no longer living on a Native reserve, but in the city of Dartmouth, across the harbour from Halifax.

THE YOUNGER GENERATION: DENISE'S STORY

Denise, born in 1969, is Donna's daughter. She now lives on Indian Brook Reserve. She works as executive assistant to the Vice Chief of Indian Brook Band Counsel. She lives with her father, her brothers and sisters, and her two small sons. Denise has attended both community college and university. She hopes to return to university once her children are older.

Denise's view of social values within her family has evolved over time very much like those of her mother and grandmother. She believes that she has more freedom than previous generations had. She feels there are no pressures for women to marry and that children are by choice, which does not necessarily have to include marriage.

Denise's mother has been an important role model for her because she was able to do exactly what she wanted. She explained that her mother had the strength to leave her husband and create an independent life.

Denise's father has been a Royal Canadian Mounted Police (RCMP) Officer for the last seventeen years. His position is one of authority within the Indian Brook Reserve. In the past Denise felt that she did not live up to her father's expectations. However, she has been able to come to terms with her relationship with her father: "I used to let my father's expectations of me bother me. I felt I let him down and could not get back to the spot I was before. I have overcome that and have learned to accept myself for what I can or cannot do."

Denise enjoys her job as the executive assistant to the Vice Chief of the Band Counsel. She likes the freedom it allows her. Her time is flexible, and she is able to take time off to be with her children. The atmosphere is relaxed, and she has the freedom to organize her own workload. Denise hopes that when her children are older, she will be able to complete her degree and go on to work with a large accounting firm.

Like her mother, Denise does not perceive herself to be a Canadian. She stated, "I am a Maritimer; I only think of myself as a Canadian when I watch hockey." Like her grandmother, Sun Rose, Denise did not express the desire to develop a strong relationship with her family. Independence seemed to take precedence. However, when being interviewed, Sun Rose was surrounded by family. Many of her grown children were at the house, playing cards and enjoying each other's company. Love for children was a taken-for-granted presence.

All women expressed their need for autonomy, freedom of choice and an ability to control their individual destinies while being rooted within Mi'kmaq culture. The fact that all three women expressed the desire to become independent is not surprising within a cultural group that for so long has been dictated to and controlled by the federal government and its patriarchal values.

CREATIVE POSITIVE CHANGES
WITHIN PERSONAL SPHERES

◄○►

The Older Generation: Margo's story

MARGO WAS AN ONLY CHILD, born in 1917 in Toronto, Ontario. Her mother was an office worker prior to marriage and a homemaker after Margo was born. Her father was a trade school teacher. Margo acquired a Bachelor of Arts and Education. She married an Anglican priest, moved to Nova Scotia and became a wife and a mother. Margo has five children, six grandchildren and one step-grandchild. She is now retired and living alone in an eight-room house along the banks of the LaHave River in East LaHave, Lunenburg County, Nova Scotia.

The Second World War had a profound effect on Margo's life. Her husband was injured during the war and much later died from the results of his injuries. At the time of her husband's death in 1965, there were few social support systems in place to help her heal. There was financial support, but no social mechanism to help her learn to cope with widowhood. When her husband was alive, she had been defined as an Anglican priest's wife. This meant that she lost her independent identity, and her position prevented her from developing any close relationships within the community. It had always been important to keep up a good front. When Margo's husband died, her desire to continue with a good front did not die with him. With time, she was able to develop as an individual. Much later she cultivated friendships with women in her community. Margo senses that women today are not as defined by their husband's social position as she was.

Margo had few support systems within the family unit, because when she married, her husband took her from Ontario to Nova Scotia, far away from her original family. When she was growing up as an only child, she learned a great deal from her extended family, especially about educational opportunities. This knowledge that education was the means to change one's social position became an important element in Margo's development. During her university years in Toronto, at Victoria College, Margo formed friendships with a group of women who played a significant role in her life. The university became her community, completely separate from her family. The Dean of Women, an important role model, introduced Margo to many different social views. Margo considered this to be a turning point in her life.

Although Margo experienced a personal awakening in university, it was many years later that she would challenge female stereotypes. Not long after the death of her husband, she was diagnosed with cancer. While receiving treatment she could no longer have her hair permed. Long after she stopped receiving treatment, she decided to continue wearing her hair straight. "Not having a perm was my resistance to stereotypes."

Margo may have resisted popular culture later in life, but in university she embraced it. While she was in university, female students incorporated a fashion that set them apart from women who were not in university. Margo began to wear saddle shoes and large flowing shirts, which were different from the skirt-and-jacket suits worn by women in the workforce.

After university, when Margo married an Anglican priest, she changed her religious affiliation from the United Church of Canada to the Anglican Church of Canada, thereby creating a need for her to alter her religious traditions. It also became compulsory for her to attend church. It was not until the death of her husband that she felt religion was a matter of choice for her.

Margo worked as a receptionist with Toronto Hydro, but her time in the labour force was short. Sexual division of labour was very much a part of Margo's married life, with her husband providing the income. Her role had not changed from that of her mother, with women playing a significant role in the unpaid workforce. She considers her role as a caregiver to have been "a labour of love." This was not to say that she was not in the public eye. There were strong social expectations that she had to be a good mother and a good wife.

Margo describes herself at the present time as a woman respected within her community and feels that she, as a person, has become more aware of social issues. Looking back over the events that have shaped her life, it was D-Day, her husband's death, the birth of her children and the knowledge that she is often alone in life that have all been significant. Her friendship with other women has been important to her, because it enables her to be a part of the social realm.

THE MIDDLE GENERATION: JACKIE'S STORY

Jackie was born in Lunenburg, Nova Scotia, in 1948. She was the middle child of five. Jackie moved to Halifax in 1964 when she was sixteen and has remained living there. She continued her education and has received a Bachelor of Science degree and a Bachelor of Education degree. She now derives her livelihood from working at the Post Office. Jackie has divorced, and she has two daughters who are still in university.

Jackie perceives her life to be very different from that of her mother, Margo, even though she took on the similar roles of wife and mother in society. For Jackie, growing up and becoming a teenager in the 1960s when women were redefining their place in society, was a frightening time. She described it as "a scary place" with "so many changes" in women's roles. Sometimes it was "difficult to keep up." She often felt pulled between the old value systems, that were still in place, and the new value systems, that were challenging the status quo. Her daughters, born in the 1970s, do not have to deal with this transition, because they grew up with new values and ideals.

Jackie challenged the stereotypical roles of mother and wife very differently from her mother and at an earlier age. She accepted the ideals of marriage and being a mother only as a means of running away from her family, in a way that was socially acceptable. Later, when she became separated from her husband, she confronted these role expectations. For Jackie, divorce was a turning point in life. Throughout her life she had felt she was different, but it was not until after her separation that Jackie confronted her lesbianism and what that meant to her and to society. After many years of healing, she has now developed a solid relationship with her lover, a loving relationship with her children and a lasting relationship with her in-laws and ex-husband. She does not perceive this to have been an easy struggle, and she believes that the women's movement has been instrumental in providing the support and knowledge that she was not alone in her battle to develop as a healthy lesbian woman.

She believes that her relationship with the wider society will always be uncomfortable and hopes her children do not have to struggle, as she did, to find themselves. She worries that being a lesbian may harm her children socially, because many in society have not yet accepted homosexuality. She protects them from social ridicule by not playing a dominant role in the community.

Jackie interpreted her expectations for her children to be very different from her mother's expectations for her. She felt that her mother would have preferred her to have become a nurse or teacher. However, when Margo was interviewed, she felt her own expectations of her children were that each would become his or her own person. Jackie hoped her children would not become involved in marriage or long-term love relationships until they have fully developed as independent selves. She also stressed the need for women to have an equal power balance within a relationship and never to betray themselves within that relationship.

Jackie's most significant role model within her family was her grandfather, because, like her, he enjoyed working with his hands. He gave her the knowledge that such abilities were important attributes in society. Jackie had gone to university because both parents had expected it; there was no question of alternatives. Yet university was not the gratifying experience for her that it was for her mother. Jackie does not believe that her two degrees have enabled her to pursue a career or have helped to develop her physical working skills.

Her role in the labour force has been more active than her mother's. However, she feels that her need to earn a living has not always been a positive experience. When the children were young, she worked part-time because she felt they needed her. When they were teenagers, she worked shift work and often worried about leaving them alone at night. She now likes her work and feels that it fulfills her needs. She is comfortable at work because she can dress in casual clothes and often works with her hands. She still has dreams of finding work that will fulfill and challenge her both physically and mentally.

The women's movement has played a significant role in Jackie's life.

Its world views have fostered and enabled her personal development. Its popular culture in the '60s allowed her the freedom to dress in blue jeans.

Overall, the factors that have changed Jackie's life have been more positive than negative. Because of a changing world view and the women's movement, she has been able to develop as a fulfilled person.

THE YOUNGER GENERATION: MAGGIE'S STORY

Born in Halifax in 1973, Maggie is the oldest in a family of two step-sisters and one natural sister. She has always lived in Halifax. Her mother and father are both university-educated. Maggie is currently finishing an honours degree in science at Dalhousie University and has been accepted in a combination master's and doctorate program in Ontario. She is single and has no children. She currently lives with her mother in the centre of Halifax, a two-minute walk from Dalhousie University, in a three-bedroom flat that belongs to Jackie's inlaws.

Maggie's world view often reflects her mother's. However, her life experiences frequently differ. The structure of Maggie's family is not the same as her mother's and grandmother's. Her family consists of a large extended family made up mostly of her father's relatives. Maggie perceives her extended family to be full of love, whereas Jackie found her home to be unloving, and Margo had to cope with a mother who suffered from depression. Maggie feels that her family has instilled positive values, that she has had choices in her life and that there has been no pressure at home to comply with female stereotypes.

Being a part of university life has been as important for Maggie as it was for her grandmother. It gives her a sense of belonging to a community, a place for her to create friendships and to accomplish dreams.

Because of the women's movement, Maggie has been able to pursue a non-traditional female profession. She also does not feel the need to fulfill certain kinds of "women's roles." She likes to do laundry, however, saying it makes her feel grounded and is "a tie to the women of the past." Popular fashion did not affect her as much as it did her mother and grandmother, but she senses that the 1960s' refusal to adopt stereo-typical women's fashion has enabled her to create what she sees as her own style. Technological changes, such as television, have become part of the popular culture and have had both positive and negative impacts on her life. She, like Margo and Jackie, senses that the media has brought women's issues to the forefront.

Maggie, like her mother, believes spirituality is important and not necessarily found in the current religious structure. Unlike her mother, Maggie recognizes the role that religion has played in her life, by building self-confidence and leadership qualities. She stated that her religious views and beliefs have developed over time. She does not believe in "God," but believes that religion played an important role in society. Such views are very different from those of Margo, who believes that she had "outgrown it," and Jackie, who does not identify with organized religion.

As Maggie prepares to move to Ontario for graduate studies in science, she feels that everything in her life is changing. She is no longer with her boyfriend, and friends seem to be coming and going. She feels a lack of motivation and a loss of confidence because of the instability in her personal life. She knows that this is not what her mother had hoped for her. She is also questioning her sexuality and perceives herself to be bisexual. Unlike her mother, her choice of sexual partners has not had any social repercussions yet, because so far all have been male.

Maggie believes that she has benefited from the women's movement and that it has opened doors of opportunity for her. She believes that many of the struggles that her mother and grandmother have encountered are no longer necessary because of changes in society brought by the women's movement.

MANY FACES OF FREEDOM

◄o►

MY DAUGHTER, MY MOTHER and I sat around the dining-room table as I conducted the group interview. We laughed a lot, and agreed to disagree. All of us were born in Nova Scotia and feel loyal to our province, although my daughter and I feel that we are Canadians first. We all considered our grandparents, uncles, aunts and their children to be our extended families. We thought that the interview was a worthwhile experience, and hope to have more discussion like this with other members of our family, also on tape.

My mother, whom I will call Alice, was born in 1910 as the seventh child from a family of eleven children (three sisters and seven brothers). Her mother was a teacher, and her father worked for the Canadian National Railways (CNR). She moved to New Glasgow and Truro, to accommodate her husband's occupation, and after his death, to Halifax. Alice has been a widow for over twenty years. Her family always maintained close ties. Today, she has one sister and two brothers living, two in Stellarton and one in nearby Westville, and she lives with her daughter and son-in-law in Dartmouth. Only two of her siblings ever moved from Stellarton, and one of those returned. She has one son and one daughter, and three grandchildren — two boys and a girl.

Like my mother, I was born in Stellarton, but I grew up in a much smaller family — with my mother, father and one younger brother. My mother stayed at home while I was growing up, and my father worked as an operator for the CNR. I went to school in New Glasgow and Truro. My husband and I moved to southern Ontario in 1964 and lived there until 1981, when we moved back to Nova Scotia. Our two children now have families of their own, and our first two grandchildren will arrive this year. My brother and his family live in Dartmouth, not far from us.

My daughter, Valerie, was born in Truro in 1966. Like me, Valerie grew up in a family with one younger brother, mother and father. She went to school in Belleville, Ontario, and Bridgewater, Nova Scotia. Although her family lived in southern Ontario where she grew up, Valerie says "we had cousins in Ontario and my grandparents were up a lot, and we came down [to NS] so we still seemed like we had extended family ..." Valerie and her husband expect their first child this fall.

We began our discussion by asking each other, "How is your generation different from other generations?" My mother answered, "We had freedom and respect. Men tipped their hats when they met a woman on the street, and removed their hats when they entered a restaurant." She believes that these former customs showed a respect for women that is lacking today. I feel that "my generation seems like an in-between generation, where a lot of things changed. Women went out in the workplace more than they had before." My daughter said, "The first thing that comes to mind is that my generation has had more opportunities and that there is more equality between the sexes than there ever has been in the past."

I was surprised by my mother's remark that her generation "had freedom and respect." I had mistakenly thought that her generation had less freedom than mine or my daughter's. Of course, freedom can be defined in many ways. Thinking about it, I realized that I am not so free at all. I have to work whether I want to or not and so does my daughter. While we have other freedoms, like choosing the size of our families by using reliable birth control methods, and having our drivers' licences, we are not as free as my mother's generation to walk at night without fear, or even to use language freely. My mother also pointed out that women's domestic tasks were "eased somewhat in regard to laundry and cooking." I remember, in fact, the great relief I felt when we finally had our own washer and dryer and did not have to visit laundromats anymore. Also, I did not have the worry that my daughter will have: that my children could be harmed, or even disappear, on their way to school. And another big difference is the taken-for-grantedness of daycare centres now. My grandchildren will grow up in a completely different way from any other generations of my family. So freedom becomes a precious commodity that permeates many facets of our lives.

As we discussed the distribution of household tasks, we observed a trend towards more sharing as the years progressed and these tasks changed. In my mother's time, "heavier chores were assigned to the males. Preparing meals, attending to household chores were assigned to the females." As I was growing up, my father was the breadwinner and my mother stayed home, doing all the household work and most of the child-rearing. My daughter remembers that I did most of the household chores when she was younger, although today my husband does as many or more chores than I do. My husband shared in child-raising much more than my father had done. In my daughter's home, she still does more household work, but her husband shares the cooking equally, and now that she is pregnant, he does more of the other work. She expects her husband to share the responsibility of raising their children equally. Correspondingly, I believe that the way our partners/ husbands were raised, and particularly the influence of *their* mothers, plays a significant role in the way household tasks are shared. For example, my father grew up living apart from his family and did outdoor chores. Also, his poor health later on affected his contribution to sharing chores. After my husband left a job in which he worked three shifts, he began to share more of the housework. Growing up, he was expected to help with chores at home, and I believe this is part of the reason he does more now. In my son-in-law's case, his mother did everything for him. He is just beginning to take on more of the housework. I don't think these influences can be discounted when considering changes in male–female roles. Along with technology, then, sharing tasks has come to lighten the load for women, to perhaps give them more freedom. But whether this freedom is truly "free" is debatable. What becomes of this free time?

We discussed gender differences in the broader society. Both my mother and I remember that women seldom went into a liquor store, and my mother said, "We never expected to see a girl in a pool hall." Taverns were male domains; there were no washrooms for women. Today, as my daughter says, going to the liquor store "is a rite of passage for everybody."

As we considered our expectations for our daughters regarding marriage or career, or both, other generational differences emerged. My mother had hoped I would "have a respectable husband." I hoped that my daughter "would have a career that would allow her to live a comfortable life if she chose to live independently." My daughter hopes that her daughter will "have a happy life." We all did not want any harm to come to our children and felt that we would interfere in any relationships that we considered dangerous. We then mentioned our hopes for our granddaughters. My mother hopes "they continue to retain their moral values" and that they choose "decent, Christian people." I wish they have "happiness and good health and the realization of their own expectations for themselves." And my daughter hopes that "they get a chance to listen to these tapes. I think that each of us carries on from the other. I like that idea." Obviously, there is change in attitude here, and once again the strong influence of the church has lessened in the younger generations. Also, the freedom for women to choose whatever lifestyle they wish today is a significant change from the expected roles of wife and mother.

We all feel that education is very important and would all have pursued higher education had circumstances permitted. My mother explained, "High school was as far as I could go. At that time to become a teacher ... they were short of teachers ... you had to study for a year at home and write provincial exams on those studies. Then I went and spent the summer in Halifax and went to teacher training." She did not attend Normal College because she would have lost a whole year. My mother continued, "I taught for four years until I married." Today, my mother says, "I would go higher if I had the opportunity."

I continued the conversation: "There were no student loans available when I was a teenager. I knew no women students in engineering or medicine. My friends and relatives who went to university in the 1960s became nurses and teachers. I did not go to university until I was in my forties, and we were back in Nova Scotia, although I had taken several correspondence courses from Waterloo University while I lived in Ontario, and which I was given credit for here. I obtained an honours English bachelor's degree and a Master of Arts in English, but these degrees have not enabled me to establish a career. I am disappointed with the outcome of my efforts. I had high expectations for myself and felt so enthusiastic and optimistic when I finally got to university. If I could go on, I'd get my PhD. However, I took my present job after two years of fruitless job searching because it has a good pension and medical plan and I felt time was not on my side in continuing my education or holding out for another job."

My daughter mentioned, "I couldn't have gone to university without student loans. If I could go back, I would have saved money to go to school so I wouldn't have the student loan I do now. I have a BA in music and now work as a library assistant. I love my job but there's no room for advancement."

Unfortunately, none of us were truly free to pursue our educational dreams. Finances and family concerns interfered with the process.

Religion has always been important to the way we live. We are all practising Roman Catholics. My mother said, "It's had an important influence on my life." I believe "it influences decisions that you make about the way you act and behave and bring up your family and every aspect of your life." My daughter commented, "I don't follow all the things in my religion. I go to church for myself and I take what I want or need from it. Maybe I exclude things that other people say you shouldn't; [they say] if you're going to follow religion you should take it as a whole, but that's not the way I look at it." We also discussed controversies such as women being priests and changes in the church. For example, there were no altar girls until my daughter's generation. My mother mentioned, "there are things which I thought could be eliminated and which are being eliminated now. It was just customs more or less. When I was young for instance, we wouldn't want to go in unless we had a hat on. I think that was style."

Obviously, the church plays a significant role in controlling women's freedom. The control of a patriarchal church in a patriarchal society has been detrimental to advancing equality between men and women. The stand taken on birth control is particularly difficult for many women (and men) to accept. However, I believe people are independently sifting through the regulations and taking comfort from the church while not necessarily following every "rule." This change of attitude can be seen in the remarks of my family. Continuing in a similar vein, we discussed women's spiritual roles in society. My mother feels that because "women are not at home with their children" society suffers since discipline and moral values are declining. I believe that "women influence the attitudes of their children and thus keep society in line." My daughter thinks that "more men are taking an active role" in child-rearing, which will benefit the larger society.

Because my mother does not want her real name used, my daughter and I respect her wishes and will use other names also. I believe this shows another change — the safeguarding of family privacy is not as important to us. No doubt because her family was a prominent one in a small community, my mother still feels the need to protect the family's "good name," a need my daughter and I do not share. I'm sure this is a reflection of the changes in society towards more openness and towards franker discussions about matters that were once taboo. Another example of this is the openness with which my daughter and I discuss her pregnancy, a matter which I would never have discussed with my mother. This is another way in which a once "private" topic has become a natural and legitimate one. However, I do feel that within our family, we still have a tendency to protect each other from the "outside world."

Finally, the topic of feminism brought our discussion to a close. My daughter commented, "I prefer the word equalist to feminist. We don't need emphasis on one sex or the other. We don't have to do what men have done to us in order to make us all equal." My mother interjected, "Men have been abused as well. Maybe not physically, but mentally." My daughter continued, "Women didn't have the vote. Things are open to me that never were before. I certainly appreciate what the women's movement has done." My mother disagreed, "Do you think that is a result of the women's movement? That was coming anyway. Some of these things have been instigated by men, too, I think." I said, "I heard about radical types. Now I see women working together to try to improve their lives, especially in Third World countries. It does mean equality." My daughter believes that "nobody can say that they haven't benefited from the women's movement. Nobody." My mother stated, "I can't say that I have." My daughter argued, "That's why you have the vote." My mother felt, "That wasn't altogether the women's movement though." My daughter suggested, "Well, if women hadn't acted to have the vote, they wouldn't have got it." My mother said that she thought that "the men co-operated." My daughter stated, "But that is not the same at all." I agreed, "Only because they were forced to." Thus our discussion closed most appropriately, I think, because we came full circle. Our opinions of how our generations are different are quite evident in the above remarks.

IMPORTANCE OF SELF-WORTH

—◁O▷—

The Older Generation: Isabele's Story

ISABELE IS MARRIED AND LIVES in Dartmouth, where she has resided for the past twenty-eight years. She was born in Truro in 1916 as the fourth child, with seven sisters and four brothers. Her mother was a cook and a homemaker. Her father was a farmer for much of his life. He also did maintenance work and sold property.

Isabele grew up in a Catholic home where there was no division of chores between the genders. Her parents divorced when she was seven years old. Because of this, everyone in the household helped her mother with the chores. Isabele said, "There was work to be done, whether you were a boy or a girl, it did not matter." Isabele's grandmother also lived with them and did her share of the work. Isabele felt very close to her family when she was growing up, and when she became older and had her own family, this closeness carried over to them.

When Isabele got married, things really changed for her with regard to household chores. She was responsible for taking care of all the bills, cleaning the house, raising four children and sometimes working for twelve to sixteen hours a day at her job. She was a head waitress for twenty-two years. Her husband did the painting and any outside work, plus his regular employment. Whether in or out of the home, Isabele felt that women contribute a great deal of unpaid labour to their families and to their communities. When asked if she felt the need to fulfill certain kinds of women's roles, she replied, "Women do everything, men just go out to work."

Today, at age seventy-nine, Isabele enjoys family get-togethers, an active life with her husband and events at two senior citizens clubs; she plays bingo and cards and bowls twice a week. She has one surviving sister living in Massachusetts and lives close to her daughters and many of her nineteen grandchildren. Her family has been an important source of protection from the wider society and helps "keep her going." She only wants happiness and peace for all of them.

Isabele did not feel that the women's movement had affected her life in any way. She was a liberal women, as it was. For example, she felt that there was no job that she would consider to be exclusively for men or women. "It's up to the individual and whatever they are capable of doing," she said. What Isabele may not have realized was how much her life and her self-concept as a strong woman was influenced by the fact that she was a beneficiary of the first women's movement. Her daughter, Debbie, recognized it implicitly when she described her mother as "probably ahead of women's lib."

THE MIDDLE GENERATION: DEBBIE'S STORY

Debbie is married and lives in the Dartmouth area, where she has lived most of her life, except for a three-year period in England and six months in Ontario. She was born in Halifax, across the harbour from Dartmouth, as the third of four girls. Her mother, Isabele, was a head waitress and also a homemaker. Her father was a fish filater, a cook in the army during the war and later a government labourer; he is now retired. Debbie has been a homemaker except for a short time when she worked as a clerk in a muffin shop. She raised six children, five boys and one girl, one of whom has died. She has two grandchildren and two step-grandchildren.

Debbie grew up in a home where women did all the chores around the home. Her mother raised the four girls while her father went "out to work." Debbie explained that "it was the women's role to look after the home and family." Debbie today still does the majority of the homework, but her husband does the painting, cooks frequently and helps with the dishes. Debbie had always looked after the bills and banking until recently when her husband started doing some of it. Now, women's and men's roles are less strictly differentiated.

Debbie chose her mother as her role model, and they are still close today. She identified her mother as "a capable and empowered woman" and believes that if her mother had been "born into politics," she would have been a leader "in the forefront."

During the time when Debbie was at the age that she could have started a career, she was raising children. She said, "I felt the need to be a wife and mother. Society and family expected me to be, and I didn't want to be a nurse or a secretary." The women's movement was just beginning to make waves at this time. Debbie did not work in the paid labour force until after her last child graduated from high school. She then went to work as a clerk in a muffin shop for five and a half years.

Debbie has mostly done unpaid work, particularly homemaking and raising six children. She says, "If women do these things, they volunteer; they don't expect to be rewarded. It is women's nurturing side." She explained, "I never received any benefits for it. The only cheque I will ever receive is the old age pension cheque, and by the time I get there, they won't have it anymore." She felt that women today are more fortunate because men are more involved in childcare, which removes some of the burden.

Debbie enjoys visits from her children who live nearby and misses those who are at a distance. Since she got her driver's licence at the age of thirty-six, she has enjoyed independence and a new sense of freedom. She said, "When I got my licence it felt great, and it still feels great to be able to drive." Debbie was thirty-six in 1975, when Canada celebrated International Women's Year with its "Why Not" campaign.

THE YOUNGER GENERATION: MICHELE'S STORY

Michele is married and lives near Dartmouth in Cole Harbour. She was born in 1970 as the youngest in the family and the only girl. Her mother, Debbie, was a homemaker and a clerk for five and a half years after Michele graduated from high school. Her father was in the military for twenty-one years. He retired from the military and worked in Marine Maintenance for twenty-two years.

Michele grew up in what she called a "traditional" household: her father went out to work and her mother raised the children and was seen as a consistent pillar of strength. Michele believed that she had more social freedoms than all of her five brothers. She was able to drive the family car and "get away with a lot more" because her brothers were much older. Michele is now married and has no children. She stated that today, "my husband and I both do the domestic tasks; it's fifty-fifty." Michele does not feel the need to fulfill certain "traditional" women's roles.

After high school and working in retail for a few years, Michele decided to take a course in hairdressing, and since then has been working as a hairdresser from her home. She loves her work as a hairdresser. Michele believes that there are many choices and opportunities for women today. She explained, "I don't feel there are any jobs exclusively for men or women; they can do anything they want to." Although Michele felt her era was very liberal, she still believes that women contribute a great deal of time and energy doing unpaid work. She says, "Women need to receive more recognition and appreciation, but I don't necessarily believe it to be financial rewards."

Michele said that the women's movement has played a significant role in her life. She credits it for allowing her to have more choices and more benefits professionally. She believes society accepts and respects women more today than it did years ago. She explains: "The media attention to women has made me stronger and more confident, and I feel I can speak out about my beliefs; media gave me a vision of reality." She feels that the women's movement and media attention have helped to make her life easier than that of her mother and grandmother. Much of the struggle was already done by the time Michele came of age.

Today Michele enjoys working and spending time with her family, husband and friends. She said that at times she finds it difficult to balance all her activities, but she feels very fortunate to be a young, capable woman who can do it all.

CHANGING ROLES
AND OPPORTUNITIES

◄◦►

THE THREE GENERATIONS

How have expectations about women's roles in society changed over three generations? What do we learn when all of the stories we collected in Nova Scotia are compared? In this final section, we group women's concerns and experiences into themes and categories. We illustrate what we have learned through the lives of three generations of women in one family. At the time of the interviews in 1995, Lillian was in her early eighties, her daughter Mary was in her late fifties, and her granddaughter Nancy was in her mid thirties.

Lillian was born in 1913, the ninth child in a family of six girls and eight boys. Her mother was a housewife and her father a blacksmith and cooper. Lillian has a Grade Six education. She was married, divorced, remarried and is now widowed. Lillian was a chambermaid at a hotel after her divorce. She then was a housewife after she married her second husband, who was a tradesman. She has one daughter, two granddaughters and two great-grandchildren. She lives on St. Margaret's Bay, not too far away from her only daughter, Mary, who lives in Halifax.

Mary was born in 1937 and grew up as an only child. She began her work as a secretary after completing three years of education at a commercial school. She also did four years of university extension courses. She is now retired from her job as a personnel advisor, and she currently lives in Halifax with her husband who is retired from the navy. She has two daughters, one grandson and one granddaughter.

Nancy, born in 1959, is the younger of Mary's two girls. She owns a house in Ottawa, but she has been living with her parents in Halifax while she completes her Master of Nursing degree. Nancy has worked as a nurse since 1979, after completing a nursing diploma program in Sydney, Nova Scotia. She did her Bachelor of Nursing degree at Dalhousie University in Halifax. She has been married but is now divorced. She has a boyfriend who lives in Toronto. Nancy plans to return to her job in Ottawa, as a nurse, when she is finished her master's degree.

WOMEN'S EXPECTED ROLE

How have women's roles changed over the lifetimes of these three generations of women? In some respects, it has become easier to be a woman. When Mary was growing up in the 1940s and 1950s and becoming a young adult into the 1960s, she had to work twice as hard as the men did to be recognized. Today, more recognition and support for women in the paid labour force has been institutionalized in programs and women have more educational opportunities. Women are now able to fulfill roles they never imagined, such as managerial positions.

In other ways, being a woman is harder because many women have both home and work responsibilities. Nancy commented that women today are away from the house more frequently and, in a sense, have more freedom. However, increased responsibilities with respect to finances, work and professional commitments are added to home responsibilities. Society expects more of women — achievements both in the outside world and within the household.

Women who decide to work solely in the home often lack respect because their work is not valued. Despite the work of Canadian groups such as Mothers are Women, contemporary society is still not successful even in counting women's unpaid work, let alone rewarding it. Women today prefer working in the paid labour force. As Lillian reflected, "It's completely different today. Years ago people didn't mind workin' for a home for anything. Today nobody wants to work. They all want to sit behind a desk." Work in the home is no longer considered a valid occupation in a society increasingly preoccupied with individualistic and hierarchical values, including greed.

FAMILY AND COMMUNITY ROLES

Family roles have also evolved from earlier generations when household responsibilities were divided along a very rigid sexual division of labour. Lillian remembers that when she was growing up in the 1920s, everybody had his or her own job to do in the family. Although work was shared, the girls' responsibilities involved inside work with the mother. She recalls the hard work of helping her mother to look after younger children while the boys did outside jobs with their father. Conversely, Mary suggested that her responsibilities as a child in the household were limited, as her mother did all the work inside, while her father had a job outside. Nancy described the family in which she grew up as one in which the responsibilities were more shared and in which the sexual division of labour, although not rigid, was still evident. Other than cooking, her father did little housework. He became more involved in household chores when he retired.

Generally families were not seen to interfere with their children's choice of husband or friends. When things were not going well for Lillian and Nancy in their marriages, both family and community were there to support them. Societal standards with respect to cohabitation have become more relaxed; Nancy feels no pressure to marry her current boyfriend.

Unlike many of the other women in the two older generations, Lillian and Mary did not feel "involved" in their communities. They were not "joiners." Perhaps Lillian did not feel she had much in common with others, being divorced and a single mother, at a time when such positions were discouraged, and being of the working class. Mary's values and aspirations with respect to work were not necessarily consistent with the goals of stay-at-home moms, who, she stated, seemed to make up these community organizations. Nancy saw herself as a member of various communities — the Dalhousie student community, the YMCA and various professional associations. However, like her mother and grandmother, she has never been very involved in the community in which she lives or in any equality-seeking women's organizations.

RELIGION

Religion and spirituality have played a significant role in the lives of many of the older women. It was important socially. Lillian, for example, looked forward to Sunday School when she was a child and continues to attend church when she can get there. Like most of the younger generation, Mary and Nancy did not regularly attend church, but both have religious beliefs. Nancy, however, was uncertain what the church and religion means and what God does. She explained, "Since the separation and divorce I haven't been back to church ... I know there's a place for it, and someday I probably will ... I still believe that there's a God, but what He is and what He does totally befuddles me ... I've always had questions, ever since I was a kid. A lot of it doesn't make sense and a lot of it is just a belief."

These women all agreed, as did most other participants, that women play important spiritual, moral and ethical roles in society. Some women would characterize God as "She."

CHANGES IN EDUCATIONAL ROLES

Like most families, education level increased with each generation, and this indicates an improvement of educational opportunities over time. Lillian stated that her opportunities were lost when she left school to help her mother at home: "I felt I was guilty if I didn't stay home to help. Poor old Mom was working herself to death ... She's your mother, so you want to help her." Otherwise, Lillian would have stayed in school to acquire a better education. Education in her time was necessary for men but not for women. Today, Lillian suggested, education is equally important for both. Mary originally wanted to be a nurse, but because of financial difficulties, her educational opportunities were limited. She attended commercial school and became a secretary. Later she took university extension courses. Conversely, Nancy thought that her opportunities were not at all limited. "Just because you're a woman ... now you can do whatever you want to do ... The educational opportunities are there, whatever you want to make them."

WORK OUTSIDE THE HOME

Work outside the home gained in both importance and in widened opportunities during the three generations. Most middle-class women of the first generation did not identify with the paid labour force. Some of them worked for short periods, between the end of their schooling and getting married. Their identity was derived from their family status, from their husband's position in the labour force and not from their own. A woman's success was measured by her ability to marry a man who would support her financially. Poor women, whose husbands' wages could not support them, worked in order to support the family's livelihood.

Both Mary and Lillian had entered the paid labour force out of necessity. After Lillian was divorced, she had to go to work to support her daughter. She worked as a chambermaid in a hotel in the city, and her daughter Mary lived with an aunt and uncle. When Lillian met her second husband, he encouraged her to quit. So she stayed home, as befit a respected married woman of her generation.

Mary began to work for similar reasons. Before she was married, she had gone to work to support herself because her stepfather had asked her to leave the house. When Mary was married, she planned to work only for a couple of years for extra income. However, after beginning to work, her intentions changed. Mary continued to work because she enjoyed it. She was dedicated to both her career and to her family, foregoing much of her social life. Her husband was away quite frequently so she was left to care for the children.

Mary began in the workforce as a secretary and, with ambition and determination, she was able to progress in her career. She thought it was very important that everybody, including women, receive recognition for equal work and that women can be equal to men — at least in the business world. As she said,

> I think today women have the same skills, but they were never really able to demonstrate them. They weren't allowed to work in fields or roles that allowed them to show the qualities they had, whereas today it's more commonplace ... When I first started out, I had to work twice as hard ... I still believe that two people — it doesn't

matter what gender they are — if they are doing the same job they should get the same recognition, and that means pay as well as pats on the back.

Nancy felt no societal pressures to stay at home. She has been part of the paid labour force since she was a teenager. Her current work on her master's degree will further her career. She already has worked as a nurse in various hospitals and in a nursing home.

Work was very important for Mary and for Nancy. It was part of their identity. They entered the paid labour force along with many other women. A number of factors contributed to this increased participation, including economic necessity, increasing education of women, growth in service industries that employ a large number of women, technology that eased home responsibilities, smaller families, new societal attitudes, women's demonstrable skills as workers, the women's movement and an expanding economy.

FEMINISM AND THE WOMEN'S MOVEMENT

The youngest generation was most clear about feminism and its value. To Nancy, feminism meant equality, having rights and being able to voice her opinions without repercussions. She considers herself a feminist and explains, "You have to have both the knowledge of the workings of society and that women are treated as second-class people. And if you don't have that, you wouldn't even know of the need for feminism ... You have to have the knowledge to notice the discrepancy that exists in society."

For Nancy, the women's movement was the most important political and social event that has affected her life "by bringing forth the inequalities that women face on a day-to-day basis. That's probably shaped my life. It's made it okay — better — to be the person that I am."

At first, the oldest generation was unsure what feminism was and did not know how to define it. When we related the women's movement to women winning the vote, however, Lillian understood immediately and spoke of voting in the past as being a "man's thing." She also felt that women are able to do things equally as well as men. She had come to understand that the feminist movement also supported ideas of education and work outside the home for women. When asked if she thought that she had benefited from the feminist movement, Lillian replied, "Sure we did; don't you?" When we asked specifically if she had benefited personally, Lillian was less sure and said, "Well, I don't know about that ... I don't think so, but there's well-educated people today — women — that I think could run all over the men (laughs). Men have learned there's more in women's brains than in theirs lots of times." We asked: "So the women's movement has really helped women advance in society?" Lillian replied: "Sure ... The men are taking a back seat in lots of places. Oh yeah ..."

Mary had many contradictory things to say with respect to the women's movement and feminism. At first she repeated that she only thought of feminism in relation to gender: "I just think of it as being female as opposed to male — just gender." This apolitical conception then changed as she continued: "I don't believe in this ... women's role where you get on the bandwagon, you burn the bra and you shout and scream and yell ... [there is] no place for that anywhere." She did not consider herself to be a feminist and stated that equal recognition is not solely a feminist ideal. Although Mary thought that feminist organizations may have done some damage in promoting the women's cause, she stated that they have contributed to it: "A lot of it has changed because of these so-called feminists, and a lot has changed just by better management practices." Mary's contradictory ideas about feminism are often expressed by the phrase, "I'm not a feminist but ... (which would be followed by a statement that a feminist might make)."

Early on, "radical feminism" seemed to turn many people against feminism, especially people who were trying to be accepted in the society. Mary thought that it was only when feminists began to relax their approach that they gained more respect from the general society and were able to make greater gains in achieving their goals of equality. The older women in the middle generation like Mary were more likely to express these contradictions and distance themselves from feminism than the more strongly feminist younger women of this generation. Sandra, for example, thought feminism means a woman can do any job a man can do and is as intelligent.

DEFINING ONE'S PLACE

The importance of freedom, independence and defining one's own place by creating new opportunities were important themes. The significance for Lillian, Mary and Nancy of maintaining their own sense of identity was clear. They valued their independence and ability to find security in their own way. Lillian's divorce enabled her to escape a situation that had denied her the right to be valued as a person. For Mary, having a career and tangible security, such as a second car, provided her with independence. She stated that security was important for her generation because when she was younger, she did not have many material things. So a car meant security. Mary was probably also influenced by the fact that after her parents' divorce, her mother's employment opportunities were limited because of her lack of education. Mary did not want to be left in a situation in which she could not function on her own. For Nancy, her divorce reinforced the importance of improving her knowledge and having her own house, as these symbolize independence.

MAKING CHANGES

Both Mary and Lillian seemed to see oppression in the lives of their own mothers and to have made changes in their own lives on the basis of the problems they perceived. Lillian, in her own family planning, acted on the knowledge that a large family of fourteen into which she was born is hard work and means self-sacrifice. She also did not want to place on her daughter the kinds of implicit demands her mother placed on her with respect to helping with child-rearing. Lillian only had one child. Lillian encouraged Mary to achieve educationally. Knowing of her mother's lost opportunities in life in terms of education and career may have influenced Mary's decision to strive to be the best she could be in her career. For Nancy, her mother was a good role model of women's success in a male-dominated society.

While Lillian's family has a greater decrease in number of children than most in her generation, the average number of children per family in our sample dropped from eight to three in that one generation.[19]

Lillian reflected on her conscious decision to limit her number of children because of her own experiences of growing up within a large family and its work implications for mothers and daughters. Future research may ask such questions of other women and may also seek to understand why the change happened in Lillian's generation and not that of her mother, for example. Contextual factors such as the women's movement, the Depression and the Second World War may have been important in raising such issues to the consciousness of Lillian and those of her generation and hence been factors in that change.

As these stories emerged, it has become clear that women today have many opportunities as a result of the struggles of earlier generations. The women's movement has helped women to make their own choices and to maintain their own identity. It has advanced ideas about sexuality and birth control. It has helped men to see that women do make a difference. Despite this, there still remain certain societal expectations that women wittingly or unwittingly follow. Women still tend to work in traditionally female occupations, experience some pressure to marry and bear the major caregiving responsibilities. Nonetheless, an evolution of women's roles is evident through these women's stories.

Notes

1. Sylvia Hamilton uses the census to suggest that forty-nine female and fifty-five male slaves were in Nova Scotia in 1767, living mainly in Halifax but spread through twelve of the thirty townships surveyed. This is 0.7 percent of the 13,374 population at the time. See her "Naming Names, Naming Ourselves," in Peggy Bristow, Dionne Brand, Linda Carty, Afua P. Cooper, Sylvia Hamilton, and Adrienne Shadd, eds., '*We're Rooted Here and They Can't Pull Us Up': Essays in African Canadian Women's History* (Toronto: University of Toronto Press, 1994) for a historically oriented focus on Afro-Nova Scotian or Black women.

2. James W. St. George Walker, personal communication with the author, July 1999. See James W. St. George Walker, *The Black Loyalists: The Search for a Promised Land in Nova Scotia and Sierra Leone, 1783–1870* (New York: Africana Publishing Company, 1976), and *A History of Blacks in Canada* (Hull, QC: Ministry of State for Multiculturalism, 1980). See also Pearleen Oliver, An Historic Minority: The Black People of Nova Scotia (Dartmouth: Metrographic Printing Services Limited, 1981), written and published at the request of the African United Baptist Association of Nova Scotia.

3. More information on the significant contributions by Black Nova Scotian women can be found in the works of Black Nova Scotian artists such as the singing group Four the Moment — see the article by that name in Angela R. Miles and Geraldine Finn, eds., *Feminism: From Pressure to Politics* (Montreal: Black Rose Books, 1989, pp. 345-352); the poet and teacher Maxine Tynes whose books *Borrowed Beauty* (1987), *Woman Talking Woman* (1990), *Save the World For Me* (1991) and *Door of My Heart* (1993) are all published in Porter's Lake, Nova Scotia, by Pottersfield Press; and the writer and film maker Sylvia Hamilton whose works include "African Nova Scotian Women: Mothering Across Generations," in Sharon Abbey and Andrea O'Reilly, eds., *Redefining Motherood: Changing Identities and Patterns* (Toronto: Second Story Press, 1998); "Naming Names, Naming Ourselves," in Bristow et al., eds.,'We're Rooted Here and They Can't Pull Us Up': Essays in African Canadian Women's History; "African Baptist Women Organize: The Women at the Well," in Linda E. Carty, ed., *And Still We Rise: Feminist Political Mobilizing in Contemporary Canada* (Toronto: Women's Press, 1993); "A Glimpse of Edith Clayton: A Traditional Basketweaver" and "Mothers and Daughters, A Delicate Partnership" with Marie Hamilton, both in *Fireweed: A Feminist Quarterly* (Winter/Spring 1984); and "Our Mothers Grand and Great: Black Women of Nova Scotia," *Canadian Woman Studies/ les cahiers de la femme* (Winter 1982). Sylvia Hamilton's film, *Black Mother Black Daughter* (Halifax: National Film Board of Canada, Atlantic Centre, 1989) portrays the strength, ability and knowledge of generations of Black women who have kept their heritage alive through oral history and struggles to create and preserve their community. For short biographies of (mainly women) teachers in racially segregated schools in Nova Scotia, see Doris Evans and Gertrude Tynes, *Telling the Truth: Reflections: Segregated Schools in Nova Scotia* (Hantsport, NS: Lancelot Press, 1995).

4. Information for this section comes mainly from *The Canadian Encyclopedia* (Edmonton: Hurtig Publishers, 1985, 1988), especially sections on Nova Scotia by

NOTES

J. M. Beck, on Black Nova Scotians by James W. St. George Walker and on slavery by Robin Winks; George Peabody, *The Maritimes: Tradition, Challenge and Change* (Halifax: Maritext, 1987); the Nova Scotia Department of Tourism and Culture, *Nova Scotia: The Doer's and Dreamer's Complete Guide* (Halifax: Nova Scotia Department of Tourism and Culture, 1994); and from our primary research. See also Margaret Conrad, Toni Laidlaw, and Donna Smyth, *No Place Like Home: Diaries and Letters of Nova Scotia Women, 1771–1938* (Halifax: Formac Publishing Company, 1988.) For research on contemporary immigrant women in Nova Scotia, see work by Evangelia Tastoglou and by Helen Ralston.

5. For a history of specific resource industries, see L. Manchester, *Canadian Fisheries* (Montreal: McGraw Hill, 1970); M. Parker, *Woodchips and Beans: Life in the Early Lumberwoods of Nova Scotia* (Halifax: Nimbus Publishing, 1992); J. Hoegg-Ryan, *Coal in Our Blood: 200 Years of Coal Mining in Nova Scotia's Pictou County* (Halifax: Formac Publishing, 1992). For an understanding of some of these resource industries at the end of the twentieth century, see Richard Apostle and Gene Barrett, *Emptying Their Nets: Small Capital and Rural Industrialization in the Nova Scotia Fishing Industry* (Toronto: University of Toronto Press, 1992); Peter J. DeVries and Georgia MacNab-Devries, *"They Farmed Among Other Things..." Three Cape Breton Case Studies* (Sydney, NS: University College of Cape Breton Press, 1983).

6. For a description of sun-drying fish, see Ellen Antler, "Women's Work in New-foundland Fishing Families," *Atlantis* 2 (Spring 1977), 106–113.

7. See Barbara Blouin, *Like a Second Mother: Nannies and Housekeepers in the Lives of Wealthy Children* (Halifax: The Inheritance Project, 1999).

8. This pattern, described in Linda Christiansen-Ruffman, "Newcomer Careers: An Exploratory Study of Migrants in Halifax" (PhD dissertation, Columbia University, 1976), was found to continue. Nova Scotia's migration statistics reflect the recessions of the early 1980s and 1990s when its residents returned home. See Canada, *International and Interprovincial Migration in Canada 1961–62 to 1975–76* (Ottawa: Industry, Trade and Commerce, 1977), and the annual editions published in 1978 and 1982, as well as Statistics Canada's publications *Quarterly Demographics* (Ottawa: Supply and Services, 1991–1995) and *Canada: A Portrait* (Ottawa: Supply and Services, 1989).

9. For a description of its development, see Patricia Baker, Linda Christiansen-Ruffman, and Ann Manicom, "Creating Feminist Spaces in the University," in Ann Shteir, ed., *Graduate Women's Studies: Visions and Realities* (North York, ON: Inanna, 1996).

10. Its major industries include fishing, iron and steel, coal mining, farming, tourism and the arts. A number of internationally known artists and musicians, such as Rita McNeil and Natalie MacMaster, have their roots on the Island. Celtic influences remain a popular source of inspiration for Cape Breton musicians.

11. Five western Canadian women legally challenged women's right to be considered "persons" who could hold public office as Canadian senators. In 1928 the Supreme Court of Canada unanimously ruled that women were not "persons." The women appealed to the British Privy Council who reversed the decision on October 18, 1929, writing that the practice of excluding women from public office is "a relic of days more barbarous than ours." The victory of the so-called

Persons case is now celebrated every October when the Canadian government presents the Persons Award to five Canadian women who have made an outstanding contribution towards improving the status of women in Canada.

12. Cheris Kramarae and Paula A. Treichler's *A Feminist Dictionary* (Boston: Pandora Press, 1985), p.160, quotes from Rebecca West from *The Clarion*, November 14, 1913: "... I only know that people call me a feminist whenever I express sentiments that differentiate me from a doormat."

13. Typically, creators of Women's Studies found that sexist biases distorted knowledge creation at all stages of the research process. The "important questions" assumed male realities. Patricentric concepts and indicators as well as population and sampling decisions excluded women by design. Men's words were considered authoritative, and even women's sex roles were doubly interpreted through male eyes of interviewee and researcher. Analytic biases made more than small differences in sociological findings: hypotheses became their opposites. Patriarchal forgetfulness and blindness led to inappropriate inferences which passed through editors as legitimate scholarship, as they still do today. See the citations in "Developing Feminist Sociological Knowledge: Processes of Discovery," chap. 1 of Linda Christiansen-Ruffman, ed., *The Global Feminist Enlightenment: Women and Social Knowledge* (Madrid: International Sociological Association, 1998), 13–36.

   Even feminist scholarship is not immune, as I noted in an article presented in 1982 and published in 1989, which theorized two components of patriarchal knowledge as the patricentric syndrome and the either/or syndrome in scholarship. See Linda Christiansen-Ruffman, "Inherited Biases Within Feminism: The 'Patricentric Syndrome' and the 'Either/Or Syndrome,' in Sociology," in Angela Miles and Geraldine Finn, eds., *Feminism: From Pressure to Politics* (Montreal: Black Rose, 1989), 123–145. In the 1990s, these biases persist as does the "abstraction syndrome."

14. Feminists discovered that some traditional research practices prevented women's voices and women's knowledge from being heard and began to develop alternative, more participatory research designs. See Maria Mies, "Liberating Women, Liberating Knowledge: Reflections on Two Decades of Feminist Action Research," *Atlantis* 21, no. 2 (Fall 1996), 10–24; Patricia Maguire, *Doing Participatory Research: A Feminist Approach* (Amherst, MA: The Center for International Education, School of Education, University of Massachusetts, 1987); Sandra Kirby and Kate McKenna, *Experience, Research, Social Change: Methods From the Margins* (Toronto: Garamond Press, 1989); and Shulalmit Reinharz, *Feminist Methods in Social Research* (New York: Oxford University Press, 1992). Our methodological approach recognizes that everyone is affected by the world around them and emphasizes both the value of individual subjectivity, and individual agency, and the importance of the geographic, structural and cultural contexts.

15. The two men in the class were given the option to interview men of three generations, so that they could also enhance the research potential of their grounded knowledge. They decided to interview women.

16. Students did not feel that the general questions were precise enough, and some students wanted to ask different questions. Thus the seminar developed its own questionnaire as an interview guide, which was used in different ways. One student

treated it as a guide for a focus group interview with two other generations from her family. She found it helped to bring out contradictions although much was unsaid to protect feelings. Other students conducted one-on-one interviews, with all but one telephone interview done face-to-face. The lengthy interview schedule was completed on the same day or with time lags up to a week apart. Some researchers did not give the questionnaire to participants; some gave it to them ahead of time and others shared it during the interview. For all researchers the questionnaire served to guide the interviews but was not restrictive; the interviewer was free to ask clarifying questions, and the person being interviewed was encouraged to add comments throughout. Most interviews were audiotaped to enable students to be more attentive to women's voices. Participants then reviewed draft reports to ensure that we had not misrepresented their stories. We discussed issues of attribution and confidentiality. In the tradition of oral history, some families are named, and in the more sociological tradition, some families are given pseudonyms. Since one woman did not want her family to be identified, the class decided on collective authorship. For a copy of the questionnaire specific to the Nova Scotia project, write to Changing Landscapes Project, Linda Christiansen-Ruffman, Department of Sociology/ Women's Studies, Saint Mary's University, Halifax, NS B3H 3C3.

17. The above is an edited and revised version of their introduction to Nova Scotia and their analysis of three generations. Parts of their introduction, such as their description of Nova Scotian weather, have been omitted. No changes have been made to the final section, what is now called the Conclusion.

18. For example, we could investigate the historical requirement for some women to leave their job at marriage or the pattern of naming women over the decades, or both, which reflected men's treatment of women as property in the past. A number of sources in archives and libraries could be used, such as government records, minutes of groups, newspapers, other media and diaries.

19. If this reduction in number of sisters and brothers between families of the first and second generation reflects a trend in the larger society, it is curious that such a major historic change is not better known. It is neither named nor noted, except in Québec, where it is part of the Quiet Revolution. It is ironic, but probably not surprising to feminists, that what appears to be a historically dramatic decrease in birthing may have been eclipsed while public attention was focused on another demographic pattern of this century, that of the "baby boomers." More research is needed into this broader concept of family planning.

Study Questions

1. What were some of the similarities you noticed among members of each of the three generations? What are the major generational differences? To what extent do the preliminary findings capture themes from other provinces? Do the chapter headings also point to themes that have come

up elsewhere? If so, describe the similarities. If not, how would you account for the differences?

2. How did we arrive at the dates for our three generations? Are they all similar or different from the generational dates from other chapters in this book? How do they differ from dates that might come out of a study which you and your age cohort might do?

3. In another study how might we decide where one generation begins and another one ends? How might the Nova Scotia findings about differences in the middle generation help us to decide? What differences do these theoretical and methodological decisions make for our research and our understanding of the world?

5. In many ways, the women in this chapter are "ordinary" women. Although no one was active in women's organizations, several of the women were influenced by women's movements for social change. In what ways do you think they were influenced?

6. How do you think the lives of women in the first generation would have been different if the women had been born fifty years later, in the third generation? Give reasons for you speculation. How do you think your life would be different if you were born fifty years from now?

QUESTIONS FOR
GENERAL STUDY

1. Investigate the earth, the place of land where you live. Who has lived there before? How has the life on that place of land changed? From whose perspectives do you see the landscape?

2. How has immigration affected your family?

3. Consider the idea that culture is the site where values are produced or reproduced, or both. Choose one of the stories in this book and locate where the women reproduce the values of their culture and where the women change them. Can you identify a place where a woman must accommodate a change which she does not want?

4. What are the differences between domestic power and public power in women's lives?

5. What access have you had to political information and ideas? Where have you formed your values and beliefs? Are there alternative sources for information and ideas? What conditions affect the existence of these?

6. Pick a quote from any part of this book and apply it to your own life, showing why it can be applied to the particulars of your own experience.

7. The following are autobiographical exercises. The American writer Flannery O'Connor said that anyone who had lived beyond the age of eight has enough to write about for the rest of her or his life. Nonetheless, sometimes it's difficult to get started on an autobiographical account. Here are some exercises to help you generate the material for your own autobiographical account:

   a. Think of your greatest accomplishment to date. Write about it and investigate if it has elements that are related to your gender.

   b. What's in a name? Investigate the origins of your name, why it was chosen for you, and what hopes were inherent in the choice?

   c. Draw a circle. Divide it into five-year segments of your life. For example, if you are twenty, you will divide the circle into four portions each representing five year segments. In each segment make notes of the major happenings in that period of your life. Pick out the segments in which gender plays an important role and write about them.

d. Some of the subjects that often lead us into considering the impact of gender on our lives are childhood games, childhood chores, clothes, puberty, how we feel and felt about our bodies, friends, important women in our lives, school, what we thought we would become. Brainstorming on any or all of these should generate material for autobiographical writings.

e. What has made you the person you are? Draw a circle and divide it into seven sections. Put the following headings on the sections: gender, ethnicity, race, religion, sexual orientation, degree of ableness and other (this is a category for you to create/fill in). In each section, explain how you categorize yourself and how this category has affected your position, choices and hopes in life.

f. If you are learning feminist theory in your Women's Studies course, pick a theory and test its validity by applying it to your own life and that of women in your family.

8. How may we theorize landscape? Do the various chapters conceive of "landscape" as geographical or social or historical or all three? In each of these cases how is "landscape" gendered and how do these gendered dimensions of landscapes interrelate?

9. What are different ways to theorize generations? For example, what are different ways of thinking about generations historically? Which are historically important signifiers of generations in the social life of your community? What about provincially? nationally? globally? How would "generations" look differently from these different social perspectives? Now think of generations differently, focused on the chronological ages of individuals you know. How do they differ from the dates in the book? What are the implications of this concept of generations? What are the different ways in which you might "date" generations using each of these criteria?

10. What are other ways in which a researcher might define generations? What are the theoretical implications of defining generations differently, or what are different meanings of the word "age"? In what ways does the idea of changing landscapes capture these differing meanings of generations?

11. Roles and identities of individuals are, in many ways, defined for us by social structures and cultures into which we are born. In every generation, some changes are possible to what is taken for granted as impossible. Imagine yourself as a member of a previous generation, before a particular change for the advancement of women. What taken-for-granted ideas would have enforced the status quo and prevented women from "going against the times"? How did patriarchal society and its social relationships

with its structures, ideologies and cultures enforce the subjugation of women in that era? How do you think change was able to come about? What changes do you think should come about at present?

12. Sociologists have often distinguished between private troubles, experienced only at the individual level, and public issues, which have often gone through a process of having been put on the public agenda by groups such as women's organizations. Use the case studies materials from the chapters to illustrate this distinction and discuss the processes by which private troubles become public issues. Discuss an example from present times of the process. Are there troubles faced by women today which are on their way to becoming public issues?

13. We often learn a lot about the problems of our own lives by comparing our life and its patterns with others. Describe your reflections on your own life after your readings in this book. (Advanced students might be interested in speculating on similarities and differences in the types of questions that the different chapters raised for them.)

14. Collect stories from three generations of your own family or from the family of a friend. What similarities and differences did you find with the book (a) in terms of the methodologies and (b) in terms of the findings about generational differences?

APPENDIX

WOMEN'S CHANGING LANDSCAPES IN CANADA:
THREE GENERATIONS OF WOMEN COMMENT ON THEIR LIVES

*The Canadian Project for the Commonwealth
Secretariat's Submission in Beijing*

Date:_____

Demographic Questions

1. Name: _____

2. Date of Birth: _____

3. Place of Birth: _____

4. If born out of Canada, year of immigration: _____

5. Number of sisters and brothers, and where subject is in family:

_____

6. Mother's name and occupation: _____

7. Father's name and occupation: _____

8. Education: elementary __ ; high school __ ; college __; university: under-grad __ / graduate __ ; professional school __ ; training program _____; other (please specify): _____

9. Current occupation or employment: _____

10. Married __ ; common-law __ ; single __ ; separated __ ; divorced __ ; remarried __ ; widowed __ ; lesbian couple __

11. Number of children, gender and ages: _____

12. Number of grandchildren, gender and ages: _____

Questionnaire

I. FAMILY, AFFILIATIONS, RELATIONSHIPS

1. What was your family of birth like? (Or the family in which you grew up, if that was different.)

a. Were males and females treated differently in your family? If so, in what ways?

b. What role did an extended family play in your life?

c. Who in your home-family situation was your most important role model and why? Would you make the same choice of role model now?

2. What are your current family-home arrangements?

a. What are the domestic tasks to be done, who does them and why? Is this different than the way domestic tasks were addressed in your family of birth?

b. What are and have been the most gratifying elements of family life for you in the past and now?

3. How important has romantic love been in your life?

a. What have been the most important romantic relationships in your life?

b. Did your family or community, or both, have any influence on your choices in love and on what happened in these relationships?

c. Would you attempt to influence your daughters' (or other young women's) romantic relationships? If so, under what circumstances?

d. How do you understand "romantic love"?

e. Over your lifetime, have you observed differences in the kind of love relationships and expectations women have?

4. Has friendship been an important factor in your life?

a. Could you describe your most important friendships?

b. Have you experienced differences in friendships with men and with other women?

II. Growth, Dreams, Learning

1. What educational choices have been available to you throughout your life?

2. Did you feel a need to fulfill certain kinds of "women's roles" in your life? If so, why?

3. To what extent did the era in which you grew up and its fashions, customs and events shape your life?

4. How much did other people's expectations of you affect your choices? And your own expectations of yourself?

5. Have your attitudes to your own capabilities changed in your lifetime? If

so, how and why?

6. Would you make different educational choices now than you did in the past? If so, what would they be and why?

7. Have spirituality or religion been important in your life? If yes, in what way?

8. Have your religious views and beliefs changed much in your lifetime?

9. Do you think women have a particular religious/spiritual role to play? If so, what is it and why?

10. Describe yourself at age fifteen.

11. Describe yourself now.

III. WORK

1. Do you regard any kind of work as being exclusively suitable to men or women? If so, what? If not, why?

2. Have you ever worked in the paid labour force? If so, when, what?

3. Have you ever experienced inequity in the work place? If so, what did you do about it?

4. Have you had any difficulties reconciling family life with work "outside" the family? If so, what are they?

5. Have you ever experienced sexual harassment in the work place? If so, what did you do about it?

6. Have you had any important mentors or role models at work? If so, who and in what situations?

7. Describe the best and worst things about your current job.

8. Do you feel well informed about financial matters and in control of your own finances?

9. If you could choose, what job would you most like to have?

IV. LOCATION AND POLITICAL PARTICIPATION

1. How would you describe your race, ethnicity, religion, sexual orientation, social class and level of ableness?

2. Which of the above factors have most affected your life, and how?

3. Have your ideas about these factors in your life changed over time? If so, how?

4. To what extent is your life affected by your region and community? Does the place where you live mean a lot to you?

5. Are there specific places or political events that have changed your life in significant ways?

6. Have you been active in volunteer organizations? If so, which ones, and what did you do?

7. Have you been involved in a woman's organization? If so, which one and what did you do?

8. How important are women's work and women's organizations to the life of your community?

9. Have you been active in the political life of your community? In what way?

10. What does the word "feminism" suggest to you? Has media attention to women affected your life in any way?

11. Are there any particular groups of women with whom you feel a sense of identification?

V. REACTIONS

1. How have you found this interview?

2. Is there anything you would like to add?

3. When you look back on your life, what stands out as the most important social change affecting you in your lifetime?

differences in generation, age, culture, region.
social class come out.   similarities ...

* Family   past and present.

  Work.   in home and pay

  Education   opportunities, achievement.

  Religion.   affect on life

  Political Involvement, Women's Group, Friendship.
      (Importance of)

Idea of what feminism is. what issues they feel are important today, their past and present.
hope and goal.   · 316 ·

CONTRIBUTORS' NOTES

LINDA CHRISTIANSEN-RUFFMAN is a Professor of Sociology at Saint Mary's University. She is an initiator and the graduate co-ordinator of the Inter-University Women's Studies Program at Mount Saint Vincent University, Dalhousie University and Saint Mary's University. She has served on the board of the Canadian Research Institute for the Advancement of Women (CRIAW) and has presided over the Canadian Sociology and Anthropology Association. She remains active with CRIAW locally and is a member of CRIAW's Global Feminism committee. She is a member of the International Sociological Association executive, representing them at the United Nations. She is co-editor and co-author of *The Global Feminist Enlightenment: Women and Social Knowledge* (ISA, 1998) and is one of the founding editors of the electronic journal *Feminist Strategies Féministes*.

HUGUETTE DAGENAIS was born in Montréal. She is a Professor in the Department of Anthropology at Laval University in Québec City. She has been very active in feminist studies at Laval University as co-founder and first director (1982–86) of the Groupe de recherche multidisciplinaire féministe (GREMF), co-founder and first director (1986–97) of *Recherches féministes*, the only francophone feminist research journal in Canada, and the holder (1993–97) of the Chaire d'étude sur la condition des femmes. Among her numerous publications are *Women, Feminism and Development*, which she co-edited with Denise Piché (Montréal: McGill-Queen's University Press, 1994); *Science, conscience et action. 25 ans de recherche féministe au Québec* (Montréal: Remue-ménage, 1996); editor of *Pluralité et convergences. La recherche féministe dans la francophonie* (Montréal: Remue-ménage, 1999); and co-editor with Anne-Marie Devreux of *Ils changent disent-ils* (1999), a joint issue of the Québec-based *Recherches féministes* and the Paris-based *Nouvelles questions féministes*.

KEITH LOUISE FULTON is a professor of English and Women's Studies at the University of Winnipeg, where she co-ordinates the Women's Studies Program. Her focus is on writing by women, in particular, that writing that contributes to feminist understanding. She is a co-editor of *Atlantis: A Women's Studies Journal* and was the Margaret Laurence Chair in Women's Studies at the University of Winnipeg and the University of Manitoba from 1987–1992.

GRETA HOFMANN NEMIROFF co-taught the first Women's Studies course in a Canadian university in 1970 and has been teaching, researching and writing on Women's Studies ever since. From 1991–96 she held the Joint Chair in Women's Studies at Carleton University and the University of Ottawa. She is an active participant in the struggle for women's rights and human rights through membership in various organizations. Currently, she is the Co-ordinator of Women's Studies at Dawson College in Montréal, where she also teaches English and Humanities, and is president of the Montréal-based Sisterhood is Global Institute. She has written numerous articles and stories, and has written and edited several books. She is mother to three adult children.

CHRISTINE ST. PETER is Chair and Associate Professor in the Women's Studies Department of the University of Victoria. For the past sixteen years she has been working to create Women's Studies and feminist scholarship at the University of Victoria and in national organizations. From 1995–98, she was co-editor of *Atlantis: A Women's Studies Journal,* and is currently a member of its editorial panel. Her book *Changing Ireland: Strategies in Contemporary Fiction* is forthcoming from Macmillan Press, England.

ELIANE LESLAU SILVERMAN is a historian and head of the Women's Studies Program at the University of Calgary. She has been active in the women's movement in Canada at the local and national levels for thirty years, and expects to continue forever agitating for change even as she continues writing about women. Her mother, Charlotte Leslau, was an active feminist from the age of six, and her daughters, Lisa and Monique, are also committed feminists and strong women. Dr. Silverman has based most of her scholarly writing on interviews with women, because her hope is that women's voices will be heard in our common world.